For Jan
and the future of his generation

Masculinities and Crime

Critique and Reconceptualization of Theory

James W. Messerschmidt

Foreword by R. W. Connell

Rowman & Littlefield Publishers, Inc.

ROWMAN & LITTLEFIELD PUBLISHERS, INC.

Published in the United States of America
by Rowman & Littlefield Publishers, Inc.
4720 Boston Way, Lanham, Maryland 20706

British Cataloging in Publication Information Available

Library of Congress Cataloging-in-Publication Data

Messerschmidt, James W.
Masculinities and crime : critique and reconceptualization of
theory / James W. Messerschmidt.
p.   cm.
Includes bibliographical references and index.
1. Criminology.   2. Sex role.   3. Masculinity (Psychology)
I. Title.
HV6030.M473   1993   364—dc20   93-7809   CIP

ISBN 0-8476-7868-7 (cloth : alk. paper)
ISBN 0-8476-7869-5 (paper : alk. paper)

Printed in the United States of America

The paper used in this publication meets the minimum requirements of
American National Standard for Information Sciences—Permanence of
Paper for Printed Library Materials, ANSI Z39.48–1984.

Contents

Foreword

R. W. Connell

This is a vivid and original analysis of crime. It is also a vivid and original discussion of masculinity and gender relations. The combination of the two defines its importance.

Masculinities and Crime is part of a conceptual revolution in the social sciences, reflecting profound changes in our understanding of everyday life. James Messerschmidt is writing at a time when questions of gender and sexual politics, femininity and masculinity, have been brought out of obscurity and seen as key issues in our society.

This is not the first time such issues have been addressed in social science. When people speak of "second wave" feminism, they are making an indirect acknowledgment of a "first wave," which in its day had a major impact on understandings of society. The "woman question" of the late nineteenth century was not seen as the concern of women alone. It was actively debated also by men, in public life and in intellectual circles.

Practitioners of the newly invented science of "sociology," which at the time mainly meant evolutionary speculation about the past and future of human society, were decidedly interested in such issues. For instance, Lester Ward, the first American sociological theorist of note, whose book *Dynamic Sociology* was confiscated and burned by the Tsarist regime in Russia supposedly because its title suggested "dynamite" and "socialism" to the authorities, wrote hundreds of pages about what we would now call "sexuality," "gender," and "gender relations," and what he called "the phylogenetic forces."

In the early decades of the twentieth century, that kind of speculative sociology reached an intellectual crisis and was displaced by a new kind of social science. This was a more mundane and also more specialized enterprise, whose core was the social problems of industrialized societies, especially problems of social control and management. Criminology developed as a typical branch of this new social science, and one of its most typical features was the way it pushed questions of gender to the margin.

One of the first accomplishments of Messerschmidt's book is to show what this marginalization meant for the way criminology understood crime. As he points out, the question of gender was not obliterated. It is, indeed, too conspicuous a feature of crime in industrial capitalist civilization to be absolutely ignored.

What happened, rather, was that the issue of gender was treated in a way that depoliticized it, that removed it from the realm of the problematic to the comfortable zone of the taken-for-granted. Messerschmidt deftly shows the different forms this removal took, in classic works of criminolgy. I find particularly illuminating his demonstration of the importance of assumptions about biological differences in character. This emerges not only in the crass forms we see in Lombroso and in the modern-day Lombrosos of the pseudoscience of "sociobiology," but also in much more subtle and intricate ways in theorists whose main intention is to illuminate the social. The ideology of "natural difference" is extraordinarily pervasive.

Messerschmidt's capacity to see these things *in* criminology is dependent on his ability to take a conceptual standpoint *outside* criminology as it has been traditionally understood. Readers may find it surprising that a book on crime spends a good deal of time working through theoretical debates about the nature of gender and patriarchy. I would urge those who do find this surprising, not to skip this part. It is not a detour, but an essential part of the argument.

The commonest alternative to the concept of biological difference is the concept of "sex roles." The notion of a sex role seems to acknowledge the social character of gender, the extent to which masculinity and femininity are cultural conventions, not fixed by the genes. It suggests there is real significance in dressing babies in blue and pink, giving little boys footballs and little girls dolls, steering young men toward machinery and young women toward cosmetics, promoting images of "real men" and nurturant mothers.

But as Messerschmidt shows, the notion of sex roles is inadequate for the analysis of the real world. It typically rests on an unexamined notion of natural difference on which society is supposed to elaborate. It drastically simplifies complex cultural processes and negotiations. Perhaps most importantly, it consistently obscures questions of social power and inequality—between races, between classes, and between genders.

Messerschmidt, therefore, explores accounts of gender that *do* recognize issues of power and inequality, almost all of which have been produced by feminists. Unlike most men, Messerschmidt is highly aware of the complexity of feminist thought and the variety of currents within feminism. He traces those currents that have fed into the recent American debates about men's power and criminality. He notes how the school of thought that at first most strongly emphasized issues of men's social power, later moved back toward a kind of biological essentialism; and how the school of thought that, at first, had most to say about material inequalities, got tangled in conceptual dilemmas about the priority to be given to the "systems" of patriarchy and capitalism.

This is, I think, an accurate and helpful account of problems that have emerged in the attempt to understand gender as a social structure. It is an extremely difficult set of problems; no one should underestimate the difficulty, or think we have anything more than a partial understanding of the issue. But because the issue matters so much, it is necessary to press ahead with whatever tools we have. And Messerschmidt does move on, from his review of the difficulties in familiar theories of gender, toward a more sophisticated position.

The key to this is the recognition (by no means a new one, but persistently underestimated in the heat of political struggles around issues of sexual politics) that gender is a *complex* structure, not a one-dimensional one. Messerschmidt emphasizes that the social structure of gender incorporates different types of relationships between people, which can usefully be sorted out into substructures: the gender division of labor, the structure of power, and the structure of sexuality.

He also insists, as an important current of modern social theory does, that social structure does not exist "outside" everyday life. Structure exists in (and only in) personal practices. At the same time, personal practice does not float free of structure, but is always grounded in the structures in play at a given time and place.

Messerschmidt uses this concept of an interplay, or mutual constitution, between structure and action to get a grip on the important but very difficult problem of the relationship between class, race, and gender. This is an issue on which socialist feminism came to grief, and is often posed without very much being offered by way of a solution. Messerschmidt treats these structures as simultaneously present in, and determinant of, the same social action—not as structures that govern each its own chunk of social reality. This is, I think, a much more fruitful approach, and Messerschmidt shows its fruitfulness in many examples throughout the book, which are shown repeatedly to involve an interplay of class, gender, and race.

It is this conception of structured action that is the key to the reconstruction of criminology that Messerschmidt is attempting in this book. He proposes two great reversals of our usual way of thinking.

The first is contained in his focus on masculinity. This is a deceptively simple move, not at all as obvious as it seems in retrospect, once the move has been made. As the history of crimonology traced in the early part of the book shows, criminologists have long recognized that most crime was the affair of men, without seeing this as a problem. It was women's lack of criminality that was seen as the intellectual problem—a classic illustration of the way patriarchal ideology takes men as the norm and understands women as departing from it (deviants from the deviance, so to speak).

To say that men and masculinity are the intellectual problem is to insist on "studying up" rather than "studying down," to focus on those who hold the more privileged position in the gender order. This is not a stance that comes easily to those who share the position of privilege.

Though Messerschmidt's writing makes it seem easy, we should not underestimate the difficulty of making problematic one of the foundations of one's own being in the world. It is not an accident that the tentative critiques of masculinity that emerged among men influenced by the new left, counterculture, and feminism in the 1970s, were followed in the 1980s by a cultural backlash of impressive proportions. This ranged from the cult of hypermasculine violence in the movies (*Rambo* and the like), to the attacks on "soft men" and attempts to create a masculine cult by figures such as Robert Bly with his "mythopoetic men's movement." Messerschmidt's message is not likely to be a wildly popular one. Let us hope that truth still has a chance of prevailing in the marketplace.

The second reversal of common ways of thinking is contained in the way Messerschmidt conceives the relation between masculinity and crime. Conventional thinking, when that link is noticed, conceives of criminal behavior as an *expression* of masculinity: thinking that the person's gender is logically *prior to* the behavior, already settled, and can be understood as the behavior's cause.

Messerschmidt proposes something quite different from this, consistent with his concept of structured action. He draws on the research that has shown gender as something constructed in social action, as something done, accomplished, in the everyday actions of social life. Masculinity is not something that is preformed or settled. It is something that has to be made, and criminal behavior is one of the means for its making. A great deal of crime makes sense only when it is seen as a resource for the making of gender, and in most cases, that means it is a strategy of masculinity.

In some cases, this is very easy to see. Assaults on gay men, for instance, whether by gay-bashing youth groups or by the police, are commonly accompanied by abuse of the gays' effeminacy—the bashings are explicitly an assertion of heterosexual masculinity. In other cases, it is less blatant, but the connections are still there to be found.

Of course, there is not just one masculinity. There are a variety of masculinities, or ways of enacting masculine gender. And there is a wide range of settings in which the job is done: urban and rural communities, among working class and ruling class, among white men and black, at workplaces and in the home, and so on.

In the second half of the book, Messerschmidt takes on the task of working through that range and variety and showing how the gender dynamic plays out in different types of crime. Here he shifts from mainly conceptual argument to the analysis of concrete cases, though the framework of ideas is still in play.

Since "street crime" is very much an affair of young men, Messerschmidt spends a full chapter on youth. He draws out the importance of class situation in the shaping of youth groups and the kinds of criminality that emerge in them. Here he makes two important contributions to the emerging sociology of masculinities.

The first is his emphasis on the collective processes, the internal social life of the youth groups, in the making of masculinity. Competitions for prestige (including sexual prestige and access), social support for activities such as theft, are key features of the situation, not incidentals. Messerschmidt's vivid account of street robbery as a social process and a kind of work is a notable illustration of this principle. Indeed, there is a strong sense that it is the group, not the individual, that is the bearer of a particular form of masculinity.

The second point is the importance of a "public masculinity," in the *arena* provided by group life. To say that certain violent masculinities involve performance in an arena is not to suggest they are just being acted, that it is an insincere performance of a "role." The performance may be so sincere that it is literally a matter of life and death. Yet, it is still structured by the collective enactment.

I am impressed by Messerschmidt's analysis of the Central Park "wilding" rape case. Many people have been struck by the detail of the youths' high-spirited celebration during the rape and after it, as they left the victim, for all they knew, to die. This of course was manna to racist critics of black youths' savagery. Messerschmidt makes us understand how this derives from a group dynamic of masculinity in a context of racial antagonism and class deprivation.

Class and ethnicity are not just abstract dimensions of difference in this approach. Messerschmidt treats them in terms of the concrete situations and settings that they create, and the different kinds of masculinity constructed in response. The masculinity of the pimp, the factory worker, or the corporate executive is made with different kinds of resources, and different kinds of crime arise as a result. Types of crime thus have a situational logic, and the picture of gender is made both more complex and more realistic. Corporate law-breaking, for instance, is shown to be not an aberration—the product of a few bad apples—as business ideology would have us suppose. It is, on the contrary, the rigorous consequence of the cultivation of a particular kind of masculinity, embedded in a particular milieu of competition and hierarchy, among the managerial elite.

It is one of the great strengths of Messerschmidt's analysis that he does not focus only on the spectacular displays of masculinity in crime found in working-class and underclass milieux. He follows the logic of "studying up" in terms of class and race as well as gender, looking at the crimes of privileged men, and showing how the same principles allow us to understand these too.

In doing this, Messerschmidt contributes to another emerging theme of research on masculinity, the importance of institutions. Gender is not just an aspect of personality, a feature of the individual—though that is how the ideology of "natural difference" reads it. As we have already seen, it is an aspect of group life and collective processes. We live in an organizational world, a world of corporations, governments, world-spanning media, and technological systems. It would be most surprising if this were not also an important dimension of gender.

The case Messerschmidt addresses most closely is the case of the state. This is, of course, an essential theme of criminology, since a "crime" is defined by state action (i.e., the enactment of a law), and the state provides the apparatus of police, courts, and prisons for processing infringements of its rules.

It is increasingly acknowledged that the state is, in a profound sense, a gendered institution. This is obvious from a glance at its personnel, with men having a near-monopoly of policymaking positions. Even the Clinton presidency's attempt to have an administration that "looked like America" produced a cabinet overwhelmingly male; as a sardonic critic put it, the administration does look like America— men on top. Women are a large proportion of public sector employees, but are overwhelmingly in feminized occupations, such as secretary, nurse, and elementary teacher. The organizational culture of different parts of the state reflects this makeup.

Not only is the state gendered in this sense, it also acts in gendered ways, pursuing policies to do with issues of sexual politics. The Reagan-Bush administration's pursuit of right-wing agendas on abortion and homosexual rights is a conspicuous recent example of this, but is in no sense exceptional. States routinely, and extensively, regulate family relations, regulate sexuality in pursuit of religion or population policies, enforce or modify the gender division of labor, define and redefine legal rights (including citizenship) in terms of sexuality and gender, and so on. This amounts to a large area of state activity, when it is all added up.

In the final part of the book, Messerschmidt develops a fascinating account of the ways this gendered organization and its regulatory activities produce gendered crime and criminality.

Certain categories of crime are obviously the product of attempts at regulation. "Status offenses" involving girls are a significant example—it is familiar that the criminalization of girls involves regulation of sexuality in a way very different from the criminalization of boys. The history of such offenses was shaped by political mobilizations, especially the interplay between middle-class feminism and social purity campaigners, which reshaped the prostitution industry as well as creating social control systems directed toward youth.

The state, of course, is not monolithic; there are struggles within it as well as attempts to shape it from without. It is important to acknowledge this, to understand the politics of law, and to overcome the common tendency to treat the state as an abstraction, or as something beyond the human scale. One of the virtues of Messerschmidt's approach is that he consistently tries to see the state in terms of the concrete settings and particular groups involved in state action.

Indeed, his analysis of the police, as agents of state power in criminal matters, is one of his finest pieces of writing. He offers a vivid account of the realities of police working life, and the different styles of police masculinity that come into play—street cop versus office cop, for example. Police crimes, such as gay-bashing, find a place in this analysis alongside police law enforcement. Messerschmidt's argument is sensitive to the economic situation of the police as workers, and also to the emotional pressures of their role in social control and physical violence. It is also aware that the conditions of the doing of masculinity in police work change over time, for instance, with the increasing presence of police officers who are women.

This final section of the book, for me, raises two very large issues, one of theory and one of practice. The state is a strongly gendered institution and pursues with large resources agendas of sexual politics. But its *effects* on gender and gender relations often seem to be very different from what is (at least apparently) intended.

In the regulation of violence among working-class youth, for instance, state power seems repeatedly to provide an object against which a violent, resistant masculinity can be defined. This happens in relation to state power as realized in the school as much as it does in relation to the police. The impact of state activity, over time, thus seems to be the *incitement* of masculine violence as much as its control or suppression.

Paradoxical effects of this kind are impossible to explain via sex-role theory and its concept of "socialization." They are much closer to the way psychoanalysis understands the formation of personality. The problem Messerschmidt leaves us with is how we can understand such dialectical, contradictory processes at the social level as well as the level of psychodynamics; for his evidence leaves no doubt about the importance of collective processes here.

Messerschmidt's convincing demonstration of the importance of a politics of masculinity in understanding state action leaves a practical dilemma about reform. Across the range of social conflicts and problems he surveys, which in different ways get swept up into the category of crime, reform *must*, repeatedly, involve state action. But the state itself, as it is currently constituted, is a major part of the problem.

How can we expect democratic reform of gender relations from an institution that is dominated by those who benefit from the present gender order? What kind of reform process could possibly transform the gendered character of the state, without being trapped by the politics of social control in which the state is enmeshed? (What politician would survive, with a policy of taking the police *off* the streets?)

These questions are not rhetorical; they are the kinds of strategic questions that will have to be addressed, as the implications of studies like this one sink in. They do have answers, immensely complicated and long-drawn-out answers, of course, as is always true of practical politics. It is one of the great merits of Messerschmidt's work that it helps us see the shape of these strategic issues more clearly.

This is a clearly argued but complex book, addressing major issues in social theory as well as the concrete subject matters of crime and masculinity. Messerschmidt has built his argument carefully, constantly working from the facts but also working with imagination and passion. I hope the book gains a wide readership. We need such guidance to issues as tense, and as ominous, as these.

Acknowledgments

During my work on this project, a number of people gave me support and encouragement and shared their ideas, criticisms, and editorial suggestions. In particular, Piers Beirne, Bob Connell, Tony Jefferson, Nancy Jurik, Gray Cavender, Meda Chesney-Lind, and Bob Miller took much time away from their own work to provide me with detailed and careful comments on the entire manuscript. Additionally, numerous people were kind enough to read specific chapters of the manuscript at various stages of its development and to offer valuable comments: Candace West, Betsy Stanko, Cheryl Laz, Barbara Perry, Ken Polk, Christine Bowditch, Dusan Bjelic, and Peter Lehman. I thank all of these people and hope that I have justified in these pages the time, intellectual assistance, and support they have so generously and graciously provided.

Jon Sisk, editor-in-chief at Rowman and Littlefield, recognized early on the importance of this topic and has been both very supportive and committed to the book throughout the entire process. I thank him and his staff—especially Lynn Gemmell, Lucretia Lyons, and Lynda Hill—for everything.

I also thank my colleagues in the Department of Sociology and Criminology at the University of Southern Maine and Dean Richard Stebbins and Provost Dave Davis for supporting my work by allowing release time from teaching and awarding me an important sabbatical. Moreover, the staff of the Interlibrary Loan Services at the University of Southern Maine's Luther Bonney Library—in particular, James Brady and Cassandra Fitzherbert—provided invaluable assistance in obtaining materials from other libraries.

Finally, I am especially grateful to Ulla Eurenius for her warmth, comfort, support, and criticism, and to Erik and Jan Messerschmidt, whose interruptions continue to remind me that the personal is indeed political.

Part of Chapter 1 was first published as "From Marx to Bonger: Socialist Writings on Women, Gender, and Crime" in *Sociological Inquiry*, 58 (4) 1988: 378–92, and is reprinted (with revision) by permission of the University of Texas Press.

Part of Chapter 6 was first published as "Feminism, Criminology, and the Rise of the Female Sex 'Delinquent,' 1880–1930" in *Contemporary Crises*, 11 (3) 1987: 243–63, and is reprinted (with revision) by permission of Kluwer Academic Publishers, © Martinus Nijhoff Publishers, Dordrecht.

Chapter 1

Gender and Criminological Theory

It is no secret who commits the vast majority of crime. Arrest, self-report, and victimization data all reflect that men and boys both perpetrate more conventional crimes and the more serious of these crimes than do women and girls. Men also have a virtual monopoly on the commission of syndicated, corporate, and political crime (see Beirne and Messerschmidt, 1991: 547–48 for a more thorough discussion of this evidence). Indeed, gender has consistently been advanced by criminologists as the strongest predictor of criminal involvement. Gender explains more variance in crime cross-culturally than any other variable, and this "appears so *regardless* of whether officially known or hidden ("true") rates of crime are indexed" (Harris, 1977: 3–4). This fact recently led Judith Allen (1989: 19) to submit that the capacity to explain the high gender ratio and gendered character of crime "might be posed as a litmus test for the viability of the discipline." As an explanatory variable, then, gender would seem to be critical. Yet, as Frances Heidensohn (1987: 22) observes, "most criminologists have resisted this obvious insight with an energy comparable to that of Medieval churchmen denying Galileo or Victorian bishops attacking Darwin."

Although Heidensohn's emphasis on "resistance" may be excessive, there is little doubt that, although traditionally written by men and primarily about men and boys, major theoretical works in criminology are alarmingly gender-blind. That is, while men and boys have been seen as the "normal subjects," the gendered content of their legitimate and illegitimate behavior has been virtually ignored. So remarkable has been the gender-blindness of criminology that whenever the high gender ratio of crime is actually considered, criminology has asked "why it is that women do not offend?" (rather than "why do men disproportionately commit crime?"): The result has been a portentious, biologically based, misrepresentation of women (Cain, 1990: 11). In short, women and girls have attracted the attention of crimi-

1

nology only as a special category that allegedly explains the gendered nature of crime.[1]

Feminism challenged the overall masculinist nature of criminology by pointing to the repeated omission and misrepresentation of women in criminological enquiry. The result of this critique has been twofold: increasing attention to women and girls in criminological theory and research and, when criminology speaks of gender, it speaks almost exclusively of women, with little or no attention to the impact of gender on men. Although throughout the history of the discipline a handful of criminologists have addressed the influence of gender on men/ boys and crime, they have consistently employed an antiquated and fallacious "sex-role theory" that evolved in the 1940s with the work of Talcott Parsons. In short, when it comes to men and masculinity, the discipline of criminology is, quite simply, inept. Let us look more closely at my claims.

Gender-Blind Criminology

The well-known conventional criminological theories are glaringly unable to account for the gendered nature of crime. A few examples should suffice.

Robert Merton's (1938) theory of anomie suggests that there is a lack of fit in U.S. society between the culturally defined goals (economic success as measured by monetary rewards) and the socially structured legitimate means (education and paid work) to achieve those goals. In U.S. society, Merton argues, the emphasis is placed on the goals, not the means to attain them, and the legitimate means are not distributed equally in terms of social class. In other words, the "American Dream" urges all U.S. citizens to strive for economic success, while distributing unequally the legitimate opportunities to succeed. This inherent social structural contradiction results, Merton argues, in the adoption of "deviant" and illegitimate means to pursue economic success.

Although Merton's thesis has attracted many to explain the class differences in crime—and it is seen as "perhaps the consummate male theory of deviant behavior" (Smith and Paternoster, 1987: 148)—anomie theory is clearly inadequate for understanding the high gender ratio and gendered character of crime. Given the fact that economic opportunity structures are less open to women, and that women seem to strive for the same goals as men, as Morris (1987: 6–7) shows, if we pursue the logic of Merton's argument, there should actually be more crime by women and less by men! Similarly, Travis Hirschi's (1969) popular "control theory" is incapable of deciphering the gendered nature of crime. Most criminological theories use conformity as the norm and concentrate on explaining criminal behavior. Such theorists ask why people offend, and then proceed to study men and boys as the normal subjects. Hirschi's control theory assumes that crime is normal and it is conformity that is problematic. He differs from traditional criminology by asking why people conform. For Hirschi, humans are by nature amoral, yet their antisocial tendencies can, in fact, be controlled. Society, according to Hirschi, develops ways of controlling its members by inhibiting their "drive" to deviate.

Hirschi identifies four factors as critical to controlling deviation: (1) *attachment* to parents, school, and peers; (2) *commitment* to conventional lines of action; (3) *involvement* in conventional activities; and (4) *belief* in conventional values. To address the gendered nature of crime then, control theory would have to show that women and girls maintain higher levels of commitment to conventional activities, values, and people than do men and boys and, as a result of that commitment, engage in higher levels of legitimate behavior. Hirschi presents no such data.

Interestingly, Hirschi began his research project with a sample of both boys and girls, yet remarkably and without explanation, he rejected girls and concentrated his study on boys. As Ngaire Naffine (1987: 66) points out, it would have made more sense to focus on the girls (and reject the boys) as the obvious substantially more law-abiding gender, especially considering Hirschi's "own argument that criminologists should reorient their thinking by making conformity, rather than criminality, the central object of study." Thus, Hirschi's control theory, as initially conceptualized, is incapable of explaining why men and boys engage in more crime and more serious types of crimes than women and girls.[2]

Consider now labeling theory. Labeling theorists, following Lemert (1967), distinguish between "primary" and "secondary" deviance to understand the process of criminal engagement. Primary deviance entails those pervasive acts that "everybody" engages in but are held to be less significant because they have little impact on an individual's self-image. Primary deviants, in other words, do not consider themselves deviant. Only when societal reactions (i.e., public labeling) to primary deviations occur do individuals evolve a deviant self-image.

Because of continuous labeling, primary deviants eventually accept their labeled identity as a deviant, and henceforth act in accordance with the societal reaction. That is, they are well on their way to a career in secondary deviation.

For labeling theorists, however, acquiring a deviant self-image from labeling is determined by one's power to counteract potential labeling contacts. As Edwin Schur (1979: 276) states, "those with the least power are most susceptible to deviantizing," whereas those with social power are much more able "to avoid initial identification as a deviator, . . . to avoid or reduce stigma even after being so identified," and to "influence the outcome in the course of official 'processing.' "\ Given the fact that men exercise greater power in society than women and following the logic of labeling theory, men should therefore have increased opportunity to counteract official labeling and, as a result, have a lower rate of crime than women.

Correspondingly, conflict theorists, such as Austin Turk (1969: 70), argue that "the greater the power difference in favor of norm enforcers over resisters, the greater the probability of criminalization." Although this is certainly pertinent for class and race, the gender variable causes problems: men clearly exercise greater power than women and are subjected to criminalization more frequently than women.

Finally, there is nothing in other criminological perspectives, including Marxist criminology (as I have shown elsewhere, Messerschmidt, 1986: 1–24), or in the new critical criminologies—such as realism, peacemaking, or postmodernism—that explains why criminal behavior is committed primarily by men and boys (see MacLean and Milovanovic, 1991).[3]

Misrepresenting Women

Notwithstanding the foregoing, the gendered character of crime has not been totally ignored by criminologists. Although criminology has for the most part been gender-blind, the high gender ratio of crime actually has been addressed by some criminologists. Nevertheless, instead of asking how the social construction of masculinity, for example, connects with crime, these theorists generally have asked why is it that women do not offend? Moreover, this question has been asked through an androcentric lens, so that men and boys are the yardstick against which the conduct of women and girls is measured. As Maureen Cain (1990: 2) puts it, "women and girls exist as Other: that is to say, they exist only in their difference from the male, the normal."

What follows is a brief discussion of the work of three past criminologists who addressed the gendered character of crime, Cesare Lombroso, Wilhelm Bonger, and Otto Pollak, and one contemporary theorist, John Hagan, to demonstrate that although their intellectual schemes differ in fundamental ways, it is this very difference that makes what they share more significant. Let us begin with the "father" of criminology, Cesare Lombroso.

Lombroso

The work of Lombroso actually set the stage for asking why it is that women do not offend. Lombroso is well known for his strict biological determinism and, thus, his conception of the born criminal, or individuals whose atavistic qualities indicate a throwback to earlier evolutionary periods.

Lombroso collected anthropometric data on a sample of men in prison and compared them to a control group of soldiers. According to Lombroso, since the group of prisoners had more "atavistic" characteristics than the soldiers—such as "enormous jaws," "high cheek bones," "prominent superciliary arches," and "handle-shaped ears"—criminals could be identified and categorized simply from observing and counting their "degenerative physical stigmata." Criticisms of Lombroso's biological determinism eventually led him to an eclectic conception of causality that included both "atavistic" characteristics and social and environmental conditions (Beirne, 1988).

Lombroso (1911: 181) also recognized that "all statistics show that women are much less criminal than men." He reasoned that this is because of women's special biology. In *The Female Offender*, Lombroso and his son-in-law, William Ferrero (1895: 151), concluded that women's lesser criminality is explained by their "piety, maternity, want of passion, sexual coldness, weakness and an undeveloped intelligence." When women do commit crime, it is of a different type than that of men, likewise because of women's biology (Lombroso, 1911: 184–185):

> That women less often are engaged in highway robbery, murder, homicide, and assault is due to the very nature of the feminine constitution. To conceive an assasination, to make ready for it, to put it into execution demands, in a great number of cases at least, not only physical force, but a certain energy and a certain combination of intellectual functions. In this sort of development women almost always fall short of men. It seems on the other hand that the crimes that are habitual to them are those which

require a smaller degree of physical and intellectual force, and such especially are receipt of stolen goods, poisoning, abortion, and infanticide.

What Lombroso did then was to construct a general theory of crime based on men. Yet eventually he understood that such a theory could not be applied universally to men and women. Consequently, to salvage his theory, Lombroso required an explanation of the gendered nature of crime and rather than investigate the specifics of men, Lombroso scrutinized women, or those who deviated from his general theory (Allen, 1989: 22).

Bonger

A number of criminologists who wrote during this time engaged in a "critique" of Lombroso (see Beirne and Messerschmidt, 1991: 305–311). These criticisms have been catalogued *ad nauseam* elsewhere and are not repeated here. However, socialist criminologists—who have received scant acknowledgment—also wrote during this time and criticized Lombroso. These socialist "criminologists" differed from Lombroso, however, only in their greater attention to economic conditions. Notably, the writings of Filippo Turati, Bruno Battaglia, Napoleone Colajanni, August Bebel, Achille Loria, Paul Lafargue, and Wilhelm Bonger analyzed crime purely in economic terms (Greenberg, 1981; Messerschmidt, 1988).

Arguably the most prominent of these early socialist criminologists was Bonger, who, in *Criminality and Economic Conditions* published in 1905, was one of the few to address the high gender ratio of crime. According to Bonger, by reason of a capitalist economic system "egoism" arises in all members of society; however, certain people in all social classes (the class of criminals) develop a "criminal thought" from this egoism that eventually leads to crime. All forms of criminal activity, such as economic, sexual, political, and pathological crimes, are linked to egoism: self-interest above the interest of others.

Following Marx, Bonger concentrated on the mode of production, arguing that it determines whether or not members of a society will be altruistic or egoistic. It is the capitalist mode of production that "has developed egoism at the expense of altruism" (Bonger, 1916: 40). Thus, for Bonger, capitalism creates egoism, which leads a number of people of all social classes to adopt criminal thoughts and eventually engage in criminality. Bonger assumed that there are criminals and noncriminals, two different classes of behavior, one of which is motivated by "criminal thoughts."

Socialists were the first to introduce the idea that crime under capitalism is, in part, correlated to economic conditions. In so doing, they went significantly beyond biological explanations by attempting to demonstrate the relationship between crime and the social organization of capitalism.

However, in the nineteenth and early twentieth centuries, most socialist writings on crime concentrated on lower working-class criminality. If these socialists who wrote on crime maintained a form of economic determinism, when it came to the question of gender, their attention was, like Lombroso's, clearly directed at women, not men. And women's position was explained, as we will see, through a combination of biological and economic factors. Moreover, in their eagerness to identify the economic forces that encouraged such crimes as prostitution, socialist theorists denied women any role other than that of passive victim. Socialists carried into their theoretical explanations the Victorian image of women as sexual innocents who fell into illicit sex. They assumed, as did other criminologists of the time, that any sex outside marriage was so improper and degrading that no woman could choose prostitution. Socialist emphasis focused on how a capitalist economic system turns "good" women into "bad" women, damaging their prospects for marriage and proper womanhood. This, of course, encompassed a condescending view not only of prostitution, but also of women.

Like Lombroso, Bonger recognized that the gendered nature of crime threatened his class-based theory. Accordingly, Bonger went somewhat beyond other socialists, while simultaneously allying himself with Lombroso by proposing an explanation for why women commit less crime than men. Discussing strength and courage, Bonger (1916: 472) concluded that "the average woman of our time has less strength and courage than the average man, and consequently, commits on the average fewer crimes than he." Moreover, women are not involved in "sexual crimes" because of "the fact that most sexual crimes cannot, from their nature, be committed by women," and "the role of women in sexual life (and thus in the criminal sexual life) is rather passive than active" (p. 473). Bonger failed to offer any reason for women's passivity other than implying an inherent quality; this is also apparent in his portrayal of women as lacking in courage.

Although differing from Lombroso in his closer attention to social conditions, when it came to women's low crime rate, Bonger felt that biology, not capitalism, lay at the base. This biological base, plus their social position in capitalist societies, caused women's low crime rate.[4]

Bonger acknowledged the subordination of women as a contributing factor, yet made it clear that women were not as subordinate as were proletarian men. In fact, Bonger contended that although the consequences of women's social position was in many respects "harmful to the formation of character," these detrimental effects were "probably counterbalanced by those which are favorable," that is, marriage and the family (p. 478). It is this institution that protects women from the outside harmful effects of capitalism. As Bonger (p. 478) states, "her smaller criminality is like the health of a hothouse plant": it is the hothouse that protects her from harmful influences.

Bonger also argues that women engage in less property crime than men because prostitution is more financially rewarding. He finds poverty correlated with involvement in prostitution, simultaneously attributing this form of crime to an "immoral environment." Bonger (p. 329) here is clearly class biased:

> the ranks of prostitutes are in a very large measure recruited from the less well-to-do classes, or where the neglect of children has assumed enormous proportions, and not from the more favored classes where the children are carefully guarded and kept away from unfavorable influences.

Bonger then blames this immoral environment on working-class women. Because working-class women work outside the home in the paid labor market their children become demoralized (p. 318):

> The development of capitalism has led to the paid labor of married women, and consequently to one of the most important causes of the demoralization of the children of the working class. When there is no one to watch a child, when he is left to himself, he becomes demoralized.

Thus, if women were home, where they are supposed to be, children would not become demoralized, and young girls would not become prostitutes. Bonger did not, of course, regard wage labor by men as the onset of the dissolution of the family as the agency of child socialization. He objected to the extraction of mothers/wives from the family context but did not apply the same objections to the extraction of fathers/husbands from that context. For Bonger, then, the gender division of labor is "natural," and the demoralization of children, although connected to capitalism, in the end is partly the fault of women. By working outside the home, women call into question their "natural" place in the division of labor, and in this way help to cause youth crime.

Pollak

In 1950, Otto Pollak (1950) addressed the high gender ratio of crime in a manner significantly different from Lombroso and Bonger. Whereas Lombroso and Bonger argued that women's biology created a "weaker sex" and, therefore, less crime committed by women, Pollak argued that women's crime most likely equals that of men's, but because women's biology interacts with certain social conditions, "the criminality of women is largely masked criminality" (p. 5). This is so for a number of reasons.

First, Pollak felt that women are "addicted" to crimes that are easily concealed, such as shoplifting, thefts by prostitutes, domestic thefts, abortion, and perjury. Consequently, the crimes women commit are more often underreported. Second, women are biologically more deceitful than men and, therefore, more prone to criminal concealment. Pollak (p. 10) states that this "natural" deceit derives from the biological fact that a man "must achieve an erection in order to perform the sex act and will not be able to hide his failure," yet for women:

> lack of orgasm does not prevent her ability to participate in the sex act. It cannot be denied that this basic physiological difference may well have a great influence on the degree of confidence which the two sexes have in the possible success of concealment and thus on their character pattern in this respect.

In addition, Pollak declares that women conceal menstruation every four weeks. Thus, the biology of women and its impact on sexuality and menstruation make "concealment and misrepresentation in the eyes of women socially required and commendable acts, and must condition them to a different attitude toward veracity than men" (p. 10).

Pollak was not, however, only a simple biological determinist. Like Bonger, he linked gender inequality with women's "masked" criminality. As Pollak (pp. 2–3) states, "the lack of social equality between the sexes has led to a cultural distribution of roles which forces women in many cases into the part of instigator rather than of the performer of an overt act." In other words, because of women's social position in society, they are more often accomplices than perpetrators of crime.

Further, Pollak (p. 3) argues that the division of labor places women in the primary role of homemaker and mother, furnishing women "thereby many opportunities to commit crimes in ways and by means which are not available to men and which reduce the public character of many offenses." This social position then helps keep women's crime hidden from public view.

Finally, Pollak maintained that because of gender inequality, women are actually the beneficiaries of "chivalry" on the part of workers in the criminal justice system. This allegedly results in less detection of women's crime (p. 151):

> One of the outstanding concomitants of the existing inequality between the sexes is chivalry and the general protective attitude of man toward women. . . . Men hate to accuse women and thus indirectly to send them to their punishment, police officers dislike to arrest them, district attorneys to prosecute them, judges and juries to find them guilty, and so on.

For Pollak (p. 11), then, this interplay between biological and cultural factors results in a "greater lack of sincerity in women than in men" and the reality that "almost all criminals want to remain undetected, but it seems that women offenders are much better equipped for achieving this goal than are men."

Pollak's thesis has been subject to extensive criticism. For example, Heidensohn (1985: 120) notes that Pollak's "explanation" is ahistorical, unsociological, and "more ideological than empirical." Moreover, Heidensohn (pp. 120–121), Smart (1976: 46–53), and Klein (1973: 25–26), all show how he advances sexist assumptions to underpin a theory of "hidden" crime. In addition to these salient criticisms, a comparison of the work of Lombroso, Bonger, and Pollak shows how criminologists with completely different intellectual agendas unite in a masculine and steadfast scrutiny of women, not men. For these criminologists, women are the Other—those subjected to an exhaustive and all-embracing criminological gaze—while the specifics of men are disregarded. Each, in his own way, contributed to what has become a tradition in criminology: the investigator should inspect and examine women, not men, to explain the high gender ratio in crime (Allen, 1989).

Although I am critical of the masculine nature of Lombroso's, Bonger's, and Pollak's work, my criticisms have been shaped by an historically specific understanding of gender, a perception chiefly derived from aspects of contemporary feminism. Accordingly, there is no assumption here that these criminologists were somehow expected to transcend their time and place. In at least one respect, Bonger and Pollak did surpass others: they recognized gender inequality and attempted to integrate that appreciation into their individual theoretical frameworks. Yet we must concomitantly acknowledge the historical and social context in which they wrote—their sensitivity to and, indeed, particular notion of gender was unmistakably prefeminist. Thus, we should not be surprised at the product of their work: it demonstrates that the kinds of questions asked, the meaning of concepts used, and the ultimate conclusions reached, reflect the social and historical setting in which we all write.

Eventually, more sociological constructs were used to explain women's low crime rate. Yet these were usually related to home and family factors (Smith and Paternoster, 1987: 141). For example, by the 1960s, Ruth Morris (1965: 265) was arguing that girls commit less youth crime than boys because, through socialization, girls are continuously faced with "a much more stringent social disapproval of delinquency than are boys." Consequently, Morris (1964) concluded that when girls do engage in youth crime, they are more likely to come from families that experience social conditions favorable to faulty socialization, such as broken homes, those with family tensions, and those that do not teach proper personal appearance and grooming skills. A more contemporary version of "why women do not offend as much as men," John Hagan's (1989) "Power-Control Theory," follows this sociological tradition of concentrating on women and girls in the family.

Hagan

Hagan argues that in western industrialized societies, an instrument-object relationship exists between parents and children. Parents are the instruments of control and its objects are children, and this relationship shapes the social reproduction of gender. However, these power relationships vary by class and by gender. In particular, as women increasingly enter the labor market, they gain "new power in the family" (p. 156).

Hagan identifies two family structures based on women's participation in the paid labor market, "patriarchal" and "egalitarian." In patriarchal families, the husband/father works outside the home in an authority position and the wife/mother works at home. Patriarchal families, through socialization, "reproduce daughters who focus their futures around domestic labour and consumption, as contrasted with sons who are prepared for participation in direct production" (p. 156). In egalitarian families, the husband/father and wife/mother both work in authority positions outside the home. These egalitarian families "socially reproduce daughters who are prepared along with sons to join the production sphere" (p. 157).

Thus, although in both types of families daughters are less criminal than sons because daughters are more controlled by their mothers, Hagan argues that daughters in patriarchal families are more often taught by parents to avoid risk-taking endeavors, whereas in egalitarian families, both daughters and sons are frequently taught to be more open to risk taking. It is this combination of the instrument-object relationship and corresponding socialization of risk taking that affects delinquency. According to Hagan (p. 158), patriarchal families are characterized by large gender differences in delinquent behavior, while egalitarian families maintain smaller gender differences in delinquency: "daughters become more like sons in their involvement in such forms of risk-taking as delinquency" (p. 158). Thus, following criminological tradition, sons are fundamentally ignored and the gendered nature of crime is explained by a concentration on the characteristics of mothers and daughters.

Hagan should be applauded for integrating some feminist insights into a framework for understanding youth crime by girls and for developing a criminological theory that takes gender seriously as an explanatory variable. Moreover, Hagan's research is important because it demonstrates that gender is constructed differently in diverse settings (e.g., family, social class). Nevertheless, this theory has at least four major difficulties.

First, Hagan assumes that working in an authority position in the paid labor market automatically translates into power and authority in the home. Yet, although economic independence for women is an initial step toward equality, it does not guarantee a reduction in gender power and authority within the home. Indeed, the discussion of wife rape (see Chapter 5), which offers sociological evidence that many victims of this crime hold professional-level jobs, demonstrates that in ignoring the role of gender power within so-called egalitarian families, Hagan's theory betrays a simplistic notion of egalitarianism.

Second, although the biogenic base appears missing, the problem for Hagan, like Lombroso, Bonger, and Pollak, still lies in women. As Meda Chesney-Lind (1989: 20) recently noted, the conclusion of power-control theory is that "mother's liberation causes daughter's crime." In other words, women who defy traditional femininity and work outside the home in the paid-labor market increase the chance their daughters will become delinquent. However, in spite of women's labor force participation rate increasing in the past decade, during the same time the delinquency rate of girls (as measured by both self-reports and official statistics) has remained quite stable (Chesney-Lind, 1989).

Third, a comparison of Hirschi's "control theory" with Hagan's "power-control theory" shows the covert masculine nature of criminological theory. As Ngaire Naffine (1987: 67) has so carefully demonstrated, Hirschi's conforming boy is depicted as "an admirable character; he is an energetic, intelligent and rational being." When we consider the conforming girl in Hagan's theory, however, we find (p. 69):

a grey and lifeless creature. She is passive, compliant and dependent. Gone is Hirschi's rational and responsible agent, intelligently evaluating the risks and costs of crime. Conformity is now described as "compliance." The law-abiding female is biddable rather than responsible. . . . Hagan's female seems unable to construct complex and caring relationships, even with her mother who subjects her to her control. In Hagan's words, she is merely the "object" of her mother's instrumental training to be compliant. Hagan is explicit about the status of the female as a manipulated thing.

In short, Hirschi and Hagan perpetuate what criminology has always done, and that is to devalue women and girls and value men and boys, even when they exhibit the same social behavior.

Finally, empirical tests of power-control theory suggest that it is not a sufficient explanation of the gendered nature of crime (Hill and Atkinson, 1988; Singer and Levine, 1988; Jensen and Thompson, 1990). For example, the most recent test of the theory, by Merry Morash and Meda Chesney-Lind (1991), reports that (1) gender differences in youth crime appear in families regardless of whether or not they are "patriarchal" or "egalitarian"; (2) the quality of the relationship with the mother is very important in explaining low levels of youth crime, particularly for boys; (3) the experience of negative sanctions from the father explains youth crime for both genders; and (4) social class rather than risk taking socialization is a much better predictor of youth crime for both boys and girls.[5]

Thus, we see that when the gendered nature of crime was addressed, criminological attention focused on women and girls. As feminist criminologists have painstakingly shown, this concentration terribly misrepresented women and girls while glorifying men and boys (Smart, 1976; Klein, 1973; Heidensohn, 1985; Naffine, 1987). In addition, this feminist critique of criminology also revealed that the traditional celebration of women's difference from men as the cause of the gendered nature of crime actually concealed criminology's belief in women's inferiority and, therefore, served to reinforce such subordination.

Moreover, women have not simply been misrepresented in criminology's effort to understand the gendered nature of crime, but, for the most part, they have been omitted completely from criminological discourse. As stated earlier, criminology has traditionally been written by men and about men and boys (although not *gendered* men and boys). Not unexpectedly, feminist criminologists subsequently analyzed women's and girls' crime in order to correct the traditional masculine mythologies (Crites, 1976; Bowker, 1978, 1981; Datesman and Scarpitti, 1980; Price and Sokoloff, 1982; Rafter and Stanko, 1982; Miller, 1986; Chesney-Lind and Shelden, 1992). Logically, feminist criminologists rejected well-known, purportedly general and comprehensive criminological theories, as they did not apply to women's and girls' criminality (Leonard, 1982; Naffine, 1987).[6] As Eileen Leonard (1982: 1–2) states:

Theoretical criminology was constructed by men, about men. It is simply not up to the analytical task of explaining female patterns of crime. Although some theories work better than others, they all illustrate what social scientists are slowly recognizing within criminology and outside the field: that our theories are not the general explanations of human behavior they claim to be, but rather particular understandings of male behavior.

Paradoxically, the justification for a special theory of women's and girls' crime rests on the assumption about difference—that women's lives are fundamentally different from men's and that it is precisely this difference that requires illumination.[7] I discuss the idea of difference in relation to theory building and feminism more fully in Chapter 2. For now, let us turn our attention to the criminological focus on "sex roles" and their theoretical relation to crime by men and boys.

Sex Roles, Masculinity, and Gendered Crime

Criminology has been marked by a long history of masculine bias, yet men as men and boys as boys have never been the object of the criminological enterprise. While criminological theory and research have concentrated on men and boys as the normal subjects, the *gendered* man and boy, like women, has been notoriously hidden from criminological history. Moreover, although criminology has failed to explain adequately women's and girls' crime, this does not mean that criminology effectively explains the criminality of men and boys. Indeed, what has not been ignored has been viewed fallaciously.

Following in the footsteps of Lombroso, Bonger, and Pollak, yet beginning to concentrate on men and boys, criminologists have relied ultimately upon an essentialist framework to explain the high rate of crime for men and boys. That is, the presumption has been that a natural distinction exists between men and women. Accordingly, what unites criminologists who focus their specific theoretical attention on men and boys is that their frameworks ultimately ascribe to men certain innate characteristics. These form the basis of gendered social conditions—the "male sex role"—that leads to specific sexed patterns of crime. In other words, biogenic criteria establish differences between men and women and society culturally elaborates the distinctions through the socialization of sex roles. These sex roles, in turn, determine the types and amounts of crime committed by men and women, and by boys and girls. Consider first a few notable prefeminist theorists of this genre.

Sutherland

It was Edwin Sutherland who, in the 1930s, rejected biogenic perspectives on crime by arguing that through interaction and communication within certain intimate personal groups, individuals learn the techniques, motives, drives, rationalizations, and attitudes necessary to commit crime. For Sutherland, criminal behavior is learned in exactly the same way as conforming behavior. Thus, a particular person comes to engage in criminal behavior "because of an excess of definitions favorable to violation of law over definitions unfavorable to violation of law" (Sutherland, 1947: 6).

Differential association is Sutherland's theory of criminal transmission, in which one learns patterns of criminal behavior through social interaction. Individuals become criminal because their association with criminal behavior patterns outweighs their association with noncriminal behavior patterns in terms of frequency, duration, priority, and intensity. Sutherland held that his theory was applicable to all criminal behavior, conventional as well as white collar. Sutherland's theory continues to appeal to criminologists because, among other reasons, it eschews the idea that people commit crime because of biogenic tendencies. Yet, as we will soon see, when it came to gender, differential association was not the complete social theory of crime Sutherland claimed it to be.

In 1942, Sutherland (1942: 19) first recognized the important criminological fact that nothing "is so frequently associated with criminal behavior as being a male." Yet Sutherland (p. 19), although not providing an explanation himself, added that "it is obvious that maleness does not explain criminal behavior." In other words, just as all lower working-class people do not commit crime—and, therefore, a simple causal analysis of poverty is problematic—so, not all men and boys engage in crime, so a causal analysis of "maleness" is problematic.

It was not until 1947 that Sutherland attempted an explanation of why boys engage in crime more often than girls. Anticipating power-control theory, in the fourth edition of *Principles of Criminology*, Sutherland (1947: 100–101) argued that the higher rate of crime for boys can be explained by the differences in care and supervision of boys and girls. As Sutherland (p. 101) asserted, inasmuch as boys and girls live in the same poverty-ridden neighborhoods, social environment does not:

> explain the relatively high rate of boy delinquency and relatively low rate of girl delinquency. The significant difference is that girls are supervised more carefully and the behavior in accordance with social codes taught them with greater care and consistency than is the case with boys. From infancy girls are taught that they must be nice, while boys are taught that they must be rough and tough; a boy who approaches the behavior of girls is regarded as a "sissy." *This difference in care and supervision presumably rested orginally on the fact that the female sex is the one which becomes pregnant.* The personal and familial consequences of illicit pregnancy lead to special protection of the girl not only in respect to sex behavior but in reference to social codes in general (emphasis added).

Thus, boys are more likely to become delinquent because they are not as strictly controlled as girls, and are taught to be "rough and tough." As is self-evident, Sutherland's explanation of boys' delinquency rested on the assumption that socialization is grounded ultimately in biological differences between men and women.

Sutherland's differential association explanation of incest also exhibits his cryptic essentialism. Arguing that fathers who engage in incest with their daughters are concentrated in "families in which mothers have died, are sick, or are for other reasons not available for legitimate sex relations," Sutherland (1944: 33–34) asserted that these men often spend an increased portion of their time in "low resorts" where they "have more contact with various forms of illicit sex behavior, and this may include contact with a pattern of incest." Yet contemporary evidence existed that showed that mothers whose partners were dead or sick or who, for whatever reason, were "not available for sex," almost never engaged in incest (Allen, 1989: 27). Inexplicably, Sutherland failed to address why fathers engage in incest but mothers do not. Despite his explicit sociological perspective in other areas, when it came to gender and sexuality, Sutherland's account is biogenic. As Allen (p. 27) asks:

> Does Sutherland assume, and is the reader to assume, that only men would be expected to have the active response to unchosen celibacy of criminal incest? In the absence of other specification, it appears that Sutherland exhibits here an unexamined, hydraulic and essentialist understanding of male sexuality. Historically this understanding requires, in the shadows, passive, receptive female sexuality. For him, it seems there were no questions to ask about women and incest. Paradoxically, he thereby explored nothing about men and incest.

Parsons

Sutherland's overall emphasis on biologically based sex roles must be understood in the intellectual context of the 1940s, when concepts of sex roles became fashionable in U.S. sociology. It was chiefly the work of Talcott Parsons that popularized this concept, arguing that sex roles link men and women into a conjugal family unit that helps integrate the overall social system. Dichotomous sex roles structure the family: the "instrumental" role involves goal attainment, focusing on the relationship between the family and the wider society; the "expressive" role involves integration, concentrating on the internal structure and functions of the family. Men fulfill the instrumental role; women fulfill the expressive role. In turn, the family unit prepares children for adequate participation in society by teaching them the appropriate sex roles—masculine (instrumental) and feminine (expressive). Thus, when children are socialized into their proper sex role, society remains stable over generations.

Parsons reasons that these dichotomous roles are based in biological reproduction: the fact that women bear and nurse children and men do not. Therefore, women are best fitted to perform expressive roles, whereas men (absent from the reproductive biological functions noted above) are best adapted to instrumental roles. Accordingly, the family is structured in conformity with biological demands, functioning best for society when women's role is "anchored primarily in the internal affairs of the family, as wife, mother and manager of the household," and men's role is "anchored in the occupational world, in his job and through it by his status-giving and income-earning functions for the family" (Parsons and Bales, 1955: 14–15). For Parsons, the relationship between men and women is one of harmony, and the connection between masculine and feminine sex roles is complementary. Thus, it is not surprising that Parsons (p. 103) suggests the "prohibition of homosexuality has the function of reinforcing the differentiation of sex roles" and, therefore, is necessary and functional for society.

Parsons employed his functionalist perspective in the early 1940s to explain the greater delinquency of boys. He (1942: 605) argued that in the family, "girls are more apt to be relatively docile, to conform in general according to adult expectations to be 'good,' whereas boys are more apt to be recalcitrant to discipline and defiant of adult authority and expectations." In the urban family, specifically, because the father is absent most of the time performing his "instrumental role," the mother is the emotionally significant adult, the role model for both boys and girls. For a girl, this is "normal and natural . . . because the functions of the housewife and mother are immediately before her eyes and are tangible and relatively easily understood by a child. Almost as soon as she is physically able, the girl begins a direct apprenticeship in the adult feminine role" (Parsons, 1947: 171). But the boy does not have his father immediately available and, therefore, initially forms a feminine identification with the mother. He soon discovers that women are "inferior to men, that it would hence be shameful for him to grow up to be like a woman" (p. 171). The consequence of this "masculine anxiety" is the engagement of a compensatory "compulsive masculinity." As Parsons (p. 171) states, boys:

> refuse to have anything to do with girls. "Sissy" becomes the worst of all insults. They get interested in athletics and physical prowess, in the things in which men have the most primitive and obvious advantage over women. Furthermore they become allergic to all expression of tender emotion; they must be "tough." This universal pattern bears all the earmarks of a "reaction-formation." It is so conspicuous, not because it is simply "masculine nature" but because it is a defense against a feminine identification.

In short, it is this reaction-formation and resulting compulsive masculinity that creates a "strong tendency for boyish behavior to run in anti-social if not directly destructive directions, in striking contrast to that of . . . girls" (p. 172). Thus, for Parsons, masculinity is something that is internalized in adolescence and, resultingly, boys engage in more delinquency than girls.

Although Parsons' work is seriously flawed, which we will consider further on, it is important because it was the first attempt to connect masculinity with the gendered nature of crime. However, it would take the later work of Albert Cohen for Parsons' perspective to develop into a full-fledged criminological theory.

Cohen

In 1955, Albert Cohen synthesized the respective sex-roles arguments of Sutherland and Parsons into a theoretical formulation for understanding why "gangs" are dominated by boys. In *Delinquent Boys*, Cohen argued that a working-class delinquent subculture arises in reaction to discriminatory middle-class standards. Entering schools where teachers typically evaluate children in accordance with how their behavior approximates middle-class standards, boys socialized in working-class families are relatively unprepared for the challenge. Because working-class boys have internalized middle-class standards, they become "status-frustrated" and are "in the market for a solution" to their problems of adjustment (p. 119). The obvious solution is the collective repudiation of middle-class standards and adoption of their very antithesis—the public display of nonutilitarian, malicious, and negativistic delinquent behavior.

In a section of *Delinquent Boys* headed "What About the Sex Differences?," Cohen (pp. 137–138) revealed his acceptance of Sutherland's and Parsons' idea of dichotomous, biologically based sex roles, by using himself and his wife as examples:

> My skin has nothing of the quality of down or silk, there is nothing limpid or flute-like about my voice, I am a total loss with needle and thread, my posture and carriage are wholly lacking in grace. . . . My wife, on the other hand, is not greatly embarrassed by her inability to tinker with or talk about the internal organs of a car, by her modest attainment in arithmetic or by her inability to lift heavy objects.

Cohen went on to attempt, through a discussion of sex-role socialization, an explanation of why delinquency is dominated by boys. Enthusiastically following Parsons' idea that the actual socialization into the "male sex role" causes a compulsive masculinity, Cohen (p. 164) stated:

> Because of the structure of the modern family and the nature of our occupational system, children of both sexes tend to form early feminine identifications. The boy, however, unlike the girl, comes later under strong social pressure to establish his masculinity, his *difference from* female figures. Because his mother is the object of the feminine identification which he feels is the threat to his status as a male, he tends to react negativistically to those conduct norms which have been associated with mother and therefore have acquired feminine significance. Since mother has been the principal agent of indoctrination of "good," respectable behavior, "goodness" comes to symbolize femininity, and engaging in "bad" behavior acquires the function of denying his femininity and therefore asserting his masculinity. This is the motivation to juvenile delinquency.

Thus, although the nature of "male sex-role" socialization is not a smooth process, the problem of masculine anxiety in the home can be solved simply by joining the gang in the street. For Cohen, gang activity is explicitly masculine in that it emphasizes achievement, exploit, aggressiveness, daring, active mastery, and pursuit. The delinquent gang acts in ways that reflect these aspects of the "male sex role." As Cohen (p. 140) states, the delinquent response "is well within the range of responses that do not threaten his identification of himself as a male." Moreover, Cohen (p. 140) unmistakably applauds masculine behavior of delinquent boys:

> The delinquent is the rogue male. His conduct may be viewed not only negatively, as a device for attacking and derogating the respectable culture; positively it may be viewed as the exploitation of modes of behavior which are traditionally symbolic of untrammeled masculinity, . . . which are not without a certain aura of glamor and romance.

While the most highly "ego-involved region" for the boy is his performance and achievement relative to other boys, the "corresponding highly ego-involved region" for a girl is establishing successful relationships with boys. Arguably then, the delinquent subculture is a "tailor-made" solution primarily to problems of the "male role" but is an inappropriate solution to adjustment problems of the "female role." The latter is so because the delinquent subculture is "irrelevant to the vindication of the girl's status as a girl" and threatens her in that status by reason of its "strongly masculine symbolic function" (pp. 140–144).

Cohen's explanation of the delinquent subculture assumes, then, that it is the by-product of specifically working-class conditions. Yet middle-class boys, Cohen surmises, may at times engage in delinquent behavior. Although middle-class delinquency amounts to "but a fraction of working-class delinquency," Cohen contends that an adequate theory must account for delinquency in both classes (p. 157). Cohen attempts this by arguing that the masculine anxiety (discussed above) that infects the growing boy in both classes is especially accentuated in the middle class. In the middle class, families are small, children are isolated from "street life" generally as well as from adults (other than the parents), and the father is typically working outside the home during most of the boy's waking hours. In working-class families, the father is home more often, engages in distinctively masculine activities that sharply contrast with the feminine activities of the mother, and the boy is accorded greater freedom of movement inside and outside the neighborhood. Cohen argues that the working-class boy has greater daily contact with appropriate masculine role models and, therefore, is more likely to acquire "positive" definitions of masculinity that are not merely negations of femininity. Consequently, Cohen (p. 165) asserts that the working-class boy has "a richer and more positive conception of the meaning of masculinity than the mere antithesis of 'goodness,' and . . . is not so likely to resort to 'badness' simply as a device to prove to himself and the world that he is really masculine."

It is middle-class boy delinquency that stems from "an attempt to cope with a basic anxiety in the area of *sex-role* identification," whereas the motivation for working-class boy delinquency is adjusting to problems created by his *class* position (p. 168). The masculine nature of delinquency identified earlier by Cohen now becomes simply an attractive supplementary feature of the subculture of working-class boys and, inasmuch as Cohen believed that the vast majority of delinquency is committed by working-class boys, class conflict becomes the "real motor" for the delinquent subculture and gender is drained of any "analytical force, demoting it to a merely descriptive place" (Allen, 1989: 29). Thus, Cohen failed successfully to account for the gendered character of crime.

Sutherland, Parsons, and Cohen have been praised by many for allegedly rejecting biogenic, and firmly asserting sociogenic, perspectives on crime. But such praise is only partially deserved. When addressing the question of gender, biology clearly crept into each of their theories. In comparing Sutherland, Parsons, and Cohen with Lombroso, then, when it comes to gender, Matza (1969: 90) was correct when he stated that while "Lombroso said bodily constitution and to his close or careful readers muttered something about social conditions; nowadays, we say social conditions and to our close and careful readers mutter something about organic conditions."

Nevertheless, Sutherland, Parsons, and Cohen can be credited for putting masculinity on the criminological agenda. These theorists perceived the theoretical importance of the gendered nature of crime and acted upon that awareness. Yet their conclusions demonstrate the limitations one would expect from any prefeminist work. Indeed, essentialism was the accepted doctrine of the day and it took modern feminism to dismantle that powerful "commonsense" understanding of gender. Rather than being gender-blind, then, Sutherland, Parsons, and Cohen simply had a different conception of gender than exists among many social scientists today. The social and historical context in which they wrote embodied (1) a relative absence of feminist theorizing and politics and (2) an assumed "natural" difference between men and women. Accordingly, it should not be surprising that they wrote the type of theories they did—theories that ultimately helped reconstitute traditional hegemonic masculinity.

Wilson and Herrnstein

A contemporary version of the foregoing that does not simply mutter but vociferously clamors organic conditions, surfaced in the work of James Q. Wilson and Richard J. Herrnstein (1985), who argue that the gender ratio in crime can be explained by biological sex differences in aggression. Although aggression for these authors is often situationally controlled and the forms it takes are learned, Wilson and Herrnstein (1985: 121) assert that "the durability, universality and generality of the relative aggressiveness of males" explains their greater involvement in crime. For Wilson and Herrnstein, biology establishes a certain difference, but social conditions culturally fashion this basic distinction between the sexes. In this way, biological differences are amplified by the culture into socially constructed sex roles. As Wilson and Herrnstein (p. 119) state, boys and girls "start off on slightly different paths, and the biological and cultural forces that guide them thereafter produce the divergences we recognize as sex roles. The universality of a gender difference in early childhood points toward an in born sex difference."|

Wilson and Herrnstein differ from Sutherland, Parsons, and Cohen only in their explicit emphasis on biology. While Sutherland, Parsons, and Cohen surreptitiously assume a biological sex difference, Wilson and Herrnstein overtly attempt to prove one. To the important question "Why do men and boys dominate in the commission of crime?," Wilson and Herrnstein (p. 124) reply that their "best *guess* centers on the difference in aggression and perhaps other primary drives that flow into the definition of sex roles" (emphasis added). An aggressive culture, they say, embellishes a biological difference in aggression, which then leads to more crime by men and boys.

Steffensmeier and Allan

Liberal feminism, which emerged in the United States in the late 1960s and found political expression primarily in the National Organization for Women, centers its analysis of gender inequality on a sex-role perspective. Following the lead of the civil rights movement, the liberal feminist perspective identified as its major goal the extension of equal rights to women. According to liberal feminism, women are discriminated against on the basis of sex and, therefore, are deprived of the same opportunities as men and kept outside the mainstream of society (politics, business, finance, medicine, law, and so forth). Consequently, if "the problem is that women are in some sense 'out,' then it can be solved by letting them 'in' " (Ehrenreich and English, 1978: 19). The goal of liberal feminism is to remove sexist stereotypes promoted through sex-role socialization in the family, school, media, and state and, therefore, clear the way for "women's rapid integration into what has been the world of men" (p. 19).

In a recent discussion of gender and crime, Darrell Steffensmeier and Emilie Allan (1991) provide a contemporary liberal feminist position on gender differences in crime. First, Steffensmeier and Allan differ from Sutherland, Parsons, Cohen, and Wilson and Herrnstein, in recognizing the existence of gender inequality in society. They argue that this inequality (1) requires that women conform to "their assigned role as wives and mothers," (2) "produces no acceptable deviant roles for women comparable to those for romanticized 'rogue' males," and (3) "makes deviant labels for women—witch, whore, kleptomaniac—more stigmatizing than the labels typically applied to deviant men" (p. 73).

However, when it comes to men's overinvolvement in crime, Steffensmeier and Allan (p. 74) echo the essentialist tradition outlined earlier:

> Research indicates that aggressiveness has been found to covary consistently with male crime, and this trait is stronger among males than among females for reasons that are not altogether explained by culture. More importantly, perhaps, the universal observation that males are naturally stronger and more aggressive, coupled with a strong cultural emphasis on male violence in this country, generates both expectations and rewards that increase the likelihood both of male involvement in aggressive behavior and of defining male behavior as aggressive.

Thus, biology plus "gender norms" (their term) equals more crime by men.

For Steffensmeier and Allan, the adoption of masculine gender norms is a smooth and untroubled process; gone are the turbulent practices resulting from father-absence found in the work of Parsons and Cohen. Crime by men and boys is now simply an extension of biologically based gender norms, rather than the psychoanalytic consequences of functionalist socialization itself. In contrast to "male gender norms," feminine qualities, such as "warmth, nurturance, supportiveness, weakness, gentility, talking and acting 'like a lady,' self-effacement, and deference to the wants and needs of others . . . are basically incompatible with the qualities valued in the criminal underworld" (pp. 72–73).

Moreover, the " 'ethic of care' presupposes nonviolence, and suggests that serious predatory crime is outside women's moral boundaries" (p. 73). Accordingly, at base, men are the biological bad species and women the biological good species, a formula ultimately held to explain the gender ratio of crime. Finally, gender norms result in women's greater supervision in society and limited access to criminal opportunities, both of which inhibit criminality.

Liberal feminism, then, is progressive in a limited sense: there is at least an acknowledgment of gender inequality and an accompanying conditional focus on the social dimensions of behavior—that gendered behavior is learned through interaction in an unequal culture. In addition, the theoretical conceptualization of sex roles does present an opportunity for a politics of reform. Liberal feminists are persuasive when they argue (1) that sexist stereotypes are pervasive throughout social institutions in western industrialized societies, (2) that stereotypes of masculinity and femininity are socially constructed cultural ideals of inequality and, (3) that by attacking these ideals we contribute to social change. Consequently, liberal feminism is a major advance over previous sex-role perspectives, such as those expounded by Sutherland, Parsons, and Cohen.

Problems with Sex-Role Theory

Nevertheless, there are serious problems with sex-role theory as theory. Consider briefly certain of the problems associated with this theoretical perspective as identified by a wide range of scholars (Shover and Norland, 1978; Lopata and Thorne, 1978; Edwards, 1983; Connell, 1987; West and Zimmerman, 1987; Andersen, 1988).

Biological Reductionism

The idea that men are naturally aggressive is fundamentally wrong. Extensive examinations of hormonal, ethological, and anthropological studies of differences in gender aggression "do not suggest any compelling reason to accept the notion of a biological basis of aggressiveness" (Tieger, 1980: 957). Indeed, as Janet Katz and William Chambliss (1991: 270) conclude in their extensive examination of research on the topic of biology and crime:

> An individual learns to be aggressive in the same manner that he or she learns to inhibit aggression. One is not a natural state, and the other culturally imposed; both are within our biological potential. . . . Violence, sexism and racism are biological only in the sense that they are within the range of possible human attitudes and behaviors. But non-violence, equality and justice are also biologically possible.

Additionally, as Shover and Norland (1978: 1115) have shown, criminologists bring to their work on gender differences in crime a set of gendered stereotypes and then proceed to discern empirical patterns and construct theoretical explanations consistent with their beliefs. All of the featured sex-role theorists assume *ab initio* that there exist only two sexes (male and female) and, therefore, two sex roles (masculine and feminine). This assumption is grounded in a specific cultural framework that views gender as strictly dichotomous and unchanging. In their critique of research on biology and gender, for example, Suzanne Kessler and Wendy McKenna (1978) reported that as natural scientists engage in the social practice of biological research, they always begin with a conception of "man" and "woman."

Likewise, social scientists, including the above criminologists, begin with the assumption that there are only two sexes, and then proceed to find evidence supporting that assumption. Criminologists have addressed the problem of the gendered nature of crime through a theoretical lens that assumes that sex is exclusively dichotomous when no such dichotomy holds biologically or cross-culturally. For example, chromosomes are seen as an important biological criterion for determining sex. If there is at least one Y chromosome, the individual is "male," if there are no Y chromosomes, the individual is "female." Yet as Kessler and McKenna (p. 52) demonstrate, there exist people who are genetic mosaics (individuals with XXY chromosomes, for instance), so what is their sex? Chromosomal testing in the Olympic games provides the answer: all mosaics are declared men and may only participate in "male" events (pp. 52–54)! Indeed, as Anthony Giddens (1989: 286) points out, "there is not a single physical characteristic, or even combination of physical characteristics, which cleanly and completely separates 'women' from 'men'," yet biological criteria are socially constructed so as to buttress the sex dichotomy.

Regarding cross-culturally, anthropological evidence reveals that not only do men and women in other societies behave differently from men and women in U.S. society—and manage to retain their societal identities as men and women—but sex is not always dichotomous and not always assigned on biological criteria. Whereas in western industrialized societies the ultimate criteria for sex assignment is specifically *genitalia*, in several other societies it is strictly *social activities*. Martin and Voorhies (1975), for example, found that certain societies recognize more than two sex statuses and that in these societies, sex is not assigned on the basis of physical criteria (e.g., genitalia). Indeed, the Cheyenne *berdache* (Williams, 1986), the *xanith* of the Omani Muslims (Wikan, 1984), and the Tahitian *mahu* (Gilmore, 1990) are all examples of a third type of sex, which operates outside the westernized "male/female" dichotomy.

Societies, then, culturally construct varying definitions of sex and, therefore, gender does not naturally develop from biology. Bob Connell (1987: 76) nicely summarizes this view:

> Our conception of what is natural and what natural differences consist of, is itself a cultural construct, part of our specific way of thinking about gender. Gender is . . . a practical accomplishment—something accomplished by social practice. (We might add, not a completely consistent one.) This is not a matter of some bias or error in our ideas that might in

principle be corrected by future biological research. It is a fundamental feature of the way we have knowledge of human beings.

Consequently, both gender and crime are *social* phenomena.[8]

Distorting Gender Variability

Following from the last point, sex-role theory creates an artificial polarization, thereby distorting actual variability in gender constructions and reducing all masculinities and femininities to one normative standard case for each—the "male sex role" and the "female sex role." A helpful and clear example of viewing masculinity and crime through the perspective of the normative standard case is provided by Oakley (1972: 72):

> Criminality and masculinity are linked because the sort of acts associated with each have much in common. The demonstration of physical strength, a certain kind of aggressiveness, visible and external proof of achievement, whether legal or illegal—these are facets of the ideal male personality and also much of criminal behavior. Both male and criminal are valued by their peers for these qualities. Thus, the dividing line between what is masculine and what is criminal may at times be a thin one.

Oakley's argument is not necessarily incorrect; it is clear that criminal behavior (as argued in Chapters 3, 4, and 5) may indeed serve as a resource for constructing a particular type of masculinity. But there is a problem with Oakley's concentration on an alleged, single "male personality," which expeditiously explains away real variations in the social construction of masculinity. Sex-role theory concentrates on the differences between men and women, ignoring the fact that men and boys construct masculinity differently. Not only is there variability cross-culturally, but within each particular society, masculinity is constructed differently by class, race, age, and particular social situation, such as the school, peer group, family, and workplace. The variations in the construction of masculinity among men and boys are crucial to understanding the different types and amounts of crime among men. Sex-role theory requires that we examine masculinity and ignore *masculinities*: the way men and boys construct masculinity differently.

Ignoring Social Action

Sex-role theory describes men and women simply as "passive vessels into whom a variety of expectations are poured" (Andersen, 1988:

97). In sex-role theory, individuals display little if any creativity; their actions, including crime, are simply the result of their sex role. For sex-role theory, gender is simply internalized and becomes resolute and unvarying (usually by around age three to five). This ignores the fact that men and women are active agents in their social relations, and fails to account for the intentions of social actors and how social action is a meaningful construction in itself. As West and Zimmerman (1987: 127) put it, sex-role theory "obscures the work that is involved in producing gender in everyday activities." Gender is not simply shaped and established beforehand, it is accomplished through social action. Indeed, as shown in Chapters 3, 4, and 5, men and boys actively negotiate specific types of masculinity out of the social settings—and subsequent resources at their disposal—in which they find themselves.

The Question of Structure and Power

Sex-role theory fails to situate sex roles within a structural explanation of their origin. As noted, where *social* structure is missing, *biological* structure is present. Indeed, the terms " 'female role' and 'male role,' hitching a biological term to a dramaturgical one, suggest what is going on. The underlying image is an invariant biological base and a malleable social superstructure" (Connell, 1987: 50). Thus, sex-role theory eschews any social structural origins of gendered individuals and, therefore, a true sociology of masculinity and crime is lost.

Following logically from this premise, the concept sex roles masks questions of institutional and structural power processes that occur within gender relations (Carrigan, Connell, and Lee, 1987: 144). The discussion invariably centers on gender differences, rather than gender relations. In such an analysis, there is little room for tension, conflict, and power. As Veronica Beechy (1978: 165) argues, "sex role theory necessarily excludes the possibility of any analysis of the sources of social inequality." And Lopata and Thorne (1978: 719) point out that " 'sex roles' suggest a 'separate but equal' sort of conceptualization, perhaps one reason 'race roles' and 'class roles' never entered sociological discourse." However, in addition to excluding an analysis of structured inequality between men and women, sex-role theory ignores power relations among men. Clearly, certain men (in terms of class, race, and sexual preference, for example) possess greater power than other men.

Because the sex-role perspective neglects any understanding of the institutional and structural basis of gender inequality, it assumes (when interested) that simply rejecting sex roles will bring about social change (Andersen, 1988: 97). The political undertaking of liberal feminism does just this, concentrating on role change and women's rights rather than challenging power and women's liberation.

For all these reasons, then, we must reject sex-role theory as unsuitable to our task at hand. It appears that criminology is, when it comes to *the strongest predictor of criminal involvement*, an inept discipline. In order to comprehend what it is about men as men and boys as boys that impels them to commit more crime and more serious types of crime than women and girls—as well as different types and amounts among themselves—we need first a theoretical grasp of social structure and gendered power. In view of the fact that radical and socialist feminism place gendered structure and power at the forefront of their theoretical endeavors, they are the subject of Chapter 2.

Chapter 2

Rethinking Feminist Theory

The second wave of the U.S. feminist movement evolved from the civil rights and new left movements of the 1960s.[1] These latter movements illuminated the class and race inequalities in U.S. society, but ignored gender. Indeed, most women involved in both movements found themselves in auxiliary roles (for example, performing clerical work) rather than planning strategies, delivering speeches, and making movement decisions (Philipson and Hansen, 1990: 5). As a result, significant numbers of women discontinued new left and civil rights activities to direct their political experience into women-only groups. By the late 1960s, feminism in the United States had become a full-fledged movement, with a multiplicity of "organizations, local consciousness-raising groups, and political strategies intended to advocate transformations in women's status in society" (Andersen, 1988: 295).

In addition to liberal feminism (discussed in Chapter 1), radical and socialist feminism developed from this movement. Because liberal feminists concentrated on women's rights (rather than women's liberation) and limited their analysis for change to equal opportunity and role transformation, these more thoroughgoing feminist perspectives developed to explain masculine dominance in U.S. society. Radical and socialist feminism provide the overall ambiance and intellectual context for the contemporary study of men and masculinity. Indeed, the current interest by men in masculinity is indebted to many of the insights emanating from these two feminist perspectives.[2] Any attempt to understand masculinity and crime, then, must begin with a comradely scrutiny of the specific theoretical positions of radical and socialist feminism on men, masculine dominance, and crime.

Let us begin with radical feminism, a perspective that does not address the gender ratio of crime but, rather, concentrates on violence against women.

31

Radical Feminism

In the history of social thought, it is radical feminism that first brought into focus what had previously been ignored, namely, the nature of power in gender relations. The goal of radical feminism is to understand this masculine dominance and to develop appropriate strategies for its elimination. Radical feminism views masculine power and privilege—patriarchy—as the root cause of all forms of inequality; patriarchy is primary, all other social relations (such as class and race) derive from relations between men and women. For radical feminists, women were, historically, the first oppressed group. Moreover, women's oppression is the most widespread—existing in every known society—and women's oppression is the deepest form of oppression. According to radical feminism, history is an everchanging struggle of men for power and domination over women, this being the dialectic of sex (Firestone, 1970).

Radical feminism made distinctive and original contributions to feminist theory, yet was eventually eclipsed in the United States by what has become known as "cultural feminism." Let us look first at the development of radical feminism.

From Sex Roles to Biological Reductionism

Kate Millett's *Sexual Politics* (1970) is a classic radical feminist text of second-wave feminism. Millett was the first to reconceptualize the concept of "patriarchy" by arguing that patriarchy did not dissolve with the emergence of a market economy, as Max Weber (1978) and other social theorists maintained.[3] On the contrary, patriarchy is (Millett, 1970: 25):

> sturdier than any form of segregation, and more rigorous than class stratification, more uniform, certainly more enduring. However muted its present appearance may be, sexual domination obtains nevertheless as perhaps the most pervasive ideology of our culture and provides its most fundamental concept of power.

Millett (p. 25) continued: "Our society, like all other historical civilizations, is a patriarchy," a form of societal organization whereby "that half of the populace which is female is controlled by that half which is male." For Millett, patriarchy is a universal phenomenon, and every avenue of power within contemporary society—the military, the economy, the educational system, the state, and so on—is seen as entirely under the control of men. In short, masculine domination permeates the entire society and patriarchy is the social structural base of all power relations—racial, political, and economic.

Moreover, not only does patriarchy manifest itself throughout society as a whole, argued Millett, but the family is the chief institution of patriarchy. Through sex-role socialization, the family encourages its own members to adjust and conform to patriarchal ideologies and practices. Human personality is formed along the lines of masculine and feminine, lines that entail an elaborate, dichotomous, and oppressive code of conduct in which men are viewed as possessing superiority and, accordingly, are allocated public and private power. As Millett (p. 26) points out further, the creation of "core gender identities" is:

based on the needs and values of the dominant group and dictated by what its members cherish in themselves and find convenient in subordinates: aggression, intelligence, force, and efficacy in the male; passivity, ignorance, docility, "virtue," and ineffectuality in the female. . . . In terms of activity, sex role assigns domestic service and attendance upon infants to the female, the rest of human achievement, interest, and ambition to the male.

Millett rejected the biological reductionism of the sex-role theorists discussed in Chapter 1, and argued that men and women are trained to accept a social system that is divided into "male" and "female" spheres, encompassing unequal power relations.

Power in the private realm was emphasized by Millett because, for her, the foundation of patriarchy is the private and interpersonal power by which men dominate women. Whereas all social analyses had concentrated on the public nature of power in terms of class, caste, and status, Millett argued that personal relations between men and women were soundly political, based on domination and subordination. However, domination by men is not enforced by naked violence, but occurs through sex-role socialization and the personal nature of gendered power in the home. Indeed, it was radical feminists who popularized the new left slogan that "the personal is political," the idea that there exists a political dimension to personal life. Inasmuch as inequality is institutionalized throughout society, sex role socialization occurs in all "walks of life."

Classic radical feminist works, such as Millett's, did not afford violence by men a central place in their theories of masculine dominance. Early radical feminists argued that the normal functioning of masculine-dominated institutions sufficed to maintain the social control of women and to reproduce patriarchy. Nevertheless, Millett did point out that control in patriarchal society would be imperfect and even inoperable without the rule of force. Thus, in patriarchal society men were perceived by Millett as being equipped psychologically and technically to perpetrate physical violence against women, if necessary, to maintain their control. For Millett, men have historically used a variety of culturally specific methods to preserve their patriarchal power, such as Indian *suttee*, Chinese footbinding, the Islamic veil, African clitoridectomy, and rape and wife beating worldwide.

Millett's argument that patriarchy (and its accompanying forms of violence) is a cultural phenomenon, reproduced through socialization, had widespread support in the early 1970s. For example, Bonnie Kreps (1973: 236), writing in the popular anthology *Radical Feminism*, argued that modern patriarchy is based on "strictly enforced sex roles." For Kreps, certain roles are ascribed purely on the basis of sex: boys are socialized to be rough, tough, and aggressive; girls are trained to become timid and docile. Thus, patriarchy is founded on "the corrupt notion of 'maleness vs. femaleness,'" and "the oppression of women is based on this very notion and its attendant institutions" (p. 239).

In addition to patriarchal-based sex-role socialization, in the early 1970s, many radical feminists also argued that in patriarchal society sexuality is socially constructed in men's interests, thereby hindering further women's assertion of their own sexual needs. For example, Anne Koedt's (1973: 199) influencial article, "The Myth of the Vaginal Orgasm," argued that although orgasm originates in the clitoris, women have "been fed a myth of the liberated woman and her vaginal orgasm" because "women have been defined sexually in terms of what pleases men." Koedt advised women to redefine their sexuality by discarding "the 'normal' concepts of sex and create new guidelines which take into account mutual sexual enjoyment" (p. 199). Early on, then, radical feminists were reappraising women's sexual pleasure by rejecting the double standard that denied sexual assertiveness in women while celebrating it in men. The subjects of sexual pleasure and sexual assertiveness were at the heart of the radical feminist critique of "normal" heterosexual practice in the early 1970s (Segal, 1988: 80).

In addition to sexual assertiveness and sexual pleasure, sexual danger was specifically addressed by early radical feminists. However, as the discussion of Millett's work indicates, sexual danger was not central to radical feminist theory. Indeed, radical feminists limited their interest in sexual danger to examining particular forms of violence against women (Edwards, 1987: 18).

Susan Griffin's (1971) classic piece, "Rape: The All-American Crime," has been one of the most frequently cited and reprinted articles in the history of literature on violence against women, and is representative of radical feminist thinking on sexual danger during the early 1970s. Griffin systematically refuted several long-standing myths about rape, and argued that rape is inseparable from patriarchal society. Following Millett, Griffin maintained that patriarchy is based on a socially constructed hierarchy in which men dominate women and, as such, rape is neither "natural male behavior" nor universal to the human species. Rather, it is learned in patriarchal society, a culture that nurtures aggression from men and passivity from women. Moreover, because U.S. culture connects sexuality with violence, it is not illogical, Griffin went on, that rape should be quite prevalent in patriarchal society. For Griffin, rape and "normal masculinity" had elements in common, notably, an emphasis on aggression and sexual conquest. Nevertheless, for Griffin (p. 35) rape is primarily an act of violence:

> Rape is an act of aggression in which the victim is denied her self-determination. It is an act of violence which, if not actually followed by beatings or murder, nevertheless always carries with it the threat of death. And finally, rape is a form of mass terrorism, for the victims of rape are chosen indiscriminately, but the propagandists for male supremacy broadcast that it is women who cause rape by being unchaste or in the wrong place at the wrong time—in essence, by behaving as though they were free.

Griffin agreed with Millett that rape serves as an ultimate means of social control in patriarchal society, by severely limiting women's freedom and forcing women to depend on men. For Griffin, it is not necessarily the act itself, but the fear of rape that controls women: "The fear of rape keeps women off the streets at night. Keeps women at home. Keeps women passive and modest for fear that they be thought provocative" (p. 35). Finally, Griffin (p. 35) contended that "rape is not an isolated act that can be rooted out from patriarchy without ending patriarchy itself. . . . No simple reforms can eliminate rape." Thus, the views of Millett and Griffin were similar in the sense that they saw masculine dominance, power, and violence as social (not as biological) phenomena reproduced through cultural practices and processes, and the emphasis was on the similarities among men and between men and the institutions of patriarchal society; namely, masculine ideals.

By the mid-1970s, however, the radical feminist emphasis on the social nature of patriarchy and the learning of gender, sexuality, and violence was considered an unsatisfactory idealist explanation of masculine dominance and radical feminists began to search for root causes of patriarchy (Jaggar, 1983: 87). In the mid-1970s, the materialist alternative of biological reductionism became fashionable in much radical feminist thought (Eisenstein, 1983).

Susan Brownmiller (1975) was in the forefront of adding this new twist to radical feminist theory. In *Against Our Will: Men, Women and Rape*, Brownmiller advanced the idea that rape is the actual foundation of patriarchy and, therefore, propagates gender inequality by viciously subordinating women to men and limiting, indeed policing, women's social behavior. For Brownmiller, rape is not a sociological question, but a biological one. Because humans enjoy a unique form of sexuality not based entirely on reproduction, the sexual urge can occur virtually at any time, and not simply in response to a reproductive cycle. Consequently (p. 13):

> without a biologically determined mating season a human male can evince sexual interest in a human female at any time he pleases, and his psychologic urge is not dependent in the slightest on her biologic readiness or receptivity. What it all boils down to is that the human male can rape.

In addition to the unique nature of human sexuality, human anatomy also plays a critical and determinant role in rape. Brownmiller (p. 14) contends that had it not been for an accident of biology, "an accommodation requiring the locking together of two separate parts, penis into vagina, there would be neither copulation nor rape as we know it." Finally, because men are superior in terms of raw physical strength, they make use of this physical ability to overcome their biological sexual urge. It is the combination of this biological and physical capacity to rape that leads men to construct an "ideology of rape." In short (p. 14), "when men discovered that they could rape, they proceeded to do it."

This ability and resulting ideology to rape became simultaneously the mechanism of controlling women and a weapon of force against them. From prehistoric times to the present, rape, acccording to Brownmiller (p. 15), has played a crucial role in gender relations: "It is nothing more or less than a conscious process of intimidation by which *all men* keep *all women* in a state of fear." The fear created by rape has, according to Brownmiller, acted historically and cross-culturally as a means of social control. For Brownmiller, although all men are potential rapists, all men need not engage in rape for patriarchy to be sustained. The men who do rape provide the necessary means for maintaining patriarchy. Indeed, Brownmiller (p. 209) concludes that on the shoulders of rapists "there rests an age-old burden that amounts to an historic mission: the perpetuation of male domination over women by force." Rapists are seen by Brownmiller as the "front-line shock troops . . . in the longest sustained battle the world has ever known" (p. 209). Rape is the political weapon that sustains the subordination of women.

Following Griffin, Brownmiller (p. 423, 424, 439) argued that rape is an act of violence, "a hit-and-run attack, a brief expression of physical power, a conscious process of intimidation, a blunt, ugly sexual invasion" and a "deliberate, hostile, violent act of degradation and possession on the part of a would-be conqueror, designed to intimidate and inspire fear." In short, it was Brownmiller who popularized the idea that "rape is violence, not sex."

Brownmiller's theory differs from that of Millett, Griffin, and other early 1970s radical feminists in the sense that patriarchy is not a sociological phenomenon, but rather is founded in men's alleged biological ability and resulting ideology to rape. Moreover, Brownmiller argued that because rape and women's subordination seemed to exist in every known society, patriarchy is a universal system that stems from biological causes and, thus, "male" and "female" are no longer social categories constructed through socialization.

Brownmiller differs from earlier radical feminists in yet another important way: in her work, violence against women (rape) was seen, for the first time, as central to radical feminist theorizing. It was now clearly asserted by radical feminists that *violence against women is the foundation of patriarchy* and, therefore, sexual danger replaced sexual pleasure as central components of radical feminist thought.

Despite such differences, Millett, Griffin, and Brownmiller show similar views in the sense that men and women are depicted as distinctly different from each other. For Millett and Griffin, a masculine-dominated culture teaches women to be inferior to men and, therefore, limits women's potentialities, provides men with a broad range of opportunities that women do not enjoy, and trains men to exert power through physical force. For Brownmiller, it is biological conditions—and a resulting ideology of rape—that creates differences between men and women and, therefore, perpetuates masculine power, women's powerlessness, and violence against women.

Although these differences between women and men cause gender inequality, it does not necessarily follow that patriarchy is inevitable. Most early radical feminists argued that gender inequality could be neutralized by eliminating the differences between men and women. Gender polarization was to be replaced by a form of androgyny. In the anthology *Radical Feminism*, Joreen (1973: 52) defines the androgynous woman as one who:

> violates conceptions of proper sex role behavior and . . . incorporates within herself qualities traditionally defined as "masculine" as well as "feminine". . . . She has no liking for the indirect, subtle, mysterious ways of the "eternal feminine." She disdains the vicarious life deemed natural to women because she wants to live a life of her own.

For Joreen and others, if patriarchy and violence against women were to end, men and women could no longer be "masculine" and "feminine." Direct struggle against masculine dominance in both the public and private realms was deemed a necessity by early radical feminists in order to overcome women's subordination. Because the differences between men and women had been artifically exaggerated, which meant continued inequality and oppression for women, radical feminists argued that such differences should be minimized and eventually eliminated (Eisenstein, 1983). Indeed, Brownmiller (1975: 452) argued that the "ideology of rape" could be overcome through, for example, the enacting of criminal laws reflecting women's interests, the founding of rape crisis centers, the organizing of feminist groups against rape, and women generally challenging their traditional socialization "to cry, to wheedle, to plead, to look for a male protector." According to Brownmiller, even though men and women are biologically "male" and "female," masculinity and femininity as we know them must change. Accordingly, women must fight back on a multiplicity of levels to redress the gender imbalance and rid themselves and men of "the ideology of rape" (p. 454). Thus, for radical feminists, to eliminate masculine dominance, patriarchal sex roles had to be eradicated and a new society that emphasized androgyny created.

The Violent Heterosexual Male

Throughout the latter half of the 1970s, radical feminists increasingly concentrated on analyzing discrete types of violence against women: rape (Russell, 1975; Clark and Lewis, 1977), wife beating (Dobash and Dobash, 1979), and sexual harassment (MacKinnon, 1979). This literature successfully demonstrated that violence against women is widespread and omnipresent in Western industrialized societies, and it indicated a "seemingly boundless landscape of cultural misogyny" (Segal, 1990: 207).

Simultaneously, certain radical feminists began to assert that the ideal of androgyny was a myth. For example, Mary Daly (1975: 30) stated as early as 1975 that androgyny suggests "two distorted halves of a human being stuck together—something like John Wayne and Brigitte Bardot scotch-taped together—as if two distorted 'halves' could make a whole." Because of this "mythical ideal" of androgyny, rather than challenging patriarchy directly (which would prove ineffective), it was now argued by other radical feminists that women's liberation could actually be achieved under patriarchy by developing and preserving a "female counter culture"—*cultural feminism* was born.

In traditional social thought—including criminology, as discussed in Chapter 1—women were the Other, the different, inferior, and deviant species. For many radical feminists of the late 1970s (and throughout the 1980s), "femaleness" was increasingly theorized as normative, and "maleness," the Other. Rather than viewing women's difference from men as a source of their subordination (as did Millett, Griffin, and Brownmiller), cultural feminists began considering these differences a source of pride and a reason for confidence. Eventually, this position led to a celebration of an alleged essential "femaleness" and a denunciation of an avowed essential "maleness." For such cultural feminist theorists as Mary Daly, Robin Morgan, Andrea Dworkin, and Catharine MacKinnon, everything—from the workplace to the bedroom—that is "female" is good and everything "male" is bad (Echols, 1989; Eisenstein, 1983).

Given the early history of radical feminism, the foregoing development of cultural feminism should not be that surprising. The divorce from the new left and civil rights movements, the subsequent subordination of class and race to gender in radical feminist theory, the move to biological reductionism, the documented pervasiveness of violence against women, and the critique of androgyny all played important roles in the evolving nature of radical feminist theory. Alison Jaggar (1983: 94) in discussing violence against women, reasons that the "recognition that women live continually under the threat of physical violence from men has led many radical feminists to the conviction that men are dangerously different from women and that this difference is grounded in male biology." Indeed, Adrienne Rich (1976: 39, 72) argued that there are superior powers inherent in women that do not exist in men and, consequently, these powers bond women with the "natural order"; women's special powers associate her "more deeply than man with natural cycles and processes."

Two years later in *Gyn/Ecology*, Mary Daly (1978) maintained that the foundation of patriarchy is "sado-rituals," or crimes by men against women. Daly analyzed Indian *suttee*, Chinese footbinding, African genital mutilation, British witch burning, and U.S. gynecology, concluding that these are all a "re-enactment of goddess murder" and the means by which men maintain a worldwide patriarchal system. Mary Daly and Adrienne Rich both distinquish clear essential differences between men and women, in which women are entirely pure while men are exclusively evil; "maleness" is not only dangerous but inferior to "femaleness." As Hester Eisenstein (1983: 112) states, for cultural feminists, "women embody the force of light and men the force of darkness."

As we have seen, for most early radical feminists sexual danger was not central to their theories of patriarchy. Early 1970s radical feminists were much more concerned about sexual assertiveness and sexual pleasure. Yet by the late 1970s and into the 1980s, the issue of violence against women moved to center stage. This focus on "male violence" merged with the denunciation of "maleness" and a new criticism of heterosexuality, creating a condemnation of what became known as "male sexuality." In short, heterosexuality was now explicitly theorized as the underpinning essence of patriarchy and linked with violence against women.

Cultural feminists criticized the radical feminist theoretical neglect of a sexual component in violence against women, "insisting on the reality of sexual violence as an erotic experience, an end in itself" (Willis, 1984: 112). Robin Morgan (1978: 165) claimed as early as 1978 that "rape exists any time sexual intercourse occurs when it has not been initiated by the woman, out of her own genuine affection and desire." Andrea Dworkin (1980: 288) connected "male sexuality" with murder:

One can know everything and still be unable to accept the fact that sex and murder are fused in male consciousness, so that one without the other is unthinkable and impossible. One can know everything and still, at bottom, refuse to accept that the annihilation of women is the source of meaning and identity for men.

Dworkin (1979: 15, 59) argued further that "the penis" is the "hidden symbol of terror," even more significant than "the gun, the knife, the fist, and so on," and rape is "the defining paradigm of sexuality." In short, heterosexuality is "the stuff of murder, not love" (1980a: 152). Dworkin (pp. 148–149) continued:

> Men love death. In everything they make, they hollow out a central place for death, let its rancid smell contaminate every dimension of whatever still survives. Men especially love murder. In art they celebrate it, and in life they commit it. They embrace murder as if life without it would be devoid of passion, meaning and action, as if murder were solace, stilling their sobs as they mourn the emptiness and alienation of their lives. . . . In male culture, slow murder is the heart of the eros, fast murder is the heart of action, and systematized murder is the heart of history.

In her book *Intercourse*, Dworkin (1987: 128) repeats that heterosexuality is the basis of women's social and sexual subordination; intercourse and inequality are "like Siamese twins, always in the same place at the same time pissing in the same pot."

Jane Caputi (1987) recently extended culural feminist theory, arguing that serial sex murder is a heretofore unexamined form of "sado-ritual." For Caputi, the sex in sex murder is political sex, and what is unique about the modern age is that it is the "age of sex crime," or a new mode of heterosexual expression—the lust murder, the mutilation killing. The age of sex crime allegedly began in 1888 with the mutilation killings of five prostitutes by Jack the Ripper, and has continued to this day. Caputi argues that modern patriarchy is maintained through "gynocide" (systematic violence against women by men) and that the serial sex murderer is society's new "henchman" whose service is the custodianship of patriarchy. For Caputi (1989: 449), the serial sex murderer is a "martyr for the patriarchal state."

This fusion of violence and heterosexuality as the mainstays of patriarchy is most theoretically developed in the work of Catharine MacKinnon. MacKinnon (1989) argues that sexuality is a natural attribute and the primary sphere of masculine power, encompassing the expropriation of women's sexuality by men. It is the exploitative nature of heterosexuality that structures men and women as social beings in society. MacKinnon further claims that the universal system of patriarchy is maintained through heterosexuality and sexual violence—rape, wife beating, wife rape, incestuous assault, sexual harassment, and pornography. For MacKinnon, sexuality is crucial to women's subordination, and she theorizes it as the dynamic of inequality: gender derives from sexual dominance, not vice versa. The formula reads as follows (p. 131): "sexuality equals heterosexuality equals the sexuality of (male) dominance and (female) submission." MacKinnon (p. 137) adds:

> What is called sexuality is the dynamic of control by which male dominance—in forms that range from intimate to institutional, from a look to rape—eroticizes and thus defines man and woman, gender identity and sexual pleasure. It is also that which maintains and defines male supremacy as a political system.

Although MacKinnon rejects essentialism, her disclaimer is quickly negated by arguing, but not demonstrating, that this system of masculine dominance is invariant and universal (p. 151). Not surprisingly, then, MacKinnon (pp. 134–135) criticizes radical feminists, such as Brownmiller, who view rape solely as a violent crime:

> To say rape is violence not sex preserves the "sex is good" norm by simply distinguishing forced sex as "not sex," whether it means sex to the perpetrator or even, later, to the victim, who has difficulty experiencing sex without reexperiencing the rape. Whatever is sex cannot be violent; whatever is violent cannot be sex. This analytic wish-fulfillment makes it possible for rape to be opposed by those who would save sexuality from rapists while leaving the sexual fundamentals of male dominance intact.

Moreover, for MacKinnon (p. 174) intercourse is not that different from rape: "it is difficult to distinguish the two under conditions of male dominance"—as heterosexuality is simply coercive and violent sex. MacKinnon (p. 172) concludes that if "sexuality is central to women's definition and forced sex is central to sexuality, rape is indigenous, not exceptional, to women's social condition." Following the logic of MacKinnon's argument, *all* heterosexual women are victims and *all* heterosexual men are rapists.

Yet for cultural feminists, rape is only one aspect of "female sexual slavery" that derives from heterosexuality. As Kathleen Barry (1979:

220) argues, heterosexual domination "in one-to-one relationships is the basis for the cultural domination of women and female sexual slavery." Cultural feminists now link all forms of violence against women—which previously had been analyzed separately by radical feminists—under one rubric, heterosexuality. Indeed, according to Barry (p. 220), once we consider the numbers of men:

> who are pimps, procurers, members of syndicate and free-lance slavery gangs, operators of brothels and massage parlors, connected with sexual exploitation entertainment, pornography purveyors, wife beaters, child molesters, incest perpetrators, johns (tricks) and rapists, one cannot help but be momentarily stunned by the enormous male population participating in female sexual slavery. The huge number of men engaged in these practices should be cause for declaration of a national and international emergency, a crisis in sexual violence. But what should be cause for alarm is instead accepted as normal social intercourse!

Thus, for cultural feminists, the sexual slavery of women derives from heterosexuality, and both are the foundation of masculine dominance.

A significant change in radical feminist thought has emerged in the last twenty years: the emphasis shifted not only from sex-role socialization to essentialism as the base of patriarchy—and thus assigning strictly dichotomous and intrinsic natures to men and women—but also to a celebration of "femaleness" as the ultimate virtue and a condemnation of "maleness" and heterosexuality. For cultural feminists, women are good, men are bad, plain and simple. And it is this essential badness that leads to patriarchy and violence against women.

Notwithstanding, some contemporary radical feminists appear to reject this extreme cultural feminist position and to disavow a biological or essential basis to gender inequality and violence against women (Stanko, 1985; Hanmer and Maynard, 1987; Hanmer, Radford, and Stanko, 1989; Kelly, 1988). Yet much the same as earlier radical feminists and cultural feminists, they assert the primacy of patriarchy—"heteropatriarchy" according to some—over all other forms of social relations. As Hanmer, Radford, and Stanko (1989: 4) recently declared, "heteropatriarchy" signifies "a system of social relations based on male dominance, or supremacy, in which men's structured relationships to women underpin all other systems of exploitation." Further, these same authors declare that men's violence against women and children is "central to the maintenance and reproduction of *all exploitative social relations*" (p. 4, emphasis added).[4] Hanmer and Maynard (1987: 11) go so far as to proclaim that social class is inapplicable to the understanding of violence against women:

> In understanding violence against women the concept "class" is simply not a significant factor in identifying either victim or offender. Nor is it relevant in explaining why this violence occurs. . . . To put it bluntly, the realities of male violence and the sociological language of class seem entirely divergent.

For contemporary radical feminists, given that heterosexuality and violence against women are the foundation of patriarchy, there exists "no clear distinction between consensual sex and rape, but a continuum of pressure, threat, coercion and force" (Kelly, 1987: 58). All women experience sexual violence at some point in their lives, states Kelly (p. 59) and, therefore:

> a clear distinction cannot be made between "victims" and other women. The fact that some women only experience violence at the more common, everyday end of the continuum is a difference in degree not in kind. The use of the term "victim" in order to separate one group of women from other women's lives and experiences must be questioned. The same logic applies to the definition of "offenders."

In short, following MacKinnon, all heterosexual women are victims and all heterosexual men are violent. For radical feminists, men use such forms of heterosexual coercion, force, and violence to control women. As Liz Kelly (1988: 33) states in her book, *Surviving Sexual Violence*, contemporary radical feminists "understand that social control is men's purpose when using sexual violence against women."

The overall record of radical feminism contains numerous positive elements. For example, it is radical feminism that actually put second-wave feminism on the map, that secured sexual politics a permanent role in popular culture, and that moved sexuality and gendered power to the forefront of feminist thought. It is not an overstatement to say that the immense changes in women's consciousness over the past twenty years were "inspired by the issues radical feminists raised" (Willis, 1984: 92). Additionally, radical feminist research has spotlighted the nature and pervasiveness of violence against women and has successfully challenged "malestream" social thought: any serious theoretical analysis of violence against women can remain credible today only by incorporating some radical feminist insights (Liddle,

1989). However, a number of serious theoretical errors have accompanied the successes of radical feminism.

Obscuring the Differences among Men

The radical and cultural feminist focus on alleged differences between men and women acted to obscure differences among men. For example, the social experiences of African-American men differ from those of white men due to racist and classist structures that systematically disadvantage African-American men. Moreover, radical and cultural feminism obscure the fact that men exercise unequal amounts of control over their own lives as well as over the lives of women (Jaggar, 1983: 117–118). By concentrating on alleged differences between men and women, then, radical and cultural feminists fail to consider the variations among men in terms of race, class, age, and sexual preference, focusing instead on an alleged "typical male," as if he represents all men. Radical and cultural feminist theory disregards how social differences between men create, for example, varying forms of masculinity and, for example, different types and degrees of violence against women. This theoretical focus on the "typical male" leads to a "model of male agency which is at best one-dimensional" (Liddle, 1989: 762). Such an analysis regards "masculinity as more or less unrelieved villainy and all men as agents of the patriarchy in more or less the same degree" (Carrigan, Connell, and Lee, 1987: 140).

Radical and cultural feminists characterize violence against women as a consciously chosen "male" instrument for purposes of maintaining patriarchal power. Given that radical feminists correctly claim the effect of violence against women as social control, it is nevertheless invalid to assume that all men behave violently for the purpose of controlling women. As Mark Liddle (1989: 762–769) convincingly argues, this instrumentalism confuses the effects of violence and the motivations of individual perpetrators. Although some men are clearly motivated to control women through violence, not all violent men share this specific goal (see Chapters 4 and 5). Indeed, radical feminists simply bulldoze away the complexity in which gender (masculinity) is situationally and, therefore, differently accomplished throughout society.[5]

Disregarding Time and Place

Bob Connell (1987: 57) likewise criticizes radical and cultural feminism for explaining all forms of "male violence"—from violence against women to environmental destruction to the threat of nuclear war—"by the personal aggressiveness and ruthlessness of the typical man." Such theorizing, Connell (p. 58) argues, displays a misunderstanding of "the social machinery that makes a given form of masculinity environmentally destructive. In other periods of history aggressive masculinity did not result in a radically degraded environment" (p. 58). Connell's point is persuasive: the concentration on "heteropatriarchy" disallows any comprehension of how particular social arrangements give a particular type of masculinity a hegemonic position in a specific society and at a particular time in history.

This theoretical view is particularly evident in Caputi's analysis of serial sex murder, where, as discussed earlier, she targets the origin of the "age of sex crime" to 1888 and the case of Jack the Ripper. Yet her theoretical position is ill-prepared to explain why this particular type of crime emerged when it did. Caputi presents evidence that long before Jack the Ripper, explicit occurrences of sexual mutilation existed in other forms. For example, there are the histories of Caligula, Gilles de Rais (Bluebeard), Vlad the Impaler (a Dracula), "the Christian/occult world view that prevailed in Medieval and early modern Europe," and the history of mass rape, murder, and mutilation during war (Caputi, 1989: 4). Caputi (p. 4) argues further that by the late nineteenth and throughout the twentieth centuries, sex murders took on a new character:

> no longer the actual or legendary provinces of either maniacal aristocrats or the supernaturally/diabolically monstrous; nor can they be associated principally with periods of war and crisis. Rather, the rippers, stranglers, mutilators and other sex killers have become explicitly common criminals perpetrating an increasingly common crime.

However, Caputi not only fails to present solid evidence that this particular type of sex murder is in fact increasing, but also is incapable of answering the important question of specifically why sex murder assumes different forms at different times and in different places. Rather than analyzing the social changes marking transitions to different types of masculinity, she asserts that these new types of sex murder are "the logical and eminently functional product of the system of male domination" (p. 30).

Similarly, Brownmiller (1975) discusses a variety of contexts in which rape occurs and offers evidence that the incidence of rape is most likely higher under certain social conditions (for example, warfare). Yet Brownmiller's theory fails to explain why this is the case.

Indeed, she appears unable to account for changes in masculinity and how these changes create distinct types and degrees of violence against women.

Like Caputi and Brownmiller, Daly, MacKinnon, and other radical and cultural feminists argue that different forms of violence against women—from footbinding in China to pornography in the United States—all result from the same transhistorical and transcultural system of patriarchy or heteropatriarchy. As Barry (1979: 140) states, "Female sexual slavery is a global phenomenon. As a form of oppression, *it cannot be subject to either the respect or protection given to those cultural practices which mark a culture as distinct from any other*" (emphasis added).

As argued, this position disregards the specific ways in which masculinity is embedded in different societies at different times and, therefore, the different forms it takes. Thus, radical and cultural feminism, like sex-role theory (discussed in Chapter 1), is incapable of explaining the various ways that masculinity and femininity are constructed under different historical and social conditions (Kandiyoti, 1988; Connell, 1987; Cockburn, 1983, 1985). Indeed, one cannot understand why wife burning is prevalent in India but not in the United States without a thorough examination of the particular social conditions that prevail in these societies. Otherwise, it follows that Indian men are biologically predisposed to burning their wives while U.S. men are not.[6]

Historical differences in violence against women provide a telling example of the problematic nature of radical and cultural feminist theory. For example, in the case of rape, there is no reliable evidence that rape was particularly prominent in the preindustrial world. Anthropologists have shown that many gathering/hunting and horticultural societies are, or were, "rape-free" (Sanday, 1981; Draper, 1975; Shostak, 1983). And Porter (1986: 223) cogently adds that agricultural societies were so securely dominated by men that widespread acts of rape would have actually undermined their validation:

> A patriarchal order depending on such crude and violent "legitimations" would have forfeited its legitimacy. It would have shown itself to be insecure, which the social regimes of early modern Europe certainly were not. Men no more cherished the threat of the rapist in the wings to maintain their authority over women than property owners encouraged thieves to justify the apparatus of law and order.

Similarly, historical research demonstrates that rape was rarer in earlier Western industrialized communities than it is today. An extensive investigation of this material reported that in "the factory towns of the industrial revolution, women were underdogs, but these communities do not seem to have been the cockpits of rape" (p. 234). Finally, even in contemporary western industrialized societies, the incidence of rape varies. For example, the United States has seventeen times the rate of reported rapes as Britain, even though Britain is allegedly just as patriarchal as the United States (Segal, 1990: 239–240). Clearly, then, rape has not, historically and cross-culturally, played a crucial role in perpetuating masculine dominance, and radical and cultural feminist theory fails to account for these varying rates of rape.

On Heterosexuality

The radical and cultural feminist focus on the absolute primacy of sexuality is deeply problematic. Given that rape is not solely a violent act but also a sexual one—"you cannot, by fiat, take the sex out of a sexual act, it will creep back in at every point" (Smart, 1989: 44)—it does not follow that the enactment of heterosexuality in itself bestows on men power over women. Indeed, after reviewing research on men and sexuality, Segal (1990: 212) argued that it is precisely through sex that many men "experience their greatest uncertainties, dependence and deference in relation to women—in stark contrast, quite often, with their experience of authority and independence in the public world."

Additionally, rape correlates with a specific type of socially constructed heterosexuality rather than with heterosexuality *per se*. For example, Barbara Lindemann's (1984) analysis of rape in eighteenth-century Massachusetts revealed that rape was extraordinarily uncommon in comparison with today. Although in this period Massachusetts was securely dominated by men (p. 81):

> the cultural expectations about sexual behavior probably minimized the occurrence of rape. Extramarital sexual activity by men and women alike was severely condemned and frequently punished. Ministers enjoined women not to flaunt their sexual attractiveness. Men were not extolled for the sexual conquest of many women. Women were understood to be as interested in sex as men. Thus neither in marriage nor in courtship would a man believe that a woman really meant yes when she said no. The rape prototype of female enticement, coy female resistance, and ultimate male conquest was not built into the pattern of normal sexual relations.

It was not until the early 1800s that hegemonic masculinity was associated with seeking sexual pleasure through conquest and its feminine equation with sexual "passionlessness." Women's sexual appetites were no longer comparable with those of men. Women were increasingly seen as lacking sexual aggressiveness, and lustfulness was considered uncharacteristic of women (Cott, 1979: 163).[7] Moreover, there emerged a new emphasis on the physical attractiveness of women; notions of femininity shifted from meekness and spirituality to beauty and sexual appeal (Ulrich, 1983: 115–16; D'Emilio and Freedman, 1988: 43). Consequently, a new type of heterosexuality evolved in which:

> women had to conform to male tastes and wait to be chosen but resist seduction or suffer ostracism for capitulating; men, meanwhile, were free to take the first step, practice flattery, and escape the consequences of illicit sexual relations. (Cott, 1979: 172)

This new type of heterosexuality is most likely today hegemonic in form, yet research shows that other heterosexual practices exist as well. For example, Wendy Hollway (1984: 131) shows that many women and men simply desire a "one night stand" for physical pleasure from sex and neither wants a "relationship." Similarly, Dalna Heyn's (1992: 163) study of the "erotic silence" of white, middle-class, heterosexual, married women in the United States revealed that many had an extramarital affair in which the "only goal is mutual pleasure, without which it has no reason for being." Moreover, Sharon Thompson's (1990: 277) examination of African-American teenage mothers revealed that they never describe themselves as passive victims, but rather "as strong women who take their pleasure and defend their bodies and their rights." These young women described sexual appetites "as insatiable as their need for affirmation and opportunity," and this insatiability drove them "to break taboos—having oral, anal, and group sex—and being slick" (p. 274).

In all of these situations, exploitation is clearly possible, but not clearly inevitable. Moreover, to many men "good sexuality" is not simply force and conquest, but warmth, love, trust, the desire to be loved and to love as a whole person (Prieur, 1990: 145). Unfortunately, radical and cultural feminism render these men, as well as men who have supported women in their struggles for equal rights and liberation (see Kimmel and Mosmiller, 1992), "hidden from history."

Finally, if truly consensual heterosexual relations are impossible, it follows that all heterosexual men are victimizers and all heterosexual women are victims. Such a view, however, is extremely condescending not only to victims of actual rape (who are judged no worse off than all other heterosexual women) and to heterosexual women (who have the ability to say "no" to a man), but also, as Rosemary Tong (1989: 130) points out, to heterosexual women who have "the ability to say 'yes'—to engage in a nonexploitative relationship with a man."

Radical and cultural feminists would do well to put into historical perspective their assumption that "male sexuality" is essentially and, therefore, unchangeably coercive and insatiable. Contemporary Western industrialized societies have "thrust sex to the forefront of society" as never before and popular culture—from prime-time TV to pornography—is saturated with the image of masculinity as sexually unlimited and coercive (Porter, 1986: 220). Clearly, however, this form of heterosexuality is historically and socially constructed—sexuality is simply one practice through which men express and confirm a specific type of masculinity.

Thus, radical and cultural feminism reflect and reassert this historical connection of hegemonic masculinity with a coercive sexuality. The position that "male sexuality" is uncontrollable and preordained with violence whereas "female sexuality" is nurturant and serene reproduces, rather than challenges, current gender arrangements and normative heterosexuality. Contemporary radical and cultural feminism are similar to the sex-role theorists (discussed in Chapter 1) inasmuch as they uncritically build their theoretical frameworks upon the assumption that gender is exclusively dichotomous. As Tong (1989: 135) points out, through arguing that "women are *a priori* nurturing and life giving, and that men are *a priori* corrupt and obsessed with death, many radical feminists are buying into the male-dictated dichotomies they are trying to avoid."[8]

Let us now turn to socialist feminist theory, which attempts to overcome certain of the radical and cultural feminist limitations just discussed.

Socialist Feminism

During the early stages of second-wave feminism, other feminists, working from within the Marxist tradition, developed an alternative feminist perspective. In the mid-1960s, Juliet Mitchell (1966: 13) focused on "asking feminist questions but trying to come up with some Marxist answers." Marxist-feminists—as they would become known—subsequently attempted to explain women's oppression through the use of Marxist categories. Marxism was viewed as the scientific explanation of subordination, yet that explanation had historically ignored women's labor. In particular, Marxism failed to acknowledge, much less comprehend, women's work in the home.

The Domestic-Labor Debate

In 1969, Margaret Benston sought to uncover the material conditions that in capitalist societies define the group "women." According to Benston, women's work in the home entails the production of "use values," not the production of marketable commodities. In other words, the products and services produced by women in the home are meant to be consumed in the home and, therefore, never reach the market. This production of use-values in the home, according to Benston (1969: 20), is the defining cornerstone of women and, as well, of gender inequality:

> The material basis for the inferior status of women is to be found in just this definition of women. In a society in which money determines value, women are a group who work outside the money economy. Their work is not worth money, is therefore valueless, is therefore not even real work. . . . In structural terms, the closest thing to the condition of women is the condition of others who are or were also outside of commodity production, i.e., serfs and peasants.

Under the capitalist system of commodity production, Benston maintained, the material basis of women's oppression is found in the fact that women's labor in the home is not considered real work.

Benston stimulated a lengthy debate on the Marxist conception of domestic labor. Of particular importance in this debate was Wally Seccombe's (1973) article "The Housewife and Her Labour under Capitalism." Extending Benston's idea, Seccombe attempted to show that the primary purpose of the family in a capitalist mode of production is to reproduce labor power that is eventually sold to capital in the labor market. Under such economic conditions, inasmuch as the housewife does not produce surplus value, she is an "unproductive laborer." Nevertheless, as Seccombe (p. 7) puts it, when the housewife:

> acts directly upon wage-purchased goods and necessarily alters their form, her labour becomes part of the congealed mass of past labour em-

bodied in the labour power. The value she creates is realised as one part of the value labour power achieves as a commodity when it is sold. All this is merely a consistent application of the labour theory to the reproduction of labour power itself, namely that all labour produces value when it produces any part of a commodity that achieves equivalence in the market place with other commodities.

Consequently, such acts of daily maintenance and socialization as preparing meals, cleaning house, doing laundry, and caring for children are forms of "reproductive labor" and thus create value because that very labor eventually is incorporated into capital through the husband's and children's labor power.

Clearly, then, Benston, Seccombe, and others were attempting to introduce women's labor into an androcentric Marxist framework in order to demonstrate that domestic labor could be analyzed as work. Thus, women's domestic segregation in a capitalist economy could actually be explained, it was argued, through Marxist theory. The implication was that Marxism provided the conceptual tools for establishing not only that women's work in the home is a form of labor, but also that this type of labor is central in the explanation of women's special oppression. According to these theorists, the oppressor is capitalism, which exploits and benefits from women's labor.

This domestic-labor literature initially marked an advance over traditional Marxism but quickly fell into disfavor as an explanation of women's oppression. In particular, this reasoning was criticized for its failure to confront the most salient issue—social relations between men and women in the home. In other words, women's domestic labor was understood by Marxist feminists in its relation to capital, but not in its relation to men. As Sylvia Walby (1986: 20) points out, "the most important question is settled *a priori*. The interests that men, and in particular husbands, may have in the continuation and shaping of domestic work, are almost totally neglected." Indeed, the distinct premise of the domestic-labor argument was that capitalism is the problem, not men.

Socialist Feminism

The domestic-labor focus on the housewife and her apparent connection to capitalism proved an important development in the evolution of socialist feminist theory. Nevertheless, in the feminist literature of the early 1970s, an explanation for masculine dominance that did not focus solely on patriarchy was still lacking. Criticizing Marxist theory for its inability to recognize and conceptualize gender inequality, certain Marxist feminists appropriated the concept of patriarchy from radical feminism, and attempted to use it in a nonreductionist manner to explain masculine dominance and women's oppression under capitalism. For feminists writing in the early 1970s, the term "patriarchy" seemed adequately to address the profundity and pervasiveness of masculine dominance.

One of the first Marxist feminist writings to employ this concept and to juxtapose capitalism with patriarchy was Sheila Rowbotham's (1973) *Woman's Consciousness, Man's World*. According to Rowbotham (p. 117), "patriarchal authority is based on male control over women's productive capacity, and over her person." Although patriarchy existed prior to capitalism, Rowbotham argued, under a capitalist mode of production, it develops a historically specific configuration. While capitalism has "whittled away" at certain aspects of masculine dominance (e.g., women's labor in the market weakens the economic hold of men over women in the family), patriarchy has, Rowbotham continues, still "retained the domination of men over women in society. This domination continues to pervade economic, legal, social, and sexual life" (p. 122). Although Rowbotham theorized patriarchy as an autonomous system of oppression, under capitalism this system was seen by her as "an ever present prop in time of need" (p. 120). For Rowbotham, then, capitalism was primary and patriarchy secondary in the theoretical understanding of masculine dominance.

It was this continued concentration on the primacy of capitalism, as represented by Rowbotham's work, that eventually produced a break from Marxist feminism. Certain feminist theorists simply refused to accept the argument that gender relations were somehow of secondary importance to production relations. Their goal was to construct a theory that was truly socialist and truly feminist, one that undeniably required the avoidance of overstating an economic analysis at the expense of gender inequality.

A theoretical understanding of patriarchy provided the means with which to analyze gender relations outside Marxist categories and become the first step in formulating a cohesive socialist feminism. Expanding upon Rowbotham's initial conceptualization, patriarchy eventually was theorized as a system with its own history and its own forms of oppression that are independent of capitalism. Thus, contemporary Western industrialized societies were now viewed by *socialist feminists* as a composite of two equally important and discrete systems, patriarchy and capitalism, in which neither prevailed over the other. Zillah Eisenstein (1979) and Heidi Hartmann (1981) were notable forerunners in the attempt to connect capitalism and patriarchy, as equal systems, in an effort to understand masculine dominance. The goal of these self-proclaimed socialist feminists was to explain theoretically the relationship between what seemed to be two relatively autonomous systems of exploitation and oppression.

Eisenstein (1979) asserted that capitalism and patriarchy depend on each other for survival. The two systems do not merely operate adjacent to each other but, according to Eisenstein, are in fact so intertwined as to form a mutually interdependent system—"capitalist patriarchy."

Heidi Hartmann's (1981) "The Unhappy Marriage of Marxism and Feminism: Towards a More Progressive Union" attempted to overcome the weaknesses of both traditional Marxism and radical feminism. Hartmann argued that throughout its history, Marxist theory has clearly remained gender-blind and that radical feminism is ahistorical, insufficiently materialist, and ignores production relations or subsumes them under patriarchal relations.

Consequently, Hartmann theorized that patriarchal relations are distinct from and independent of capitalist relations and that both capitalism and patriarchy consist of their own system of power and hierarchy. Hartmann's theory attempted to recognize both systems without prioritizing one over the other. Patriarchy, Hartmann argued, like capitalism, has its own material base—masculine control over women's labor power—and this historically changing system of gender relations interacts with, but is not subsumed by, capitalist exploitative class relations. It is this dialectical interaction that leads to historically specific forms of masculine dominance and women's oppression. Capitalist class relations are theorized as gender neutral yet, when they interact with patriarchal relations, the result is a particular form of gendered domination.

Socialist Feminist Criminology

Socialist feminist theory significantly challenged radical feminism and traditional Marxist theory. Indeed, it appeared to transcend these perspectives whereby gender relations could now be theorized in a nonessentialist way that manifested a central role in the analysis of society. Socialist feminism established the interconnectedness of social relations and provided the framework for moving beyond a one-dimensional perception to what Joan Kelly (1979: 220) called a "double vision." From such a perspective, our personal, social, and historical experience is shaped both by class and gender relations, "relations that are systematically bound to each other—and always have been so bound" (p. 220).

Rejecting much of radical feminism, I became increasingly convinced of the validity of this double vision, and aspired in my own work to incorporate socialist feminist insights into Marxist criminology (Messerschmidt, 1986). Following Hartmann, I undertook to synthesize certain aspects of radical feminism and Marxism into a criminological theory that prioritized neither capitalism nor patriarchy. Rather, I viewed each as comparable, interacting and coreproducing each other. I pointed to the theoretical necessity of understanding how production (of food, shelter, and clothing) and reproduction (through sexuality, socialization, and daily maintenance) interact to determine the "social organization under which the people of a particular historical epoch live." In other words, a full understanding of production required a recognition of how it is structured by reproduction; conversely, a full understanding of reproduction required a recognition of how it is affected by production.

In addition to the premise that reproduction structures society equally with production, I argued that an individual's life experiences are shaped by both class and gender. Just as class experiences differ, the social experiences of men and women differ. This differing social experience shapes and limits the lives of both men and women. Consequently, the gendered nature of society becomes crucial as, in conjunction with class position, it helps determine how men and women perceive the world and act upon it.

In *Capitalism, Patriarchy and Crime* (1986), I argued that capitalism and patriarchy are simultaneously interdependent modes of social relations that constitute the most fundamental activities in society. I attempted to delineate a system of oppression involving the mutual dependence and articulation of production and reproduction. At any given moment of human activity, I reasoned, relations of both production and reproduction are present. Thus, to understand any social order, any human interaction, or any activity within a society, including crime, I premised that we must comprehend the interdependence of both forms of relations.

For criminology, the critical aspect of production and reproduction relations was the theoretical insight that their interaction leads to specific patterns of conduct, legitimate as well as illegitimate. By employing human powers to satisfy needs, relations of production and reproduction develop into linked institutions that significantly affect how members of society think and act and what each is capable of doing. Consequently, I pointed to the importance of analyzing both production and reproduction as a means of providing a more thorough understanding of how and why people in different class and gender locations act as they do in particular societies.

Patriarchal capitalist societies, it seemed to me, contain two basic groups: a powerless group comprised of women and the working classes, and a powerful group comprised of men and the capitalist class. Accordingly, individuals are affected structurally by their class and gender position in interaction. In well-behaved structuralist fashion, gender and class position were viewed simply as shaping one's possibilities. Just as there are gender-appropriate and class-appropriate forms of conforming behavior, I argued there are also gender- and class-apppropriate forms of nonconforming behavior. Very simply, criminality was theorized as related to the interaction of patriarchy and capitalism, and to the structural possibilities this interaction creates.

My socialist femininist understanding of crime had two premises. First, to comprehend criminality (of both the powerless and the powerful), we must consider simultaneously patriarchy and capitalism and their effects on human behavior. Second, from a socialist feminist perspective, power (in terms of gender and class) is central for understanding serious forms of criminality. It was theorized that the powerful (in both the gender and class spheres) do the most criminal damage to society. Further, the interaction of gender and class creates positions of power and powerlessness in the gender/class hierarchy, resulting in different types and degrees of criminality and varying opportunities for engaging in them. Just as the powerful have more legitimate opportunities, they also have more illegitimate opportunities. For example, the capitalist class and men in general have greater opportunities for obtaining high-quality education for their children, lucrative jobs, and overall social status. Likewise, they have greater opportunities than the powerless to engage in criminality more often and in ways that are more harmful to society. Criminality, then, is strongly related to the distribution of power in both the market and the home.

Capitalism, Patriarchy and Crime is one example of a type of analysis that seemed to offer advances over radical feminism and Marxism. My goal was to initiate a criminological theory that emphasized the double vision of socialist feminism. Not only would such a theory explain class differences in crime—a persistent emphasis in criminological theory—but also gender differences, a tenacious neglect in criminological theory. In other words, the double vision of socialist feminism was intended to provide an alternative and superior structural explanation of crimes committed by the powerful and powerless, men and women.

As with all forms of theory construction, however, it is important to recognize that socialist feminist theory and socialist feminist criminology are not without problems—some of which I now address briefly.

Uncritical of Marxism

Although recognizing the sex-blind nature of Marxism, socialist feminist theory is uncritical of the core elements of Marxist theory. The result is postulation of a capitalist system where genderless capitalists exploit genderless workers and a patriarchal system where men exploit women (Jaggar, 1983: 159). Consequently, socialist feminist theory merely tacked on an analysis of gender relations to an unaltered androcentric Marxism (Beechy, 1987: 113). Indeed, in a review of *Capitalism, Patriarchy and Crime*, Carol Smart (1987: 329) rightly pointed out that my theory retained basic Marxist formulations onto which grid I simply appended gender.

Ignoring Social Action

Smart (p. 328) added that my double vision of socialist feminist criminology was substantially deterministic. Crime was theorized in this work as resulting from a social system—patriarchal capitalism—external to the actor. In such a view, individuals display little or no creativity: their actions simply result from "the system." My socialist feminist criminology failed to account for the intentions of actors and for how action, including crime, is a meaningful construct in itself. I firmly agree with this limitation; yet, as I argue in Chapter 3, we cannot lose sight of the critical fact that actors are constrained by the social structural conditions under which they live.

Problems with Patriarchy

Socialist feminism embraced the concept of patriarchy in an attempt to conceptualize what Marxist theory omitted, namely, gender relations. However, most socialist feminists now admit that, despite its many insights, this theoretical effort was a dismal failure (Beechy, 1987; Acker, 1989). In particular, the term "patriarchy" restricts the theoretical exploration of historical variation in masculine dominance. Sheila Rowbotham (1981: 365) who, as we have seen, once accepted the validity of the concept, later argued that the term actually obscured "the multiplicity of ways in which societies have defined gender" and implies "a structure which is fixed, rather than the kaleidoscope of forms within which women and men have encountered one another." Similarly, Beverly Brown (1988: 410) wrote in a review of *Capitalism, Patriarchy and Crime*:

> The criticism of patriarchy *per se* tends to focus upon its character as a timeless, universal tautology that always works to reduce all gender relations to an identity of male dominance that in turn cannot be explained but simply posited.

Indeed, as I argued earlier, the concept of patriarchy explains away real variations in the construction of masculinity within a particular society and, consequently, encourages the theorization of one type of masculinity—the "typical (patriarchal) male."

Moreover, the recent argument by Sylvia Walby (1986) that a "patriarchal mode of production" is the foundation of a patriarchal "system" is likewise problematic. For Walby, the site of the patriarchal mode of production is the household: "The producing class is composed of housewives or domestic laborers, while the non-producing and exploiting class is composed of husbands" (pp. 52–53). Housewives produce labor power—the generational production of children and the day-to-day maintenance of the husband—but do not have control over the product of their labor, labor power. This results in the husband's expropriation of surplus labor from the housewife (pp. 53–54):

> He sells this labour power to an employer and receives a wage which is less than the value of the goods he has produced. He gives a portion of this wage to the wife for the maintenance of the family, and retains some for himself. The portion allocated to the wife's use on herself is typically less than the part of the wage allocated for the use of the husband on himself. In addition the housewife typically works longer hours than the man. Thus she performs more labour and receives less than he does.

Although this analysis clearly describes gendered exploitation as it exists in many households, it is questionable whether such exploitation is as uniform and systematic as Walby seems to claim. Indeed, Crompton and Sanderson (1990: 16–17) argued that because of this probable variability, the contrast more appropriately "lies between 'market' and 'non-market' *workers*, rather than male and female." Thus, while men have combined in numerous ways to exploit and exclude women, gender relations in the home are not simply analogous to class relations. Moreover, Walby, in similar fashion as radical and cultural feminists, portrays men in a one-dimensional way. As Roper and Tosh (1991: 10) point out in their critique of Walby:

> At work or home, men are simply agents of oppression. Masculinity is seen as unitary, fixed in time, and oppressive in equal degree. Without a more complete understanding of why men sought to control and exploit women, we risk returning to theories of an inherent male tendency towards domination.

Consequently, all these important criticisms indicate quite clearly that the concept of patriarchy has lost its strength and usefulness as an analytical tool.

Linking the "Systems"

To view the production of things and the reproduction of people as representing two distinct "systems"—a common feature in socialist feminist work—is to miss how "reproductive labor" is simultaneously productive labor, and vice versa. For example, much reproductive labor falls within the paid-labor market. As Alison Jaggar and William McBride (1985: 192) note:

> Not only has the production of food and clothes been industrialized, but laundering and the final stages of food preparation continue to move outside the home. Health care, including emotional care and the care of the elderly and the permanently disabled, is performed increasingly by paid workers and so is the care and education of children.

Moreover, the production of goods is for species survival and, thus, this production is simultaneously reproductive. Goods are produced not only for consumption, but reproduce the human species as well. For example, the production of a children's book, the chair that a parent and child sit in to read that book, the house that they both live in, and so on, simultaneously represent productive and reproductive labor. Consequently, production and reproduction are not separate systems; rather, each forms part of a continuous process of species survival and enhancement. Indeed, it is impossible to separate gender relations from other social relations. For example, gender relations are not confined to the private sphere and class relations to the public sphere.

Realistically, gender and class relations have been, and continue to be, produced and reproduced in all societal institutions. Yet socialist feminism has assumed, but not demonstrated, that the two "systems" are linked. This is a serious quandry for socialist feminism.

This holds true for race as well. Socialist feminist theory spoke from an unacknowledged but race-specific position and, therefore, tended to write out of history the existence of racial minorities, who are actually the majority in global terms. As Barrett and McIntosh (1985: 24) point out, by ignoring the question of race, feminist work "claims to be of relevance to all women but is in fact grounded in the specific experience of white women: it is ethnocentric." Socialist feminism constricted the possibilities of understanding how gender, class, and race are deeply embedded in all social groups and societal institutions. In short, socialist feminism failed to make appropriate theoretical connections among class, gender, and race.

The problems of sex-role theory (outlined in Chapter 1) and the criticisms of radical, cultural, and socialist feminist theory (outlined in this chapter) are important because they help us identify the prospects for theoretical growth. By examining the limits of existing frameworks, we are now in a better position to construct a theory that builds on feminist insights and, therefore, enhances our understanding of masculinities and crime. It is to this project that we turn in Chapter 3.

Chapter 3

Structured Action and Gendered Crime

Chapter 1 illustrated that criminological theory—although traditionally written by men and primarily about boys and men—has been alarmingly gender-blind. That is, gendered men and boys have never been the object of the criminological enterprise. Feminism has challenged the overall "malestream" nature of criminology by highlighting the repeated omission and/or misrepresentation of women in criminological enquiry. The result of this critique is twofold: (1) it has increased attention to women in criminological theory and research but (2) when criminology addresses gender it speaks exclusively of women, with little or no attention directed to the impact of gender on men. Although some consideration has focused on masculinity and crime, this relationship has been examined through an essentialist, antiquated, and fallacious sex-role theory.

Chapter 2 demonstrated that radical feminism is not a viable alternative theory. A feminism that insists upon alleged natural differences between women and men, and goes on to explain crime committed by men in terms of that essentialism, not only homogenizes men (as does sex-role theory) but also proves itself inadequate to explaining crime committed by men. Although radical feminism is applauded for moving sexuality and gender power to the forefront of feminist thought, we are compelled to reject all forms of essentialism and reductionism.

Similarly, because of the problems identified in Chapter 2, socialist feminism remains sketchy and insubstantial. Socialist feminism has never attained a complete theoretical orientation; thus my rationale for subtitling *Capitalism, Patriarchy and Crime*, "Toward a Socialist Feminist Criminology" (Messerschmidt, 1986). Both radical and socialist feminism have only initially articulated certain of the criteria necessary for constructing an adequate framework that comprehends the gendered nature of society and, thus, of crime. Nevertheless, despite initial weaknesses, further theoretical progress is possible. Accordingly, in this chapter and those that follow, I move beyond the earlier approaches and attempt to develop feminism in new directions.

To structure a comprehensive feminist theory of gendered crime, we must bring men into the framework. However, we should do this not by treating men as the normal subjects, but by articulating the gendered content of men's behavior and of crime. This approach requires a different theoretical lens—one that focuses on a sociology of masculinity—to comprehend why men are involved disproportionately in crime and why they commit different types of crime. In what follows, I build on the critique developed in Chapter 2 by employing the insights of Giddens (1976; 1981), Connell (1987), West and Zimmerman (1987), Fenstermaker, West, and Zimmerman (1991), Goffman (1979), and others to present new theoretical tools for comprehending crime committed by men.

At least two significant theoretical undertakings are suggested from the criticisms outlined in Chapter 2. First, it is essential to make the relevant theoretical links among class, gender, and race without surrendering to some type of separate systems approach (e.g., capitalism plus patriarchy). Second, it is crucial to construct a theory of crime that recognizes that illegal behavior, like legal behavior, personifies synchronously both social practice and social structure. Indeed, social structures do not exist autonomously from humans; rather, they arise and endure through social practice. Social structures originate, are reproduced, and change through social practice. In short, we can only speak of *structured action*: social structures can be understood only as constituting practice; social structures, in turn, permit and preclude social action.

Individuals exist within the basic structures of society, structures that circumscribe present experience and set limits on future action (Giddens, 1976; 1981). Thus, as we engage in social action, we simultaneously help create the social structures that facilitate/limit social practice. This chapter, then, examines how social action is linked to social structures, identifies specifically how gendered social structures enable and constrain actors in their everyday activity, and analyzes how this relates to crime committed by men.

Appropriate, then, is a theory that conceptualizes how gender, race, and class relations arise within the same ongoing practices (Acker, 1989: 239). For to understand crime by men, we must comprehend how class, race, and gender relations are part of all social existence rather than viewing each relation as outside, and at times encroaching upon, the other two. Crime operates subtly through a complex series of class, race, and gender practices and, as such, is always more than a single activity. Consequently, rather than identifying systems (such as capitalism and patriarchy) and then attempting to interconnect them, we must begin, as Joan Acker (p. 239) suggests, with "the assumption that social relations are constituted through processes in which the linkages are inbuilt." That is, social actors maintain and change social structures within any particular interaction, and those social structures simultaneously enable and constrain social action.

I begin by identifying the major social structures in contemporary Western industrialized societies, and then turn to the importance of social action in comprehending crime by men.

Social Structures

Social structures, defined here as regular and patterned forms of interaction over time that constrain and channel behavior in specific ways, "only exist as the reproduced conduct of situated actors" (Giddens, 1976: 127) and construct social relations of relatively durable quality yet of obvious historical variability. Class, race, and gender relations are each constituted by a variety of social structures and, therefore, structured action. Divisions of labor and power are examples of social structures extant in each of the three social relations. Social actors perpetuate and transform these divisions of labor and power within the same interaction and these structures simultaneously constrain and enable social action. The result, as depicted below in

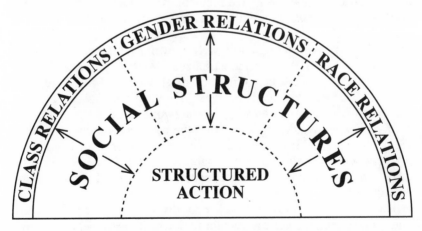

Figure 3-1. Social Relations, Social Structures, and Structured Action

Figure 3–1, is the ongoing social construction of class, race, and gender relations.

Following the important work of Bob Connell (1987) and the insights advanced by radical and socialist feminists, I propose three specific social structures underlying relations between women and men: the gender division of labor, gender relations of power, and sexuality.[1]

The Gender Division of Labor

The concept "division of labor," as socialist feminists have pointed out (Young, 1981; Tong, 1989), encompasses social relations much broader than those of class. The division of labor consists not only of class divisions of labor but also of race and gender divisions. *These three divisions of labor are produced simultaneously by the same practices.* Consequently, rather than viewing class, gender, and race as discrete "things" that somehow relate to each other, it is important to visualize these divisions of labor as mutually constituting one another (Morgen, 1990: 286). That is, throughout everyday interaction, social actors simultaneously produce these divisions.

The concept of division of labor helps to overcome the challenge of assigning equal weight to class, gender, and race as forms of domination. Examining such a division through a theory of structured action, we easily grasp how all three divisions are produced simultaneously through social action. Moreover, in viewing the division of labor from one perspective we see class, from another we see race, and from another we see gender; yet no one perspective is "complete without the other" (Acker, 1989: 239).[2] We focus now specifically on the gender division of labor, examining the concurrent presence of class and race relations.

The gender division of labor, a well-known and critical social structural feature of all Western industrialized societies, refers to the fact that the nature of labor performed for species survival is different for men and women. Historically, in Western industrialized societies labor has been divided by gender for (1) housework, (2) child care, (3) unpaid versus paid work, and (4) within the paid labor market and individual workplaces. However, this gender division of labor is not simply attached to an alleged gender-neutral class structure. Rather, like race, gender divisions are a fundamental feature of all forms of production.

The form and character of the gender division of labor have undergone fundamental historical transformation. Although gathering/hunting societies maintained highly egalitarian gender divisions of labor, a pronounced masculine-dominated gender division of labor first appeared in horticultural societies (Draper, 1975; Messerschmidt, 1986). In sixteenth- and seventeenth-century Europe, production was organized on the basis of the household unit to which all members contributed. Within an agricultural context, the household produced most of the necessities for survival and, therefore, it acted as the basic unit of production in society. In this type of relationship, as in gathering/hunting and horticultural societies, women's and children's labor were publicly visible and understood to be economically necessary (Andersen, 1988: 151). Moreover, women also dominated certain crucial skills, and in many craft guilds, women, as well as men, were members (Davidoff and Hall, 1987).

Nevertheless, by no means were women the social equals of men. Witness the Ehrenreich and English (1978: 6–7) description of who exercised authority and control in the preindustrial household unit:

> authority over the family is vested in the elder males, or male. He, the father, makes the decisions which control the family's work, purchases, marriages. Under the rule of the father, women have no complex choices to make, no questions as to their nature or destiny: the rule is simply obedience. . . . The patriarchal order of the household is magnified in the governance of village, church, nation. At home was the father, in church was the priest or minister, at the top were the "town fathers," the local nobility, or as they put it in Puritan society, "the nursing fathers of the commonwealth," and above all was "God the Father."

With the onset of industrialization in mid-1800s England, some types of production were removed from the home and organized on a large scale. Entire families—working-class men, women, and children—were compelled to labor long hours outside the home simply to survive. Thus, the productive resources of the household unit left the home and entered the wage-labor market. And with this change, the gender division of labor became more entrenched. As Hartmann (1979: 217) has shown, in the paid-labor market the dominant position of men was maintained through gendered job segregation:

> Women's jobs were lower paid, considered less skilled, and often involved less exercise of authority or control. Men acted to enforce job segregation in the labor market; they utilized trade union associations and strengthened the domestic division of labor which required women to do housework, childcare, and related chores. Women's subordinate position

in the labor market reinforced their subordinate position in the family, and that in turn reinforced their labor market position.

The working-class women and children of England worked fourteen to sixteen hours a day for less than half that paid men for working in the same jobs (Boston, 1987: 25).

By 1840, however, the wage labor of the working-class family outside the home began to change, as men working in factories lobbied for an eight-hour day for working children under the age of thirteen and for a ban on employment of children under the age of nine. The exploitation of children was viewed by men as undercutting their own wages (p. 28). Ironically, one negative effect of subsequent child-labor laws concerned parental difficulties with child care: problems with the training and supervision of working-class children (Hartmann, 1979: 217–218).

Married women who worked in the paid labor force were accused of deserting their children to "steal men's jobs," and single women in the paid labor force were criticized for growing up without the proper domestic feminine socialization it was argued they needed to be competent wives and mothers (Seccombe, 1986: 66–67). Moreover, widespread employment of women constituted a direct threat "to the job security and wage levels of skilled tradesmen" (p. 67). Consequently, working-class men and the upper classes began to recommend that women, in addition to children, be removed from wage labor in the factories. Unions controlled by men fought for and won "protective legislation" for women, limiting the number of hours they could work. Moreover, men denied women training for skilled work and eventually drove them out of trade unions (Hartmann, 1979: 226).

Consequently, for the upper layers of the white working class, a "family wage" developed that was barely sufficient to allow women to remain at home, raise the children, and maintain the family. In this way, rather than having all family members working in the labor force, men appropriated both the position of breadwinner in the labor market and the labor of women in the home. This is not to imply that men operated entirely consciously to subjugate women. Rather, operating within a particularized masculine-dominated gender division of labor, white working-class men strongly resisted the destruction of the patriarchal household unit and attempted to ameliorate the oppressive nature of the wage-labor system on "their women." In addition, although many women resisted the family-wage system, many others viewed the workplace as a desperate and dangerous place for them and for their children. Thus, along with their husbands, these women supported the family-wage system.

Likewise, such a system developed in the United States, where it was supported not only by white working-class men who wanted "their women" out of the factories, but also by "a chorus of concern . . . from reformers, ministers, conservative feminists, doctors, and other representatives of bourgeois morality, all bent on 'preserving' the family" (Zaretsky, 1978: 211). By the end of the Progressive Era (1900–1917), state policy toward the family supported the idea of a family wage: the husband as sole support of his family and a full-time mother in the home. These policies "not only reflected the outlook of the bourgeoisie but also the aspirations [though not the reality] of both men and women within the working class" (p. 212).

As seen through the lens of a theory of structured action, the family-wage system validated the husband/father as the sole breadwinner with all but sufficient earnings to maintain his wife and children who did not earn wages outside the home. The family-wage system was supportive of the class division of labor in that it helped guarantee a more stable and healthy work force as well as a reserve army of labor ready to be drawn into the paid-labor force.

Yet it also maintained, albeit in restructured form, masculine domination of the gender division of labor. This rearranged gender division of labor constituted the social construction of a new type of white-adult masculinity—full-time work in the paid-labor force as the sole breadwinner—and white-adult femininity, the full-time mother/housewife. As Jessie Bernard (1992: 207) points out, hegemonic masculinity became associated with being a "good provider": "The good provider had to achieve, to win, to succeed, to dominate. He was a bread*winner*."

This of course differed by race and class. African American men were largely excluded from labor unions, and so worked either for low wages at menial jobs or were unemployed. This is one of the reasons why so many African American married women worked in wage-labor domestic and service jobs (Ferguson, 1991: 86). Consequently, African American men were without the resources to construct a "breadwinner/good provider" form of masculinity and African-American women shaped a femininity centered on more than their own domesticity and child rearing.

Middle-class, white men, not only expected to be breadwinners/good providers, also developed masculinities centered on expertise, technical knowledge, rationality, and calculation (the "bureaucrat" and the "businessman" emerged as social types). White working-class masculinities were organized around holding a steady job, bringing pay home reliably, skill and endurance in paid labor, and a combative solidarity among wage earners (Connell, 1992: 12; Seccombe, 1986; 62). Accordingly, the family-wage system simultaneously formed practices that reproduced class, gender, and race divisions of labor, thereby constructing whiteness as a class-specific gendered phenomenon.

Separation of the center of production from the household unit to the public workplace enhanced white masculine dominance. For the first time in history, white women were thrust "to the margins of economic activity" (Young, 1981: 59). Moreover, women's work in the home was devalued, causing women to become even more economically dependent on men for survival (Andersen, 1988: 151). As Margaret Andersen (p. 151) notes:

> When the workplace became separated from the home, the family, although still economically productive, became in the long run a site largely for the physical and social reproduction of workers and for the consumption of goods. As more goods were produced outside the home, the value of workers became perceived in terms of their earned wages. The social value of women, especially those left unpaid housewives, was diminished.

Yet class, race, and gender relations were simultaneously reproduced at the site of domestic labor. Paralleling the changes in the division of labor, the number of women employed as domestic servants expanded rapidly. Most white middle-class women were in the position to hire primarily women of color to perform much of the domestic tasks of cleaning house, laundering and ironing clothes, scrubbing floors, and caring for infants and children (Palmer, 1990). As Evelyn Nakano Glenn (1992: 7) shows, these domestic servants:

> relieved their mistresses of the heavier and dirtier domestic chores. White middle-class women were thereby freed for supervisory tasks and for cultural, leisure, and volunteer activity or, more rarely during this period, for a career.

Glenn (p. 32) shows that from the late 1800s to around the 1920s, African American, Mexican American, and Japanese American women were drawn into domestic service work by a "combination of

economic need, restricted opportunities, and educational and employment tracking systems.'' White middle-class women justified employing women of color by arguing that they were especially suited for
domestic service. As Glenn (p. 14) states:

> These racial justifications ranged from the argument that Black and Mex-
> ican women were incapable of governing their own lives and thus were
> dependent on whites—making white employment of them an act of be-
> nevolence—to the argument that Asian servants were naturally quiet,
> subordinate, and accustomed to a lower standard of living. Whatever the
> specific content of the racial characterizations, it defined the proper place
> of these groups as in service: they belonged there, just as it was the dom-
> inant groups place to be served.

In short, within the context of a family-wage system, throughout
everyday interaction, social actors simultaneously produced class,
race, and gender divisions of labor in both the market and the home.
The outcome was not only the ongoing social construction of class,
race, and gender relations, but specific configurations of race/class
masculinities and femininities.

The family-wage system stabilized materially and ideologically until World War II (1941). However, with the economic developments
of the postwar period, the family-wage system and the breadwinner
power of white men have significantly diminished (although the notion
that paid work equals masculinity persists). Periodic inflation, unstable
wages, heightened individual expectations, and material accumulation
generated by advertising have compelled working-class and most middle-class families to rely on two wage earners to maintain the standard
of living previously underwritten by the single breadwinner (Burstyn,
1983: 62). In addition, the ever-increasing search for new areas of investment and development has resulted in the expansion of service and
clerical jobs. Again, ironically, these developments created conditions
that encouraged many women to move out of the home and into wage
labor to meet the demands of capital.

Outside the home, however, working women have been segregated
(for the most part) into ''female jobs''—clerical, service, nursing,
teaching, and cleaning of all kinds. And these jobs are simultaneously
racialized: white women are preferred in public positions, such as
waitress, hairdresser, and dental assistant, while women of color are
preferred in ''dirty back-room jobs as maids, janitors/cleaners, kitchen
workers, and nurse's aids'' (Glenn, 1992: 20). Thus the gender and

race divisions of labor have been restructured in the labor market so that women generally do the same type of work they do in the home.

Gendered job segregation maintains a reduced status for women and channels them generally into low-wage positions. Today, women earn approximately two-thirds what men earn, a differential wage that aids in defining women's work as secondary to men's work. Moreover, although more and more women work as wage laborers, they continue to do the major share of unpaid labor in the home (Ferguson, 1991; Folbre, 1982). Consequently, men (primarily white men) continue to benefit from higher wages in the labor market and from the work women do in the home. Indeed, the gender division of labor shapes exploitation not only in the workplace, but also in the home. And although some monogamous heterosexual relationships appear to be moving toward nonexploitive relationships (Connell, 1987: 124), I have written elsewhere that "in conditions where women labor longer than men, where their work supports men and children, where indeed men experience a net benefit from their familial affiliation to women and women a net loss in terms of labor, exploitation prevails" (Messerschmidt, 1988a: 155). In other words, under such conditions in the home, men consume more embodied labor than they produce.

More importantly, however, new forms of masculinity and femininity emerged concurrently with these changing structural conditions. Regarding the former, Barbara Ehrenreich (1989: 217–218) has shown that by the midseventies "the old notion that a working wife was a sure sign of male inadequacy was hard to find in any class." Although the notion of men as primary wage earners and the connection of paid work to masculinity persists, hegemonic masculinity is no longer based on being the sole breadwinner. Thus, although the gender division of labor is reproduced in the paid-labor market, new constructions of masculinity and femininity are emerging from the identical ongoing practices.

Relations in the paid-labor force do not merely use or adapt to gender relations. Rather, such relations are structured by gender (and race). For example, Joan Acker (1988: 478–485) has shown how wage itself is a gendered phenomenon. The idea of a "family wage" for men adequate to support a white working-class family was supported by both the unions and the state from the middle of the nineteenth century until the end of World War II (1945). In addition, however, men's wages generally have always been and continue to be higher than women's; sex segregation of economic sectors and occupations creates a wage gap; and work relations are permeated with the ongoing social construction of gender. Acker argues that all social relations (the wage being just one example) are constituted through processes in which class, race, and gender connections are inseparable. Inescapably, the gender division of labor is produced within the same ongoing practices as are other divisions of labor (Acker, 1989: 239). Understandably, then, the gender division of labor is an important structural force that shapes relations between men and women.

Gender Relations of Power

As evidenced from the brief historical discussion above, gender relations of power are embedded in, and reinforced by, the gender division of labor. Power is an important structural feature of relations between women and men. Overall, in Western industrialized societies, specific social groups possess, or are restricted from access to, material resources, a situation that places them in an unequal social relation to other groups.

Material resources, for example, help construct social structural relations of power—by class, race, and gender—and arrange individuals in relation to other individuals. A structural process is fashioned whereby "those with power can organise those who are less powerful according to their own ends" (Segal, 1990: 261). The gender division of labor (both in the home and workplace) is an example of this, embodying gender relations of power, authority and control by men, and the subordination of women.

A manifestation of gender relations of power is the obvious structural fact that men control the economic, religious, political, and military institutions of authority and coercion in society. In addition to such large-scale institutional power, gender power organizes advantage and inequality within smaller social groups and institutions (e.g., the family, peer group, and workplace), thereby providing men the legitimate authority to impose a definition on specific situations (Connell, 1987: 107). Because in gender relations the interests of men more often prevail over the interests of women, in most (but clearly not all) situations, men are able to impose authority, control, and coercion over women. Such power provides the means with which to arrange social life to the advantage of men, thus paving the way for greater legitimate and illegitimate opportunities. Connell (p. 107) provides four examples of the omnipresent, yet sometimes hidden, nature of gendered power:

Mr. Barrett the Victorian patriarch forbids his daughter to marry; parliament makes homosexual intercourse a crime; a bank manager refuses a loan to an unmarried woman; a group of youths rape a girl of their acquaintance.

These examples point out that power is not solely based on access to material resources and only occurs at the institutional level. Although material resources may clearly enhance masculine power, they are often unnecessary at the interpersonal level for the actual realization of that power. Indeed, a woman may have far superior material resources than an unemployed man, yet he nevertheless may exercise interpersonal power in the form of, for example, rape. That exercise of power is more than merely an individual embodiment; it is structural by being profoundly embedded in power inequalities: "Far from being a deviation from the social order, it is in a significant sense an enforcement of it" (p. 107). Thus, authority and control become defining characteristics not only of gender relations, but of the social construction of masculinities as well.

Power among men is likewise unequally distributed since some groups of men (in terms of class, race, and sexual preference, for instance) have greater authority and, therefore, more power than others (Connell, 1987: 109). In other words, the capacity to exercise power is always a reflection of one's position in social relations. For example, in colonial America, "white men as husbands had control over their wives and as fathers control over their children's marriages and access to family property, but Afro-American male slaves had no such patriarchal rights" (Ferguson, 1991: 113). Moreover, in late nineteenth- and early twentieth-century California and Hawaii, the majority of domestic servants for white, middle-class households were Asian men (Glenn, 1992: 9).

These examples show that class, race, and gender relations of power are produced simultaneously within the same ongoing practices and, accordingly, not only does the exercise of power over women differ among men, but also among men themselves. Heterosexual men exercise greater power than gay men, upper-class men greater power than working-class men, and white men greater power than men of color. Power, then, is a relationship that structures social interaction not only between men and women, but among men as well. As the chapters that follow will show, this differing degree of power among men significantly impacts the varieties of masculinities constructed and, consequently, crimes committed by men.

Nevertheless, power is not absolute but a contested terrain of social practice that is historically variable (Connell, 1987: 108–111). As Kathy Davis (cited in Segal, 1990: 261) has argued, power is never simply a matter of "haves" and "have nots":

> Such a conception can only lead to an over-estimation of the power of the powerful, closing our eyes to the chinks in the armour of the powerful as well as the myriad ways that the less powerful have to exercise control over their lives, even in situations where stable, institutionalised power relations are in operation.

At any point in space and time, gender relations of power promote and constrain the social action of both men and women, and conflict and resistance is pervasive. Notwithstanding, the social structure of gendered power is basic to understanding not only why men engage in more crime than women but also why men engage in different types and degrees of crime.

Sexuality

In addition to the social divisions of labor and power, sexuality is a major social structural feature of gender relations and, therefore, of the social construction of masculinity. Over the last fifteen years, an important and sophisticated historical scholarship has demonstrated three salient features of sexuality. First, sexuality is socially constructed and not biologically ordained. Beginning with Michel Foucault's *The History of Sexuality* (1978) and continuing with the important works of Jeffrey Weeks (1981, 1986) and Gayle Rubin (1984), research has consistently shown that forms of sexuality are constructed in historically specific social practices. Accordingly, sexuality varies not only from society to society but within societies themselves. Sexuality is not, therefore, a biological constant but a product of human agency.

Second, historically, certain sexual practices have been restricted. Plummer (1984) has shown that most societies define who are "appropriate" partners—for example, in terms of gender, class, race, age, and species—and restrict the human organs that may be used, the orifices entered, what is touched, with what frequency, and so on. These definitions and restrictions provide the permissions, prohibitions, limits, and possibilities with which erotica and desire are constructed (Weeks, 1986: 27). For instance, in some New Guinea societies, homosexual activities are obligatory for all men and homosexual acts are considered utterly masculine; yet such men and their society do not view them as homosexuals (Rubin, 1984: 285). Similarly, in nineteenth-century U.S. society, "two women who shared the same household and bed were usually perceived as close friends; by the twentieth century, such women were increasingly viewed as lesbians" (Vance, 1984: 8).

In western industrialized societies, it was not until the 1860s that the term "homosexual" was fashioned. Although prior to that time erotic activities between persons of the same gender certainly existed, homosexual as a distinct category of person, did not (Weeks, 1986: 33). Moreover, nineteenth-century moral reformers and sex theorists considered masturbation unhealthy, and argued that it would impair the maturation of children by leading to insanity and/or simply stunt the physical growth of children. Accordingly, many children were tied down at night to prevent masturbation, and physicians frequently performed clitoridectomy on little girls caught masturbating and employed "little metal suits of armour fitted over the genitals and attached to a locked belt as prophylaxis for masturbation" (Rubin, 1984: 268; Weeks, 1981: 51).

Third, the result of the foregoing is that in Western industrialized societies, a hierarchical system of sexual value exists, with marital-reproductive heterosexuals alone at the top, followed closely by unmarried heterosexuals, those who prefer solitary sexuality, lesbians and gay men, prostitutes, transvestites, and sado-masochists (Rubin, 1984: 279). Thus, heterosexuality is deemed normative and carries "injunctions to love and marry the right kind of person, to find such-and-such a kind of masculinity or femininity desirable" (Connell, 1987: 112). Lynne Segal (1990: 101) supports this view by adding, "the polarities of male and female, heterosexual and homosexual, are the pivot of contemporary Western thinking on sex. Sex is about sexual difference, the desire for the 'opposite' sex." Indeed, as Gayle Rubin (1984: 306) clearly argues in her work:

> economic sanctions, family pressures, erotic stigma, social discrimination, negative ideology, and the paucity of information about erotic behavior, all serve to make it difficult for people to make unconventional sexual choices. There certainly are structural constraints that impede free sexual choice, but they hardly operate to coerce anyone into being a pervert. On the contrary, they operate to coerce everyone toward normality.

The result is that "deviant" sexual identities are ridiculed, policed, and repressed; not surprisingly, heterosexuality becomes a fundamental indication of "maleness." However, it is not simply heterosexuality, but a particular type of heterosexuality. Hegemonic masculinity is currently established through an alleged uncontrollable and insatiable sexual appetite for women, which results in a "naturally" coercive "male" sexuality (see discussion in Chapter 2). As Edwin Schur (1988: 149) states, the "crucial point is that men are *supposed* to try to coerce women into sexual activity, . . . they are *supposed* to be able to perform sexually in each and every instance." Normative heterosexuality is comprehended as "the pleasure of the Phallus and by extension the pleasures of penetration and intercourse—for men"; sexual pleasure for women is simply assumed to correspond with this perception (Smart, 1989: 28).[3] Consequently, dominant ideology marks heterosexual performance as a hallmark of one's identity as a man—sexual impotence threatens not only a man's sexuality, but his masculinity as well (Segal, 1990: 211).[4]

Yet while normative heterosexuality structures hegemonic masculinity as well as specific forms of sexual incitement and inequalities between sexualities, simultaneously it is organized on the basis of gendered relations of power. For example, female sexuality has historically been limited by (1) economic and social dependence on men, (2) the power of men to define sexuality, (3) the limitations of marriage, (4) the burdens of reproduction, and (5) the endemic fact of violence by men against women (Weeks, 1986: 39). The "male" insatiable sex drive empowers men, shapes women as objects of heterosexual desire, and delineates lesbianism as mysterious, incomprehensible, and pathological (Smart, 1989: 30). As Connell (1987: 113) argues:

> A heterosexual woman is sexualized as an object in a way that a heterosexual man is not. The fashion industry, the cosmetics industry, and the content of the mass media are tangible proof of this. For instance, the glamour shots on the covers on women's magazines and men's magazines are pictures of women in both cases; the difference is in the way the models are dressed and posed. Broadly speaking, the erotic reciprocity in hegemonic heterosexuality is based on unequal exchange.

For many women, economic survival entails learning to present themselves as sexual beings. As Alison Jaggar (1983: 308–309) points out:

> male superiors penalize women who seem to be "punishing" or defying men through their appearance; much of women's paid work is sexualized; and, in the end, the best chance of economic security for most women

remains the sale of their sexuality in marriage. . . . [Women] are expected to titillate male sexuality in situations that are not overtly sexual and in overtly sexual situations they are expected to fascinate, to arouse and to satisfy men. In short, men rather than women control the expression of women's sexuality: women's sexuality is developed for men's enjoyment rather than for women's.

Simultaneous with sexual objectification, then, women sometimes "come to experience their own sexual impulses as dangerous" inasmuch as such practices may instigate and elicit an aggressive and unpredictable sexual response from men (Vance, 1984: 4). As Carol Vance (p. 4) points out, women "inherit a substantial task: the management of their own sexual desire and its public expression. Self-control and watchfulness become major and necessary female virtues." Moreover, limited access to contraception and abortion have likewise restricted women's access to sexual pleasure (Segal, 1990: 98). Consequently, while sexuality is clearly a domain of extensive exploration and pleasure for women today, it remains simultaneously a site where gendered oppression may occur—violence, brutality, and coercion—and a site of considerable gendered repression of women's desire and sexual pleasure. Thus, normative heterosexuality helps legitimize the ideology that women are dependent on men for their sexual and economic well-being and simultaneously denigrates women's relationships with other women.

Because normative heterosexuality likewise is based on power relations, not only between sexualities but also between men and women, it defines masculinity through difference from, and desire for, women. Normative heterosexuality therefore is not only a major structural feature for understanding gender, but for understanding masculinities and crimes committed by men as well.

Structured Action

Thus far I have addressed the social structural features underlying relations between women and men of western industrialized societies—the gender division of labor, gender relations of power, and sexuality—which are necessarily theorized to understand the gendered nature of crime and, more specifically, crime committed by men. Although these social structures may clearly follow different historical trajectories, they are not separate in the sense implied by the capitalism plus patriarchy framework. Through social action, these structures are constantly constructed together. For example, the gender division of labor is simultaneously sexualized and maintains gendered power relations.

However, comprehension of these social structures is only part of the gender equation. As stated earlier in this chapter, it is essential to theorize structure and action as one and the same. Giddens (1981: 171) similarly argues that a social structure consists of "both the medium and outcome of the social practices it recursively organizes." In other words, social structures are "both constituted *by* human agency and yet at the same time are the very *medium* of this constitution" (Giddens, 1976: 121). In this sense, structure is not external to the agent, nor is it simply and solely constraining. Rather, structure is implicated in social action and social action is implicated in structure, so that structure both constrains and enables social action.

To understand why men engage in more and different types of crimes than women and in differing amounts and forms among themselves, we need an adequate account of social action. We can begin by recognizing that in society all individuals engage in purposive behavior and monitor their own action reflexively. That is, we comprehend our actions and we modify them according to (among other things) our interpretation of other people's responses. Social action is creative, inventive, and novel, but it never occurs separately from, or external to, social structures. Social structures are constituted by social action and, in turn, provide resources and power from which individuals construct "strategies of action" (Swidler, 1986: 227). Social structures organize the way individuals think about their circumstances and generate methods for dealing with them.

Gendered Social Action

Critical to understanding crime by men is the gendered nature of social action. As ethnomethodologists have shown, social reality is created on the basis of taken-for-granted assumptions. For example, the experiments of Harold Garfinkel (1967) demonstrate how social interaction is contingent upon taken-for-granted knowledge and how we all obliviously and inevitably use creative, yet "relevant" and "necessary," practices to constitute social interactions and, therefore, to construct a particular social reality. Gender is especially important in this regard. Garfinkel's (1967: 118–140) discussion of the transsexual "Agnes," biologically a man who adopted the identity of a woman and underwent a sex change, shows how gender is created through interaction and based on taken-for-granted knowledge.

Garfinkel studied the methods Agnes employed to "pass" as a "normal natural female" and how Agnes acquired a public "female-ness" by utilizing the appropriate "female" skills and capacities, and effectively displaying "female" appearances and performances. Garfinkel concluded that the study of "violation cases" such as Agnes demonstrates for us what we all do: the naturalness of a world in which there are two sexes is realized through customary, yet self-regulated, management of performance and display, and is an interactionally accomplished cultural event. As Garfinkel (p. 181) puts it, "normally sexed persons are cultural events in societies whose character as visible orders of practical activities consist of members' recognition and production practices."

Kessler and McKenna (1978) take Garfinkel's insights further, arguing that all social action is constructed through taken-for-granted assumptions, or what they call "incorrigible propositions." Our belief in two objectively real, biologically created, constant sexes is a telling incorrigible proposition. We assume there are only two sexes; each person is simply an example of one or the other. In other words, we construct a sex dichotomy in which no such dichotomy holds cross-culturally or biologically. Western industrialized societies surgically "correct" the "intersexed," socially creating two opposite sexes.

Suzanne Kessler's (1990) study of the role physicians play in cases of intersexed infants shows clearly how these physicians engage in practices designed to ensure infants' physical conformity to the culturally ordained sex dichotomy. As Kessler (p. 24) expresses it:

> Although the deformity of intersexed genitals would be immutable were it not for medical interference, physicians do not consider it natural. Instead they think of, and speak of, the surgical/hormonal alteration of such deformities as natural because such intervention returns the body to what it "ought to have been" if events had taken their typical course. The non-normative is converted into the normative, and the normative state is considered natural. The genital ambiguity is remedied to conform to a "natural," that is, culturally indisputable, gender dichotomy.

The key process in social construction of the sex dichotomy is what Kessler and McKenna (1978: 1–20) call "gender attribution," or the active (though usually unconscious) way we decide what sex a person is. A significant incorrigible proposition of gender attribution is that men have penises; women do not. Thus we consider genitals the ultimate criterion in making sex assignments; yet, in our daily interactions, we continually make gender attributions with a complete lack of information about others' genitals. Our recognition of another's "sex" is dependent upon the exhibit of such characteristics as speech, hair, clothing, physical appearance, and other aspects of "personal front"—a gender display that becomes a substitute for the concealed genitalia (Goffman, 1979: 2).

Gender as Situated Accomplishment

In a series of articles, West, Zimmerman, and Fenstermaker (West and Zimmerman, 1987; Fenstermaker, West, and Zimmerman, 1991; West and Fenstermaker, 1993) distinguish "sex" (one's birth classification), "sex category" (the social identification as a woman or man), and "gender" (social action validating that identification). They agree with Goffman and Kessler and McKenna that we attribute the "correct" sex to individuals when they display the appropriate social signs of a sex category. We attempt to adorn ourselves in a culturally appropriate "female" or "male" fashion and daily, in every interaction, we engage in gender attribution—we identify and categorize people in an appropriate sex category while we simultaneously categorize ourselves for others.

Nevertheless, the concepts of gender display and gender attribution are not wholly sufficient in and of themselves. West, Zimmerman, and Fenstermaker argue correctly that *gender* entails much more than simply the social signs of a sex category. Rather, it involves a "situated accomplishment," that is, "the activity of managing situated conduct in light of normative conceptions, attitudes, and activities appropriate to one's sex category" (West and Zimmerman, 1987: 127). Thus, while sex category refers to social identification as a woman or man, gender is the processual corroboration of that identification and is accomplished in social interaction; we coordinate our activities to "do" gender in situational ways.

Crucial to the conceptualization of gender as a situated accomplishment is the notion of "accountability": "the possibility of describing activities, states of affairs, and descriptions themselves in serious and consequential ways—for example, as 'manly' or 'womanly' behaviors" (Fenstermaker, West, and Zimmerman, 1991: 294). Because individuals realize their behavior is accountable to others, they construct their actions in relation to how they might be interpreted by others in the particular social context in which they occur. Since sex category is always pertinent, an "individual involved in virtually any course of action may be held accountable for her/his execution of that action *as a woman* or *a man"* (p. 294). Because we believe there are but two natural sexes, we attempt to become one of them.

Moreover, we expect others to attribute a particular sex category to us—a sex category that corresponds to our "essential nature"—and we satisfy the ongoing task of accountability by demonstrating that we are a "male" or a "female" by means of concocted behaviors that may be interpreted accordingly. We configure our behaviors so we are seen unquestionably by others in particular social situations as expressing our "essential natures"—we do masculinity or femininity. As Fenstermaker, West, and Zimmerman (p. 294) conclude, "doing gender involves the management of conduct by sexually categorized human beings who are accountable to local conceptions of appropriately gendered conduct."

In this view, then, masculinity is accomplished, it is not something done to men or something settled beforehand. And masculinity is never static, never a finished product. Rather, men construct masculinities in specific social situations (although not in circumstances of their own choosing); in so doing, men reproduce (and sometimes change) social structures. As Giddens (1976: 138) forcefully argues, "every act which contributes to the reproduction of a structure is also an act of production, a novel enterprise, and as such may initiate change by altering that structure at the same time as it reproduces it."

Behavior by men is obviously considerably more complex than that suggested by the idea of a universal masculinity that is preformed and embedded in the individual prior to social action. Such a traditional approach to understanding masculinity (sex role socialization) was criticized in Chapter 1. In contrast, what is being suggested here is that men "come to be involved in a *self-regulating process*" as they monitor their own and others' gendered conduct (West and Zimmerman, 1987: 142). The accomplishment of gender "involves not only the appropriation of gender ideals (by the valuation of those ideals as proper ways of being and behaving) but also *gender identities* that are important to individuals and that they strive to maintain" (p. 142). Arthur Brittan (1989: 40) makes the same point:

> When one treats a male child as a boy, when one says to him that little boys do not cry, or when one indicates to him that his sexual organs are the sign of his difference from females, this cannot be a one-way process in which parents simply turn organic material into a gendered being. The male child also makes his own attributions, he does his own identity work—he is also a party to the negotiation and construction.

Masculinity personifies the construction of personal history up to a specific point in time and exemplifies the unification of self-regulated practices. These practices do not, however, occur in a vacuum. Rather, they are influenced by the gender ideals we have come to accept as normal and proper and by the social structural constraints we experience. Because men reproduce masculine ideals in structured specific practices, there are a variety of ways of "doing masculinity" (and femininity). Although masculinity is always individual and personal, specific forms of masculinity are available, encouraged, and permitted, depending upon one's class, race, and sexual preference. Masculinity must be viewed as structured action—what men do under specific constraints and varying degrees of power. As Connell (1987: 222) perceptively notes, we are "not monads closed off from others" but experience ourselves as "having shared pasts and sharing the present."

In this way, then, social relations (which are constituted by social structures) place each of us in a common relationship to others—we share structural space. Consequently, common or shared blocks of knowledge evolve through interaction, in which particular masculine ideals and activities play a part. Through interaction, masculinity becomes institutionalized, and men draw on such existing, but previously created, masculine ways of thinking and acting to construct a masculine identity in any particular situation. The specific criteria of masculine identities are embedded in the recurrent practices whereby social relations are structured (Giddens, 1989: 285).

Thus, a sociology of masculinity must first recognize that men are positioned differently throughout society and, therefore, share with other men the construction of masculinities peculiar to their position in society. Further, a sociology of masculinity must acknowledge that socially organized power relations among and between men are historically constructed on the basis of class, race, and sexual orientation. In other words, while there is a complex interlocking of masculinities, these masculinities are quite clearly unequal.

Hegemonic and Subordinated Masculinities

Several pro-feminist men have begun to employ Antonio Gramsci's notion of "hegemony" to distinguish between "hegemonic masculinity" and "subordinated masculinities" (Carrigan et al., 1987; Connell, 1987; Frank, 1987). Gramsci (1978) used the term hegemony to refer to the ascendancy—obtained primarily by manufactured consent rather than by force—of one class over other classes. Ideological hegemony, as the dominant conception of reality, is manifest throughout social institutions and, therefore, comprises "the 'spontaneous' consent given by the great masses of the population to the general direction imposed on social life by the dominant fundamental group" (p. 12). According to Gramsci (p. 12), hegemony is achieved fundamentally through consent, yet force may at times be necessary for "those groups who do not 'consent' either actively or passively."

Similarly, Connell (1987: 184) defines "hegemonic masculinity" as the ascendancy of a certain form of masculinity that is "embedded in religious doctrine and practice, mass media content, wage structures, the design of housing, welfare/taxation policies, and so forth." Connell's notion of hegemonic masculinity is constructed in relation both to subordinated masculinities and to women; it is the dominant form of masculinity to which other types of masculinity are subordinated, not eliminated, and it provides the primary basis for relationships among men. Moreover, force and threat of force may be used to help maintain hegemonic masculinity (for example, violence against women and homosexuals).

Simply defined, in any culture, hegemonic masculinity is the idealized form of masculinity in a given historical setting. It is culturally honored, glorified, and extolled, and this "exaltation stabilizes a structure of dominance and oppression in the gender order as a whole" (Connell, 1990: 94). In contemporary Western industrialized societies, hegemonic masculinity is defined through work in the paid-labor market, the subordination of women, heterosexism, and the driven and uncontrollable sexuality of men. Refined still further, hegemonic masculinity emphasizes practices toward authority, control, competitive individualism, independence, aggressiveness, and the capacity for violence (Connell, 1990, 1992; Segal, 1990). Hegemonic masculinity is substantially different from the notion of a "male sex role," because it allows us to move beyond universal and, therefore, categorical formulations of what constitutes "male" behavior. With it, we are able to explain power relations among men based on a hierarchy of masculinities and see how such masculinities are socially constructed.

The concepts "hegemonic" and "subordinated" masculinities also permit investigation of the way men experience their everyday world from a particular position in society and how they relate to and attempt to construct differently (or in fact reject) the cultural ideals of hegemonic masculinity. Because "most men benefit from the subordination of women, and hegemonic masculinity is the cultural expression of this ascendancy," most men engage in practices that attempt to sustain hegemonic masculinity (Connell, 1987: 185). Indeed, most men help maintain hegemonic masculinity (and consequently the subordination of women) by means of the practices that reflect their particular positions in society. Thus, the cultural ideals of hegemonic masculinity need not correspond to the actual personalities of most men (pp. 184–185).

> Indeed the winning of hegemony often involves the creation of models of masculinity which are quite specifically fantasy figures, such as the film characters played by Humphrey Bogart, John Wayne and Sylvester Stallone. Or real models may be publicized who are so remote from everyday achievement that they have the effect of an unattainable ideal, like the Australian Rules footballer Ron Barassi or the boxer Muhammad Ali.

Although men attempt to express hegemonic masculinity through speech, dress, physical appearance, activities, and relations with others, these social signs of masculinity are associated with the specific context of one's actions and are self-regulated within that context. Masculinity is based on social action that reacts to unique circumstances and relationships, and it is a social construction that is renegotiated in each particular context. In other words, social actors self-regulate their behavior and make choices in specific contexts. Consequently, men construct varieties of masculinity through specific practices that constitute social structures.

Structured Action and Gendered Crime

What I have argued to this point, then, is that within different social situations, there are patterned ways that masculinity is represented and enacted. Depending upon the setting, practices attempt to define and sustain specific conceptions of hegemonic masculinity, which express and reproduce social divisions of labor and power as well as normative heterosexuality. In this way, gender identity is firmly embedded in the social context and in the recurrent practices whereby social relations are structured. Masculinities are constructed through practices that maintain certain types of relationships between men and women and among men (Morgan, 1992: 67). Specific forms of masculinity are constructed in specific situations, and practices within social settings produce, reproduce, and alter types of masculinity. Thus, we "do gender" (West and Zimmerman, 1987) in response to the socially structured circumstances in which we live and within different social milieux diverse forms of masculinity arise, depending upon prevalent structural potentials and constraints. Because masculinity is a behavioral response to the particular conditions and situations in which men participate, different types of masculinity exist in the school, the youth group, the street, the family, and the workplace. In other words, men do masculinity according to the social situation in which they find themselves.

Accordingly, the chapters that follow will demonstrate the continuing vitality of the earlier argument in *Capitalism, Patriarchy and Crime*: gendered power is central to understanding why men commit more crimes and more serious crimes than women. Although crime is simply one practice in which and through which power over women can be naturalized, I must add that power relations among men determine the different types of crime men may commit. In the process of "doing gender"—socially constructing forms of masculinity—men may simultaneously construct forms of criminality. Doing masculinity, then, means creating differences from women and girls. It also means that aspects of social settings, social occasions, and social activities provide resources for "doing gender" (West and Zimmerman, 1987: 137–146).

When men enter a setting, they undertake social practices that demonstrate they are "manly." The only way others can judge their "essential nature" as men is through their behavior and appearance. Thus, men use the resources at their disposal to communicate gender to others. For many men, crime may serve as a suitable *resource* for "doing gender"—for separating them from all that is feminine. Because types of criminality are possible only when particular social conditions present themselves, when other masculine resources are unavailable, particular types of crime can provide an alternative resource for accomplishing gender and, therefore, affirming a particular type of masculinity. For, although men are always doing masculinity, the significance of gender accomplishment is socially situated and, thus, an intermittent matter. That is, certain occasions present themselves as more intimidating for showing and affirming masculinity. As Coleman (1990: 196) states, "Such an occasion is where a man's 'masculinity' risks being called into question." The taken-for-granted "essential nature" of a man or boy can be questioned, undermined, and threatened in certain contexts, those situations where he lacks resources for masculine accomplishment.

In such predicaments, sex category is particularly salient; it is, as David Morgan (1992: 47) puts it, "more or less explicitly put on the line," and doing masculinity necessitates extra effort, generating a distinct type of masculinity. Under such conditions, performance as a member of one's sex category is subjected to extra evaluation and crime is more likely to result. Crime, therefore, may be invoked as a practice through which masculinities (and men and women) are differentiated from one another. Moreover, crime is a resource that may be summoned when men lack other resources to accomplish gender.

Yet, social action is never simply an autonomous event but is amalgamated into larger assemblages—what Swidler (1986: 273) calls "strategies of action," or "persistent ways of ordering action through time." The cultural ideals of hegemonic masculinity encourages specific lines of gendered action and social structures shape the capacities from which gendered strategies of action are constructed over time. Men and boys apply the ideals of hegemonic masculinity to the situations that face them in everyday life, and in the process, pursue a gendered strategy of action (Hochschild, 1989: 17).[5]

From this perspective then, social action is often designed with an eye to one's gender accountability both situationally and in the future. Moreover, West and Zimmerman (1987: 138) point out that "many situations are not clearly sex categorized to begin with, nor is what transpires within them obviously gender relevant." Gender is not always relevant to the accomplishment of an activity, yet within the context of gendered strategies of action, behavior not situationally gender relevant may still be a resource for future gender accountability. That is, the particular social action is undertaken and designed not necessarily for that particular moment (it may not be relevant for the accomplishment of that particular action at that specific time), but with an eye to one's gender accountability at some impending time. Crime, then, can provide a resource for doing masculinity in specific social settings as well as contributing to a gendered line of action in which future accountability may be at risk (e.g., being an adequate breadwinner).

Crime by men is not simply an extension of the "male sex role." Rather, crime by men is a form of social practice invoked as a resource, when other resources are unavailable, for accomplishing masculinity. By analyzing masculinities, then, we can begin to understand the socially constructed differences among men and thus explain why men engage in different forms of crime.

Chapters 4 and 5 distinguish between public and private masculinities and the various crimes associated with these masculinities. In employing the concepts public and private, however, I neither relegate the former to the realm of the market and those facets of social life susceptible to state regulation nor relegate the latter to the realm of the home and those aspects immune from state regulation. Such distinctions have been properly criticized by socialist feminists (Jaggar, 1983: 143–148), and I have no intention of repeating that blunder here.

Nevertheless, it is axiomatic that in daily activity, we interact with others in social situations that can be categorized as public and private. That is, interaction occurs in social situations that can be understood as open to the sight, presence, or intrusion of "outsiders" (e.g., school, street, and youth group) or secluded from the vision, company, or intervention of "outsiders" (e.g., home and workplace). In the former, public masculinities and crimes are constructed; in the latter, private masculinities and crimes take place.

Chapter 4 focuses on youth crime and its relation to masculine construction in the public realms of school, youth group, and street. Chapter 5 examines public and private forms of adult masculinities and crimes in the realms of street, workplace, and family. These chapters are structured according to age for the purpose of demonstrating that the meaning of masculinity, and thus of crime, changes throughout the life course. In addition to age, however, each chapter highlights the relationship among class, race, and masculinity in the social construction of criminality.

Chapter 4

"Boys Will Be Boys" Differently

The two most significant and tenacious features associated with crime are age and gender. For example, young men account for a disproportionate amount of crime in all Western industrialized societies (Beirne and Messerschmidt, 1991; Chesney-Lind and Shelden, 1992). Moreover, although Albert Cohen's (1955) thesis on "delinquent boys" can be legitimately criticized for the reasons outlined in Chapter 1, his awareness of a relationship between the school and youth crime should not be discounted. Research has shown that youth crime declines drastically when public schools are not in session and that youth who leave school during the academic year engage in less crime than those currently enrolled (Elliott and Voss, 1974; Messerschmidt, 1979). Yet schooling is one of the chief social milieux for the development of youth crime and also a social setting that has institutionalized gender and, therefore, patterned ways in which femininity and masculinity are constructed and represented. School, then, does not merely adapt to a natural masculinity among boys. Rather, it constructs various forms of masculinity (and femininity) and negotiates relations among them (Connell, 1987: 291–292).

Similarly, there is a strong relationship between youth group activities and youth crime (Morash, 1986), and youth groups are an important social setting for the accomplishment of gender. Accordingly, in Chapter 4 I examine the reciprocal relationships among schooling, youth groups, masculinities, and crimes and attempt to illustrate how all of these are constituted through structured social action. More specifically, I explore the way social action is linked to structured possibilities/constraints, identifying in particular how the class, race, and gendered relations in society constrain and enable the social activity of young men in the school and the youth group, and how this structured action relates to youth crime.

"Boys will be boys" differently, depending upon their position in social structures and, therefore, upon their access to power and resources. Social structures situate young men in a common relation to other young men and in such a way that they share structural space. Collectively, young men experience their daily world from a particular position in society and differentially construct the cultural ideals of hegemonic masculinity. Thus, within the school and youth group there are patterned ways in which masculinity is represented and which depend upon structures of labor and power in class and race relations. Young men situationally accomplish public forms of masculinity in response to their socially structured circumstances; indeed, varieties of youth crime serve as a suitable resource for doing masculinity when other resources are unavailable. These forms of youth crime, as with other resources, are determined by social structures.

Social Structures, Masculinities, and Crime in Youth Groups

Research on youth groups indicates that what young men and women do tends to mirror and recreate particular gender divisions of labor and power and normative heterosexuality. This appears to be so regardless of class and race position. From Thrasher's (1927) early research to the works of Cohen (1955), Cloward and Ohlin (1960), Short and Strodtbeck (1965), Klein (1971), Miller (1980), Quicker (1983), Schwendinger and Schwendinger (1985), Harris (1988) and Fishman (1988), women have been found to take on secondary or "auxiliary roles" in the group if, in fact, they are involved in the group at all. Anne Campbell's (1984: 242–243) important ethnographic study of lower–working-class racial minority youth groups in New York City found that both men and women assume positions within the group that might be available to them in society at large:

> In straight society the central, pivotal figure is the male. His status in the world of societal and material success is the critical factor, while the woman supports, nurtures, and sustains him. The gang parodies this state of affairs, without even the economic infrastructure to sustain it, for the male rarely works and often it is the female who receives a more stable income through welfare. Nevertheless, the males constitute the true gang! Gang feuds are begun and continued by males; females take part as a token of their allegiance to the men.

Campbell (p. 266) argues further that specific girl groups:

> exist as an annex to the male gang, and the range of possibilities open to them is dictated and controlled by the boys. Within the gang, there are

still "good girls" and "bad girls," tomboys and fallen women. Girls are told how to dress, are allowed to fight, and are encouraged to be good mothers and faithful wives. Their principal source of suffering and joy is their men. And though the girls may occasionally defy them, often argue with them, and sometimes patronize them, the men remain indisputably in control.

What Campbell's research indicates is that the gender social structures of labor and power shape interaction in youth groups, affording young men the opportunity to arrange social life to their advantage. Although these opportunities vary by race and by class, young men exercise authority and control in terms of gender, at least relative to young women of the same race and class. The youth group, then, is unmistakably a domain of masculine dominance, a domain that reflects the gender structures of labor and power in society and the related practices by which they are reproduced.

Besides overall dominance in youth groups, normative heterosexuality is a decisive "measuring rod" for group participation. Indeed, young men often control and exploit the sexuality of young women. Campbell (1984: 245) reported that in one particular group, heterosexuality was so crucial to group membership by young women that when "dykes" were discovered, they were "multiply raped and thrown out of the club." Similarly, the Schwendingers (1985: 167) found that "sexist exploitation of girls is common to all stratum formations," from middle- to working-class youth groups.

Suspicion and jealousy being one of the most disruptive practices inside youth groups, serial monogamy is demanded and enforced. Jealousy by a young man is often interpreted by a young woman as evidence not of his control, but of his passionate attachment to her. Similarly, "the beatings that she may receive at his hands when he believes that she has been unfaithful are interpreted as a direct index of his love for her" but "his infidelity is blamed upon his desirability to other women, rather than seen as evidence of his less-than-total commitment to her" (Campbell, 1990: 174–175). Campbell (pp. 180–181) adds that both the men and women see the men as being:

> by nature, unable to refuse an offer of sex. Consequently, it is not the boy's fault when he strays but rather the other woman's. The confrontation is recast as between the girlfriend and her rival, rather than between the girl and the boy. Consequently, sexual betrayal is terminated by an attack on the rival, not on the boyfriend, who simply was following his nature.

Other research suggests similar heterosexual relations in lower–working-class (Fishman, 1988), working-class (Willis, 1977), and middle-class (Schwendinger and Schwendinger, 1985) youth groups. Accordingly, normative heterosexuality is constructed as a practice that helps to reproduce the subordination of young women and to form age-specific heterosexual styles of masculinity, a masculinity centering on an uncontrollable and unlimited sexual appetite. Normative heterosexuality, then, serves as a resource for the situated accomplishment of gender in youth groups.

Regardless of the degree of participation in youth groups by young women and the nature of youth sexuality in such groups, research clearly shows that various masculinities (as well as femininities) are constructed within these groups and, thus, the various forms of youth crime associated with those masculinities. William Chambliss's (1973) classic study "The Saints and the Roughnecks" is notable in this regard. The Saints were "eight promising young men—children of good, stable, white upper–middle-class families, active in school affairs, good pre-college students" (p. 24). They were successful in school, earned high grades (two boys had close to straight "A" averages), and several held student offices. At the end of their senior year, the student body selected ten seniors as "school wheels"; four were Saints.

As for youth crime, the Saints were involved primarily in practices that "raised hell," such as traveling to nearby cities on weekend evenings (often under the influence of alcohol) to vandalize property, engage in a variety of "pranks" and forms of "mischief," and commit minor forms of theft. The Saints, however, never fought; in fact, they avoided physical conflict both inside and outside their group. Chambliss (p. 26) points out: "The boys had a spirit of frivolity and fun about their escapades. They did not view what they were engaged in as 'delinquency.'"

Although the Roughnecks attended the same school as the Saints, they were six lower–working-class white boys. The Roughnecks avoided school as much as possible because they considered it a burden. They neither participated in school affairs, except for two who played football, nor earned good grades, averaging a "C" or lower. Moreover, these boys were involved in more serious forms of delinquency. In addition to drinking, truancy, and vandalism, they engaged in major forms of theft and violence. The Roughnecks sometimes stole as a group (coordinating their efforts) or simply stole in pairs, rarely stealing alone. Regarding violence, the Roughnecks not only welcomed an opportunity to fight, but they went seeking it, frequently fighting among themselves; at least once a month the Roughnecks would participate in some type of physical fight (pp. 27–29).

Chambliss's study is important for showing that within this particular social setting, the same school, the Saints and the Roughnecks both used available class and race resources to shape particular types of public masculinity. It is not that the Roughnecks were masculine because of their violence and that the Saints were not masculine because of their pranks. Rather, the Saints and Roughnecks were constructing different personifications of masculinity and drawing on different forms of youth crime (e.g., pranks vs. violence) as resources for that construction.

Other research indicates similar processes occurring among masculine-dominated youth groups, enabling us to build on Chambliss's data. For example, Herman Schwendinger's and Julia Schwendinger's (1985) study, *Adolescent Subcultures and Delinquency*, attempts to explain the forms of youth crime that emerge at the group level and, in so doing, identify two types of group formations that young men dominate: the "socialite" and "street-corner youth." The Schwendingers' data show that both groups construct different forms of masculinity and, therefore, exhibit varying types of youth crime. Yet the middle-class "Socs" (socialites) and the lower–working-class "Eses" (street-corner youth) both marshal gender and class resources in their struggle for power and status in the adolescent world.

Like the Saints, the Socs are "less likely to be involved in the most serious violent and economic forms of delinquency" (p. 56), drawing on school resources and various forms of vandalism, drinking, gambling, petty theft, and truancy to construct a specific type of public masculinity. Although the Eses engage in the same types of delinquent activities, the most extreme forms of violence are found among these street-corner youth. In other words, both groups of young men pursue gendered strategies of action that reflect their relative class and race/ethnicity position. Again, like the Saints, Socs have specific potentials and opportunities that help construct less violent forms of masculinity. As the Schwendingers (p. 208) point out:

> the Socs control the student organizations in their high schools, and the payoffs from this control are considerable. These advantages do not merely mean unique experiences, such as trips and contacts with prestigious youth in other schools, but also large and pleasant facilities in which to hold dances. Furthermore, their frequent control over the student

council, cheerleading squad, and student monitor system reflects their integration with prevailing systems of institutionalized power and enables them to establish an authoritative position in the eyes of other youth.

Eses have no access to such resources and power, and thus accomplish gender in a different way. For the street-corner youth, masculinity does not derive from competition for school office but from violent conflicts with other street-corner men. Carlos, a member of a street-corner gang, told the Schwendingers (p. 171), "In my territory that's the way they are now. That's the way we are. It seems to be the neighborhood that is the thing. You want to prove yourself to nobody but these people."

For both the Saints/Roughnecks and Socs/Eses, the youth group is a critical organizing setting for the embodiment of public masculinity. It is within this group that young men's power over young women is normalized and that youth crime, as a social practice within the group, constructs gendered differences, weaving "a structure of symbol and interpretation around these differences that naturalizes them" (Messner, 1989: 79). Yet, simultaneously, these findings exhibit clear differences in "doing gender" for middle- and lower–working-class boys. In fact, the above findings require a more rigorous examination of class and race distinctions.

In what follows, then, I attempt to identify certain of the chief class and race junctures in the social construction of youthful public masculinities and crimes—in particular, the important relationship between youth crime and school. The focus is on how some young men come to define their masculinity against the school and, in the process, choose forms of youth crime as resources for accomplishing gender and for constructing what I call *opposition masculinities*. I begin with white, middle-class boys.

White, Middle-class Boys

Given the success of the middle-class Saints and Socs in school, it is this very success that provides a particular resource for constructing a specific form of masculinity. In this type of masculinity, the penchant for a career is fundamental: a "calculative attitude is taken towards one's own life" and the crucial themes are "rationality and responsibility rather than pride and aggressiveness" (Connell, 1989: 296–297). Throughout their childhood development, white, middle-class boys are geared toward the ambiance and civility of the school.[1] Within the school environment, for these boys, masculinity is normally accomplished through participation in sports and academic success. This participation in (or at least avid support for) sport creates an environment for the construction of a masculinity that celebrates toughness and endurance, incessantly advocates competitiveness and shame of losing, and "connects a sense of maleness with a taste for violence and confrontation" (Kessler, Ashenden, Connell, Dowsett, 1985: 39). Yet, in addition to creating this specific type of masculinity, sport is so revered and glorified within the school that it subordinates other types of masculinity, such as the sort constructed by the "brains" who participate in nonviolent games like debate (p. 39).

Over and above sport, white, middle-class masculinity in the school is typically achieved through a reasonable level of academic success. As Tolson (1977: 34–36) argues, the middle-class family supports this trajectory: "books in the home and parental help with homework provide a continuous emotional context for academic achievement"; moreover, middle-class families also tend to emphasize the importance of obtaining the appropriate qualifications for "respectable careers" that guarantee the "security" of a "profession." As Heward (1988: 8) experienced in an English boarding school, white, middle-class parents "planned their sons' futures carefully and then pursued their plans very actively, with the aim of placing them in suitable occupations and careers." For the white middle class, then, manliness is about having a secure income from a "respectable" professional occupation. Thus, there is an important link between school and family in middle-class life, and both transmit class-specific notions of hegemonic masculinity to white, middle-class boys—a particular type of work in the paid-labor market, competitiveness, personal ambition and achievement, and responsibility.

Accommodating and Opposition Masculinities

Nonetheless, hegemonic masculinity also involves practices characterizing dominance, control, and independence (see Chapter 3). Such masculine ideals are, however, the very qualities that schooling discourages. Although white, middle-class youth generally exercise greater authority and control in school than do youth from other class and race backgrounds, research on secondary schooling reveals that adaptation to the social order of the school requires that all students, regardless of their class and race, submit to rock-hard authority relations in which students are actually penalized for creativity, autonomy, and independence (Bowles and Gintis, 1976; Greenberg, 1977; Messerschmidt, 1979). In other words, white, middle-class boys, like other boys, experience a school life that is circumscribed by institutionalized authoritarian routine.

In spite of this constraint, within the school most white, middle-class boys conform, since proper credentials are necessary to attaining careers. As Greenberg (1977: 201) notes, students "who believe that their future chances depend on school success are likely to conform even if they resent the school's attempt to regulate their lives." Within the social setting of the school, then, white, middle-class boys accomplish gender by conforming to school rules and regulations and by dominating student organizations, reflecting a wholehearted obligation to the school and its overall enterprise. White, middle-class boys "accept" school values and therefore the school exercises a prominent and influential restraint on these youth, at least within its own boundaries (Tolson, 1977: 39).

Because masculinity is a behavioral response to the particular conditions and situations in which we participate, white, middle-class boys thus do masculinity within the school in a specific way that reflects their position in the class and race divisions of labor and power. Their white, middle-class position both constrains and enables certain forms of gendered social action, and these boys monitor their action in accord with those constraints and opportunities, thus reproducing simultaneously class, race, and gender relations. Moreover, this particular masculinity is sustained as a type of collective product in a particular social setting—white middle-class schools.

However, because the school is "emasculating" in the fashion discussed earlier, white, middle-class boys who join a youth group act outside the school in ways that help restore those hegemonic masculine ideals discouraged in school. In this process of "doing gender," these boys simultaneously construct age-specific forms of criminality. Youth crime, within the social context of the youth group outside the school, serves as a resource for masculine realization and facilitates (as do such other practices as school athletics) "dominance bonding" among privileged young men (Messner, 1989: 79).

Successful "pranks," "mischief," vandalism, minor thefts, and drinking outside the school validate a boy's "essential nature." Such behaviors reflect an age-specific attempt to reestablish a public masculine identity somewhat diminished in the school, behaviors that are purposely chosen and manipulated for their ability to impress other boys. Moreover, outside the confines of the school, white, middle-class boys' masculinity is still held accountable, not to school officials, but to other white, middle-class boys. These behavioral forms help a white, middle-class boy to carve out a valued masculine identity by exhibiting those hegemonic masculine ideals the school denies—independence, dominance, daring, and control—to resolve the problem of accountability outside the school, and to establish for himself and others his "essential nature" as a "male." Indeed, most accounts of these forms of youth crime miss the significance of gender: it is young men who are overwhelmingly the perpetrators of these acts (Chesney-Lind and Shelden, 1992: 7–18). Accomplishing gender by engaging in vandalism, "pranks," and "mischief" (as an age-specific resource) incontrovertibly provides a public masculine resolution to the spectacle of self-discipline and emotional restraint in the school.

Thus we see that white, middle-class, youth masculinity is accomplished differently in separate and dissimilar social situations. For white, middle-class boys, the problem is to produce configurations of masculine behavior that can be seen by others as normative. Yet, as the social setting changes, from inside the school to outside in the youth group, so does the conceptualization of what is normative masculine behavior.

Through class appeal for educational credentials, white, middle-class boys are drawn into a different masculine construction within the school: they develop an *accommodating masculinity*—a controlled, cooperative, rational gender strategy of action for institutional success. The white, middle-class boy's agenda within the school, then, is simply to become an accomplice to the institutional order, thereby reaping the privileges it offers—access to higher education and a professional career (Connell, 1989: 295–297). In other words, as white, middle-class boys accomplish gender in the school setting, they simultaneously reproduce class and race relations through the same ongoing practices.

Being a man is about developing the essential credentials to obtain a suitable middle-class occupation. However, because the school both creates and undermines hegemonic masculinity, within the company of peers outside the school some white, middle-class boys draw primarily on nonviolent forms of youth crime, thus constructing an *opposition masculinity*—a masculinity based on the very hegemonic masculine ideals the school discourages. In short, white, middle-class boys are forming different types of masculinity that can be assessed and approved in both social settings (inside and outside school) as normal and natural. Through this specific type of youth crime in the peer group, middle-class masculinities are differentiated from one another.

The case of white, middle-class youth demonstrates how we maintain different gendered identities that may be emphasized or avoided, depending upon the social setting. White, middle-class boys construct their gendered actions in relation to how such actions might be interpreted by others (that is, their accountability) in the particular social context in which they occur. White, middle-class boys are doing masculinity differently because the setting and the available resources change.

School Success, Masculinity, and Youth Crime

Social control theorists argue that youth who develop close bonds to the school are the least likely to engage in youth crime (Hirschi, 1969; Wiatrowski, Griswold, and Roberts, 1981). Yet the considerable amount of youth crime committed by the Saints and the Socs (who were the school "wheels" and high academic achievers) outside the school justifies reasonable concern regarding this argument. Nevertheless, middle-class schools, like schools in other social settings, develop a status system based on academic success. Research has consistently shown that students who fail academically (for whatever reason) and/ or who occupy the lowest status positions in school, exhibit the highest rates of youth crime. (See Messerschmidt, 1979 for a review of this research.) Consequently, for white, middle-class boys who are not successful at schoolwork and who do not participate in school sports or extracurricular activities, the school is a frustrating masculine experience as a result of which they are likely to search out other masculine-validating resources.

This view was demonstrated in one study of an upper–middle-class, white neighborhood, described by the authors as an "environmental paradise" that "harbors mansions and millionaires as well as deer and raccoons" (Muehlbauer and Dodder, 1983: 35). The particular neighborhood youth group, which called itself "the losers," was composed primarily of boys who did not do well in school and who demonstrated little athletic interest or ability. "The losers" spent considerable time "hanging out" together at the town square, but were not at all fond of interpersonal violence and controlling turf. Rather, they engaged chiefly in acts of vandalism—such as breaking streetlamps, making graffiti, destroying traffic signs, and doing donuts on the lawns of the more affluent members of the community—as well as organizing drinking parties at public beaches and parks. Indeed, the only serious violence committed by "the losers" was the firebombing of the personal automobiles of two representatives of "emasculating" authority: the chief of police and the vice-principal of the school. Thus, the specific types of youth crime engaged in by "the losers" served as a resource for masculine construction when other types of class-specific resources were unappealing and/or unattractive (e.g., academic success).[2]

Although this opposition masculinity outside the school is clearly not the only version of white, middle-class youth masculinity, nor perhaps the most common version, it differs considerably from that of white, working-class youth, especially because of its reduced emphasis on the public display of interpersonal aggression/violence. It follows that we must consider more closely how this type of youthful, white, middle-class, masculine construction and its attendant youth crime differs from that of youthful, white, working-class men.

White, Working-class Boys

As exemplified by the Roughnecks and the Eses, white, working-class boys engage in such acts as vandalism, truancy, and drinking because, as demonstrated more precisely below, they also experience school authority as an "emasculating" power. Not surprisingly, many of these boys also turn to this age-specific resource for "doing gender" outside the school. And yet, they define their masculinity against the school in a different way than do white middle-class boys, a way that nevertheless leads to an in-school opposition masculinity as well.

"The Lads" and the "Ear'oles"

Paul Willis's (1977) classic study *Learning to Labour* demonstrates how a group of white, working-class British boys ("the lads") reject both schoolwork and the "ear'oles" (earholes, or other young men who conform to the school rules) because "the lads" perceive office jobs and "bookwork" as "sissy stuff." The lads come to school armed with traditional notions of white, working-class masculinity: the idea that "real men" choose manual, not mental labor. Because of this particular gendered strategy, schooling is deemed irrelevant to their working-class future and "emasculating" to their conception of masculinity. In other words, schooling is unmanly in a different and broader way for these boys than for the white, middle-class boys discussed above. Accordingly, the lads evolve into an unstructured, counterschool group that carves out a specific masculine space within the school, its overwhelming rules, and unnerving authority.

In resisting the school, the lads construct behavior patterns that set them apart from both the ear'oles and also the school. Because the ear'oles are enthusiastic about schooling and support its rules, they are a major conformist target for the lads.[3] One such practice for opposing the school and the ear'oles is "having a laff," that is, devising techniques to circumvent the controlled environment of the school. Willis (pp. 13, 31) describes some of these:

> Settled in class, as near a group as they can manage, there is a continuous scraping of chairs, a bad tempered "tut-tutting" at the simplest request and a continuous fidgeting about which explores every permutation of sitting or lying on a chair. During private study, some openly show disdain by apparently trying to go to sleep with their head sideways down on the desk, some have their backs to the desk gazing out of the window, or even vacantly at the wall. . . . In the corridors there is a foot-dragging walk, an overfriendly "hello" or sudden silence as the teacher passes. Devisive or insane laughter erupts which might or might not be about some one who has just passed. It is as demeaning to stop as it is to carry on. . . . During films they tie the projector leads into impossible knots, make animal figures or obscene shapes on the screen with their fingers, and gratuitously dig and jab the backs of "ear'oles" in front of them.

Another activity that distinguished the lads from the ear'oles is fighting. The lads exhibited "a positive joy in fighting, in causing fights through intimidation, in talking about fighting and about the tactics of the whole fight situation" (p. 34). Constructing masculinity around physical aggression, the lads—eschewing academic achievement—draw on an available resource that allows them to distance and differentiate themselves from the nonviolent ear'oles. As Willis (p. 34) points out, "Violence and the judgement of violence is the most basic axis of 'the lads' ascendance over the conformists, almost in the way that knowledge is for teachers." The lads reject and feel superior to the ear'oles; moreover, they construct such practices as having a laff and fighting to demonstrate their perceived masculine eminence.

In this way, then, the lads accomplish gender in a specific relational way by opposing both the school and its conformists. Whereas white, middle-class boys are more likely to oppose school outside its boundaries but conform within school, the social setting for the lads is different. *They are the opposition both inside and outside the school.* Understandably, there is no accommodating masculinity here. Because schooling is conceived as unnecessary to their future while simultaneously encompassing effeminate endeavors, the lads earn symbolic space from the school by engaging in different forms of "pranks" and "mischief" within the school itself. Such behaviors help transcend the "sissyish" quality of the school day while simultaneously distancing the lads from the conformists.[4]

But the lads also draw on forms of physical intimidation and violence to differentiate themselves from the ear'oles and the girls. For the lads, the fight "is the moment when you are fully tested"; it is "disastrous for your informal standing and masculine reputation if you refuse to fight or perform very amateurishly" (p. 35). In fact, physical aggressiveness seems to be an institutionalized feature of the lads' group. As Willis (p. 36) notes, "the physicality of all interactions, the mock pushing and fighting, the showing off in front of girls, the demonstrations of superiority and put-downs of the conformists, all borrow from the grammar of the real fight situation." These activities provide the fodder with which to accomplish their gender and to establish (for the lads) their "essential male nature." They are designed with an eye to gender accountability and resultingly construct inequality among boys by attempting to place the ear'oles masculinity beneath their own within the public context of the school. The lads are constructing an opposition masculinity as a collective practice; notwithstanding, this specific type is significantly different from the white, middle-class in school accommodating masculinity and gains meaning in relation to the masculinity of the ear'oles.

Outside the School

It is not only conformists to the school whom white, working-class youth, like the lads, attempt to subordinate in the process of doing gender. In Western industrialized societies, what have become known as hate crimes—racist and anti-gay violence—are disproportionately committed by groups of white, working-class boys, crimes that can also be understood in the way discussed above (Beirne and Messerschmidt, 1991: 562–563; Comstock, 1991: 72-92).

For some white, working-class boys, their public masculinity is constructed through hostility to, and rejection of, all aspects of groups that may be considered inferior in a racist and heterosexist society. For example, the ear'oles are considered inferior and subordinate to the lads because of their conformity to, and seeming enjoyment of, effeminate schooling projects. But other groups outside the school are also viewed as inferior by many white, working-class boys. Willis (1977:

48) found that different skin color was enough for the lads to justify an attack on, or intimidation of, racial minorities. Indeed, the meaning of being a "white man" has always hinged on the existence of, for example, a subordinated "black man." Thus, a specific *racial gender* is constructed through the identical practice of racist violence; a social practice that bolsters, within the specific setting of white, working-class youth groups, one's masculine "whiteness" and, therefore, constitutes race and gender simultaneously. White, working-class, youthful masculinity acquires meaning in this particular context through racist violence.

Moreover, for some white, working-class youth, homosexuality is simply unnatural and effeminate sex, and many turn this ideology into physical violence. As one white, working-class youth put it, "My friends and I go 'fag-hunting' around the neighborhood. They should all be killed" (Weissman, 1992: 173). Gay bashing serves as a resource for constructing masculinity in a specific way: physical violence against gay men in front of other young, white, working-class men reaffirms one's commitment to what is for them natural and masculine sex—heterosexuality. In other words, the victim of gay bashing serves, "both physically and symbolically, as a vehicle for the sexual status needs of the offenders in the course of recreational violence" (Harry, 1992: 15). Accordingly, gender is accomplished and normative heterosexuality is reproduced.[5]

White, working-class boys such as the lads construct public masculinities outside the school in other ways as well. As with the Roughnecks and the Eses, the lads also occasionally participate in various forms of theft. Because they want to take part in the youth culture (go to pubs, wear the "right" clothes, date, and so on) shortage of cash becomes "the single biggest pressure, perhaps at any rate after school, in their lives" (Willis, 1977: 39). Through contacts with family and friends, many of the lads acquired part-time, after-school, and summer jobs; in fact, Willis found that it is not uncommon for these youths to work over ten hours a week during the school year. Consequently, "this ability to 'make out' in the 'real world' . . . and to deal with adults nearly on their own terms" is seen by the lads as evidence of their "essential nature" as "males"—a practice that reproduces this specific type of white, working-class masculinity (p. 39). In addition, because of their access to paid employment, the lads involvement in theft is irregular rather than systematic, providing a little extra pocket money when needed.

Mercer Sullivan's (1989) analysis of a white, masculine-dominated, working-class youth group from "Hamilton Park" suggests the presence of analogous processes in the United States. Most of the boys in this group are from the more established and better employed white, working-class households where the "man of the house" is the "head of the house" as well as the principal wage earner. The working-class jobs held by these men have been passed down from generation to generation through masculine-dominated, family networks. The boys from these families view schooling in the same way that Willis's "lads" in Britain view schooling, and racism is pernicious and widespread among these boys. Indeed, the violence committed by these youths is based on ethnic boundaries between the predominantly white neighborhood of Hamilton Park and the adjacent African American and Latino areas.

Sullivan did not examine interpersonal violence in depth and he disregarded whether or not these youth engaged in "pranks" and "mischief" in school; rather, he concentrated on property crime outside school. Sullivan found that by the age of fourteen, the Hamilton Park boys began working steadily in part-time jobs during the school year and in full-time jobs during the summer months. This regularized work came to them in the same way work came to the lads, through connections. Sullivan found that because of these links to paid employment, the Hamilton Park youths had far less involvement in street crime than youth from lower–working-class, racial minority neighborhoods who had no such connections. Although during their early and midteen years the Hamilton Park youths engaged in factory burglary, shoplifting, and joyriding, none of them later engaged in systematic theft as a primary source of income. By their midteens, most worked at jobs paying better than the minimum wage and, therefore, "wages, not theft, provided their primary source of income during those years" (p. 179).

Because of their attachments to paid employment and a future in manual labor, periodic property crime was an important practice in the construction of their specific type of masculinity for both the lads and the Hamilton Park boys. The way they committed theft reflected their lack of dependence on stealing for income, which in turn provided a resource for constructing their "essential nature" in a specific way. As Willis (1977: 40) recorded for the lads:

> thieving puts you at risk, and breaks up the parochialism of the self. "The rule," the daily domination of trivia and the entrapment of the formal are broken for a time. In some way a successful theft challenges and beats authority.

In this specific context, then, intermittent theft is a resource that helps construct an "out-of-school," autonomous, independent, and daring opposition masculinity. And with part-time work available as a masculine resource, outside the school these white, working-class youths only sporadically turn to theft as a resource to accomplish gender. Thus, theft not only provides these youth with a resource for doing masculinity in the specific social setting of the group, it also helps construct a gendered line of action in which future gender accountability may be at risk. That is, it contributes to the wherewithal for adequate masculine participation in the youth culture.

Yet while the part-time workplace and youth group are initially seen as superior to the school—a milieu where masculinity as they know it is accepted—these working-class boys eventually find themselves locked into dead-end jobs, making less money than those who did not participate in the group and who conformed to the school. In this way, Willis's book shows how white "working-class kids get working-class jobs." The initial context, and ultimate result, of the lads' opposition masculinity in the school was an orientation toward manual labor. Through their specific construction of masculinity, the lads themselves (and, similarly, the Hamilton Park boys) thus reproduced class, race, and gender relations as the structures constituted in those relations constrain and enable their collective social action.[6]

Lower–working-class, Racial-minority Boys

Consider now how this white, working-class opposition masculinity (and the white, middle-class masculinity discussed earlier) differs from youth masculinity of lower–working-class racial minorities who engage in youth crime. Because these youth have no access to paid labor (as have the lads and Hamilton Park boys) and their parents are unable to subsidize their youth culture needs (as are the parents of white, middle-class boys), the youth gang in lower–working-class, racial-minority communities takes on a new and significant meaning inasmuch as it is here where resources are available with which to sustain a masculine identity. For many of these youths (although far from all), life is neither the workplace nor the school; it is the street.

Jean-Paul Sartre's (1963) discussion of "the project" illustrates the important attraction of the street group to many lower–working-class, racial-minority boys. For Sartre (p. 90), people make history on the basis of social structures because these conditions "furnish a direction and a material reality to changes which are in preparation; but the movement of human *praxis* goes beyond them while conserving them." What Sartre (p. 91) affirms is the explicitness of social action "which transforms the world on the basis of given conditions." For Sartre (p. 91), the project is behavior constrained by the present social factors that condition it, as well as a future or nonfuture that is visualized:

> The most rudimentary behavior must be determined both in relation to the real and present factors which condition it and in relation to a certain object, still to come, which it is trying to bring into being. This is what we call the *project*.

At any given historical period, there are what Sartre calls a "field of possibilities." Social structures (race, class, and gender divisions of labor and power, as well as normative heterosexuality) circumscribe an individual's field of possibilities and, therefore, lower–working-class, racial-minority boys are, according to Sartre (p. 95), "defined negatively by the sum total of possibles which are impossible for them; that is, by a future more or less blocked off." For these youths, each cultural, technical, or material social enrichment represents a diminution, an impoverishment—the future is almost entirely barred.

Pointing to the effects of the divisions of labor and power on these youth, Sartre defines the life of these young men as determined not by the possible but by what is impossible. Because they are, in effect, denied many resources for constructing hegemonic masculinity (i.e., paid work), these young men undergo, in Sartre's words, a "subjective impoverishment" (pp. 95–96). The resulting masculine-dominated street groups in marginalized, racial-minority communities are, in part, the result of a collective awareness of a hegemonic, masculine future that is, in terms of social possibilities, almost entirely unobtainable. It is a form of transcendence limited by class and race divisions of labor and power where individuals become aware of their position in society by perceiving what future is and is not possible for them. For many lower–working-class, racial-minority boys, the street group has become both a collective solution to their prohibitions and a life-style that sometimes takes the form of street crime. For these youths, then, street crime becomes a "field of possibilities" for transcending class and race domination and an important resource for accomplishing gender.

Opposition in School

Most white, middle-class boys envision a future in mental labor and members of the white, working-class (such as Willis's lads and Sullivan's Hamilton Park youths) realistically anticipate manual-labor positions. Consequently, these youths have resources (and a future) for masculine construction that are unavailable to lower–working-class, racial-minority boys. For marginalized, racial-minority boys, no such occupational future can be realistically anticipated and, accordingly, hegemonic masculinity is severely threatened. Under such conditions, life inside school takes on a significantly different meaning.

These youth are the least likely of all to perceive a connection between school and occupational success, a fact that Arthur Stinchcombe (1964) pointed out thirty years ago in *Rebellion in a High School*. More recently, Cernkovich and Giordano (1992: 264) reported that among many, but clearly not all, lower–working-class, racial-minority youth, "school is perceived as unrelated to future success; as a result, they see little reason to conform to the demands of the school environment." These youth search out ways to escape what appears to them an "emasculating" monotony and formal discipline better suited to "wimps."[7] Moreover, given that they do not have the resources of white, middle-class and working-class boys, marginalized, racial-minority boys are more likely to employ other means of accomplishing gender. In particular, violent behavior, as a resource for an opposition masculine construction, is more likely to increase relative to youth of other class and race backgrounds.

Disorder, including violence against teachers, is greatest in those schools serving lower–working-class racial-minority communities (Gottfredson and Gottfredson, 1985). In such schools, the young men who engage in this violence treat a teacher's insistence on a right to authority as violative of their masculine rights to autonomy, independence, and control. Because the school is seen simply as another institutional impediment to a future in hegemonic masculine ways and because they lack the resources of white, middle-class and working-class boys, these young men are more likely to turn to those hegemonic masculine ideals that remain available, such as physical violence.

Physical violence within the school is a resource employed for masculine construction. In situations where class and race structural disadvantage are severe, one's taken-for-granted "essential nature" is more likely to be undermined and threatened; therefore, gender is held more accountable. In short, at the level of personal practice, this translates into a display of physical violence as a specific type of in-school, opposition masculinity. The following is one example (cited in Mancini, 1981: 97):

> I fool around the place, throw books at the other kids. . . . I have a elastic on my hand, and pop the kids and, you know, look all innocent, like I didn't do it. . . . I break out and start laughin', couldn't hold it, so he goes and tells the vice principal. So he comes . . . and starts grabbin' on me, and, you know, take the elastic off my wrist . . . starts shakin' me up and everything. Then I start, you know, pushin' on him . . . fighting back. . . .

Another example demonstrates this willingness to use violence publicly (cited in Mancini, 1981: 97):

> We gotta wear ties at the Dubois. One day I didn't have mine on; I had it hangin' out my back pocket. The vice principal came, yankin' on my shoulder . . . he said, put it on before I pick it out and hang it around your neck. So I told him to try it. He took the tie out, tried to get it around my neck, and I snatched it and pushed him; he leaned back on the table and flipped right over it (chuckle). . . .

Thus, for lower–working-class, racial-minority boys in the process of opposing the school, doing masculinity necessitates extra effort; consequently, they are more likely than other boys to accomplish gender within the school by constructing a physically violent opposition masculinity. And in doing so, they turn to available hegemonic masculine ideals with which to construct such masculinity. This physical violence in the school is one practice that differentiates lower–working-class opposition masculinity from the other types discussed earlier.

Opposition Outside School

In addition to opposition within the school, because the school has less significance to these youths than to young men in other social classes, the street group also takes on a distinct and significant meaning in which opposition masculinity outside the school is likewise quite different from that of other youths. Marginalized, racial-minority boys are disproportionately involved in such serious property crimes as robbery and in such publicly displayed forms of group violence as "turf wars" (Steffensmeier and Allen, 1981; Elliott and Huizinga, 1983; Tracy, Wolfgang, and Figlio, 1991). The roots of this violent street crime are found in the disconcerting nature of the school and in the social conditions of poverty, racism, negated future, and power accorded men. Because of these social conditions and their attendant possibilities/constraints, young ghetto men are the most likely to commit certain types of street crime and thus to construct a different type of opposition masculinity outside the school.

Let us return now to Mercer Sullivan's (1989) ethnographic study that examined Puerto Rican (from "La Barriada") and African American (from "Projectville"), lower–working-class youth groups and their involvement in property crime. Sullivan reported that La Barriada youth are from an extremely poor neighborhood most of whose households are headed by women supported chiefly by welfare payments. Other families in the same neighborhood are supported by men holding low-wage jobs that provide an income only slightly higher than that provided by welfare.

Although most of the youth in the street group from La Barriada left school to seek employment by the age of fifteen, they were unable to obtain ordinary legitimate jobs and turned initially to systematic factory burglaries to generate a somewhat regular income. Most had become systematic armed robbers by the age of sixteen; an age marking an important transition in their lives. In other words, they needed an even more regular income since some of the youths had begun to live on their own while others simply wanted "money for recreation and to buy clothes to impress females" (p. 135).

Robberies were usually executed at knifepoint against random victims at sites some distance from the robber's neighborhood. This "robbery stage" lasted approximately two years; by the age of eighteen, most decreased or terminated altogether their criminal activity. For these youths, the most crime-intensive years were the midteens during which they were unemployed or otherwise out of the labor force. These youthful criminal careers followed a progression "from exploratory economic crime through systematic factory burglaries to street robberies to decreasing criminal involvement" (p. 139).

The African American youth of Projectville were from a public-housing project physically distant from any major center of employment. Although some households were headed by women holding low-wage health and clerical jobs, most residents of the project were supported by welfare payments. Like La Barriada youth, Projectville youth were both out-of-school and out-of-work, and simply "hung out" together on the street concocting illegal schemes for "getting" money. Because Projectville youth lacked opportunities for factory burglaries present in La Barriada, by the time they were fifteen their most prevalent illegal venture was robbery, often committed in elevators, stairwells, and unprotected spaces that separate project buildings.

How do we understand the significance of robbery in the lives of these ghetto and barrio boys? For both La Barriada and Projectville youth, personal profitmaking is an obvious motive for robbery. Yet uninterested in pulling themselves and their families out of poverty, their robbery is "a response to the disjunction between the desire to participate in social activities with peers and the absence of legitimate sources of funds needed to finance this participation" (Greenberg, 1977: 197). But how does robbery, specifically, satisfy this need?

Sullivan and others (Zimring and Zuehl, 1986: Conklin, 1972) have reported that most robberies are committed by a group of young street men. Within this collective setting, robbery is a means of getting money when other resources are unavailable, and is particularly attractive for young boys on the street. Robbery provides a public ceremony of domination and humiliation of others. Because young street boys are denied access to the labor market and are relegated to a social situation (the street group) where gender accountability is augmented, they are more often involved in crimes that entail actual or possible confrontation with others. As such, robbery provides an available resource with which to accomplish gender and, therefore, to construct a specific type of public masculinity—what Katz (1988: 225–236) terms "hardmen," or men who court danger and who, through force of will, subject others to it.

"Doing stickup" is doing masculinity by manufacturing "*an angle of moral superiority* over the intended victim" and, thereby, succeeding "in making a fool of his victim" (pp. 169, 174). Obviously, group robberies result in greater violence, both because violence is needed to "pull it off" (without a weapon the chances for a successful robbery diminish) and because "the guys" are watching and/or participating. As Ron Santiago (Hills and Santiago, 1992: 26) put it regarding his robbery days as a youth, "You know, you can't show fear in front of the guys. Either you're down or you're not down. And if you're not down, you can't hang out."

The robbery setting provides the ideal opportunity to construct an "essential" toughness and "maleness"; it provides a means with which to construct that certain type of masculinity— hardman. Within the social context that ghetto and barrio boys find themselves, then, robbery is a rational practice for "doing gender" and for getting money.

Correspondingly, the spur-of-the-moment nature of the robbery is attractive to many of these boys as a mechanism for accomplishing gender. Santiago (p. 27) explains the nature of spur-of-the-moment robberies:

> And we would either be hanging out together and somebody would come up with an idea and say, "Well, hey man, let's rob this place," or let's rob that, or let's do this or let's do that. And we'll say, "Yeah, okay, let's do it."

As an example, one evening Santiago and a few of his friends were "hanging out" and decided fortuitously to rob a Kentucky Fried Chicken restaurant (p. 34):

> We went inside and there were two customers and one guy behind the counter. Alvin grabbed the guy behind the counter and he stuck the gun to his head. I took the two customers and pushed them to the side and held the gun on them; the other guy just stood by the door. Alvin jumped over the counter and made the guy give up the money out of the safe, and threatened him, which was standard: don't call the police, don't use the phone, don't touch the alarm, or anything.

Santiago and his friends escaped with $2,700, and "that was a big haul for an off-the-top-of-your-head stickup" (p. 35). Participation in such spur-of-the-moment robberies is a resource for gender accountability since the robber's survival in such a dangerous atmosphere demonstrates the fierceness of his will; survival substantiates that he is able to "transcend the control of the system" (Katz, 1988: 231).

For marginalized, racial-minority boys, robbery reflects their structural position as the most available resource for constructing a specific type of masculine expression. Within the social setting of the street group, robbery is an acceptable practice for accomplishing gender.

The La Barriada and Projectville youths (as well as Santiago) used the proceeds of robbery for clothing and for recreational purposes: to participate in sports, to go to movies and dances, and to purchase drugs and alcohol. Sullivan (1989: 249) reported that the point of their participation in robbery was "to share in the youth culture that is advertised in the mass media and subsidized for middle-class teenagers who attend school by their parents." In other words, a successful robbery not only is a practice for "doing gender" situationally, it also helps provide the funds necessary for adequate masculine accomplishment in a class/race specific youth culture. For such youth, systematic robbery is a short-term occupation—a way of "getting paid," as these young men expressed to Sullivan—a means of altering their material circumstances while simultaneously accomplishing gender. Getting paid through robbery is an available resource for accomplishing hegemonic masculinity in a particularized way.

Comparing the white, working-class group of boys from Hamilton Park with the two groups of minority boys, Sullivan found that the former, because of access to legitimate employment, matured out of crime at a faster rate. As Sullivan (p. 209) states, "the minority youths still faced much more unemployment and the attendant possibility of continuing or reverting to their reliance on criminal income."

John Hagedorn's (1993: 11) recent investigation of white and racial minority youth groups in Milwaukee found similar processes occurring: African American and Latino gang members "matured out of the gang at a slower rate than Whites, who found steady employment in much greater numbers." White youth had access to legitimate resources with which to construct a particular form of hegemonic masculinity and, therefore, age out of crime. Most racial minority boys similarly want to age out of crime, Hagedorn found, but the racial divisions of labor and power limited access to such resources. The majority of racial minority boys interviewed by Hagedorn want to settle down, get married, and work in the paid-labor force. The following example is representative (p. 14):

Q. Five years from now, what would you want to be doing?
A. Five years from now? I want to have a steady job, I want to have been working that job for about five years, and just with a family somewhere.

Yet Hagedorn (p. 31) found that African American and Latino young men only were able to secure a provisional relationship with legitimate paid labor, if that: "A large majority of gang members bob and weave in and out of legal and illegal markets in a tragic search for a conventional life." As the following respondent indicates, he turned to low-wage paid labor and to drug dealing as resources for constructing a specific type of "provider masculinity" (p. 22):

As far as selling drugs, even though I just got out of jail, I intend to get back to it cause the job I got, they ain't paying me nothing but four fifty, and now I got a wife, now three kids, they staying in the house with me,

I got two other kids that ain't in the house with us, and trying to make ends meet off of four fifty just ain't going to work.

In addition to robbery and being less able to age out of crime, marginalized, racial-minority youth are involved disproportionately in interpersonal forms of street violence. Sampson and Wilson (1991: 1) recently identified the centrality of this issue for young African American men:

> the leading cause of death among urban black males is homicide and the lifetime risk of being murdered is as high as 1 in 21 for black males compared to only 1 in 131 for white males. Although rates of violence have been higher for blacks than whites at least since the 1950s, record increases in homicide since the mid–1980s in cities such as New York, Chicago, and Philadelphia also appear racially selective. For example, while white rates remained stable the firearms death rate among young black males more than doubled from 1984–1988 alone. These differentials help explain recent estimates that a resident of rural Bangladesh has a greater chance of surviving to age 40 than does a black male in Harlem.

As stated earlier, men in all social classes form close, specialized relationships with one another. For many lower–working-class racial minority boys, a significant focus of this bonding is the street group, where assurance of one's masculinity is established through a ritual rejection of femininity.

Masculine bonding does not so much involve having friends as constructing a particular type of masculinity for others. Young ghetto and barrio men tend to bond into neighborhood-specific street groups that provide a competitive arena in which an individual proves himself a man among men. It is here where marginalized, racial-minority boys develop strong ties with members of their neighborhood, persons with whom they are acquainted and who they perceive to be like themselves (Dunning, Murphy, and Williams, 1988: 205).

Participation in street violence, a more frequent practice when other hegemonic masculine ideals are unavailable (e.g., a job in the paid-labor market), demonstrates to closest friends that one is "a man." In fact, it is in marginalized communities where we find "a greater proportion of peer groups that subscribe to violent macho ideals" (Schwendinger and Schwendinger, 1983: 205).

Reflecting on the masculinity of her brother as the two siblings were growing up, African American feminist bell hooks (1992: 87) reports:

"In our southern black patriarchal home, being a boy meant learning to be tough, to mask one's feelings, to stand one's ground and fight."[8]

Street-group violence is based on an explicit concern with a particular type of masculine expression and validation. The struggle for supremacy over other marginalized street groups is a means with which to gain recognition and to reward one's masculinity, a means with which to solve the gender problem of accountability. As one member of a street group in the South Bronx puts it (cited in Browning, 1981: 36):

> I been raised in the gangs. Like my brothers were, only they're in jail now and one got on junk [heroin] so my mother said he's dead. Gangs are like families. Like brothers and sisters all together. We rumble because you have to show blood. Blood is strength. In the Bronx, there's a lot of blood.

Street-group warfare, based on idealized conceptions of hegemonic masculinity, principally involves maintaining and gaining status ("rep") and protecting one's territory ("turf"). Members of street groups rework these notions, representing and defining status or reputation as the ability to stand up to violent physical confrontation. Indeed, street groups confer a dubious prestige on boys with a proven ability to fight, boys for whom street fighting is an essential source of meaning and status. As Ron Santiago (Hills and Santiago, 1992: 20) states, to belong to a gang "I had to whip another kid's ass to prove my manhood."

Open expression of violence/aggression is not only tolerated in the street group but during specific times and in specific contexts it is positively sanctioned (Dunning, Murphy and Williams, 1988: 209–210). Consider one street group member who attempts to explain "rep" (cited in Allen, 1978: 46):

> We got a lot of challenges, which gave us some headway, cause that meant a lot of fights was on our ground. Now a rival gang when they just outright challenge you, always wanted to use you as a stepping stone, just like boxers do. They figure if they could chalk up a lot of wins in gang fights, then they'd be in a better position to fight somebody big.

In the street group, young men gain status, reputation, and self-respect through street-group violence.[9]

As argued, young boys from marginalized racial-minority commu-

nities are typically denied masculine status in the educational and occupational spheres, which are the major sources of masculine status
available to men in white, middle-class communities (educational and
occupational) and white, working-class communities (occupational).
This denial, deriving from the class and race divisions of labor and
power, creates the context for the more pronounced public aggressive
masculinity employed by ghetto and barrio boys. Because they are
available gender resources and because sex category is heightened in
situations of structural disadvantage, these youths come to rely more
frequently on behaviors that include fighting and other forms of physical intimidation with which to construct their masculinity.[10]

Nevertheless, openly violent behavior is confined to, and positively
sanctioned in, specific social contexts where there exist "approved"
sites for establishing this form of masculinity. Bonding with youths of
common residence, marginalized, racial-minority boys tend to develop
a collective loyalty to their community and to form territorial ownership over their turf (Dunning, Murphy and Williams, 1988: 208). A
street group's specific territory, carefully branded and protected at levels of conspicuous absurdity, defines the group and its perimeters of
activity, turf actually serves as a boundary between groups and as an
arena of status and possible conflict. Moreover, a "universal rationale
for violence among street elites is their claim to control landmarks of
a particular residential area: street boundaries, 'turf,' local food out-
lets, parks, or particular benches in parks" (Katz, 1988: 118).

Obviously, then, street groups are intolerant of "invasions" of their
space by outsiders (Murphy, Williams and Dunning, 1990: 146).
When outsiders do invade their local area, this is viewed as naturally
offensive. The following example illustrates one such invasion (cited
in Mancini, 1981: 100):

> We saw some white kids on the railroad track. So they saw us, they
> started runnin' . . . so we started chasin' 'em. We caught up with 'em,
> we grabbed all of 'em, you know, threw 'em off the railroad track (chuck-
> les) . . . and so we jumped down, and grabbed 'em again. And there were
> some empty trains over there . . . so we put 'em in the train, so we tell
> 'em to get on their knees and don't look . . . so we picked a big bag of
> newspaper (chuckle) and threw it on their heads . . . we threw 'em down,
> stomped 'em.

And as Ron Santiago (Hills and Santiago, 1992: 20) explains, "if I
went outside my neighborhood, whether I was in a gang or not, I was
prey to whatever gang was in that particular neighborhood."

Yet it is not necessarily the territory *per se* that is significant, but the local group's identification with it. As Murphy, Williams and Dunning (1990: 155) point out: "it is their *collective pride* which is threatened by the rival group. Such threats can be experienced mutually even on 'neutral' territory as, for example, when two rival groups encounter each other by chance at a motorway service station." Territory, the "zone of defense," thus becomes the "appropriate" area and reason for intergroup violence. Street groups develop a collective masculinity centered on the reality that they must rule their turf. Consequently, young marginalized racial-minority street groups adopt names that "declare an inborn right or power to rule" (Katz, 1988: 120):

> Some track the status terms of ancient and medieval royalty and aristocracy: Lords, Nobles, Knights, Pharoahs, Kings, Emperors, Viceroys, Crusaders, and Dukes. Others pick up "classy" terms of style: Diplomats and Savoys. Another tradition of nomenclature ties ghetto youth to regal levels of the animal world: Lions, Eagles, Panthers, and Cobras. Still another points upward cosmologically, to Stars and Jets.

Young men who fight more casually—regardless of the setting or circumstance, the odds, and the probability of being arrested—are often perceived by the street group as strange and somewhat mysterious (Dunning, Murphy, and Williams, 1988: 212). Just as some middle-aged, white, working-class men acquire acclaim and prestige only from "scrapping" in a bar (Dyck, 1980), marginalized, racial-minority boys in street groups acquire praise and esteem only from fighting in the street. In fact, most publicly aggressive boys behave in other settings with a substantial degree of respectability (Dunning, Murphy, and Williams, 1988: 215). For example, Mancini (1981: 98–101) found that one member of a violent street gang constructed a different type of masculinity at home: at home he appeared withdrawn, spent long hours in his bedroom (reading comic and army books), listened to records, watched television and experienced serenity doing housework for his mother.

Rape, like other violent street crimes, is basically an intraclass and an intrarace phenomenon. That is, just as young ghetto and barrio men are more likely to be robbed and physically attacked by each other, so young, marginalized, racial-minority women are more likely to be raped by young marginalized racial-minority men. In fact, Robert Staples (1982: 62), an African American sociologist, argues in his book *Black Masculinity* that the "typical rapist is a black male and his victim is most often a black female." While Staples can be criticized for exaggerating the race/rape connection, we do know that violent forcible rape is a more severe problem in a group setting, where group rapes disproportionately involve youthful offenders and where extreme forms of violence are associated significantly with group rape (Messerschmidt, 1986; Schwendinger and Schwendinger, 1983).

The "Central Park Jogger Rape" is a case in point. On the night of April 19, 1989, four young (fifteen-to-seventeen year-old) African Americans entered Central Park for purposes of "wilding," and violently beat and repeatedly raped a woman jogger. The victim was dragged unconscious to the bottom of a ravine some two hundred feet from the road where she was left for dead. When she eventually was found, she had lost three-fourths of her blood; her body temperature had fallen to 80° F; she had sustained multiple skull fractures; and there were cuts and bruises on her chest, arms, legs, hands, and feet (Stone, 1989).

All the boys who participated in the Central Park rape had constructed a similar in-school opposition masculinity described earlier. They were frequent troublemakers in school; several were constantly truant and some had been suspended for such acts as weapons' possession, fighting with other students, and physically attacking teachers. Outside the school, these youths "discovered life on the street" as a setting for obtaining masculine approval. Lacking alternative resources, these boys developed forms of social action that allowed them, as Stone (p. 34) put it, to be "wannabees," or individuals who "wanna be tough, wanna be doing things in the street."

Such group rape helps maintain and reinforce an alliance among the boys by humiliating and devaluating women, thereby strengthening the fiction of masculine power. In all Western industrialized societies, the vast majority of violent, forcible rapists are those "most removed from the confirmations of manliness derived from wealth or position; most removed, indeed, from any type of 'respectable' status or identity" (Segal, 1990: 245). Because lower–working-class, racial-minority boys have lost the institutional benefits of gender divisions of labor and power—"the economic gain in relation to women that accrues to men in employment, the better chances of promotion, the better job classifications" (Connell, 1991: 165)—these particular boys acted out hegemonic masculine ideals that could be exhibited.

Group rapists may not be concerned at all with sexual gratification *per se*; engaging in intercourse is simply a fundamental indication of "maleness." As argued earlier, hegemonic masculinity currently is partially defined through an alleged uncontrollable and insatiable sexual appetite for women, in which men are expected to perform adequately in each and every sexual situation. Indeed, heterosexual intercourse is the hallmark of one's identity as a man and inadequate performance severly threatens one's masculinity.

Accordingly, in the social situation of the gang described above, the result is a spectacular masculine display of sexual "conquest" wherein the victim suffers "the most brutal forms of physical violence" and the gang rapists "compete for status with one another" (Segal, 1990: 246). As bell hooks (1992: 94) notes, the ability to use a penis in sexual conquest brings a man as much status as being a wage earner and provider and, therefore, "even unemployed black men can gain status, can be seen as the embodiment of masculinity, within a phallocentric framework." In other words, these young Central Park rapists are reworking phallocentric heterosexuality to suit their particular social situation. They are acting out in practice what James Baldwin (cited in hooks, 1992: 111) underlines in theory:

> Every black man walking in this country pays a tremendous price for walking: for men are not women, and a man's balance depends on the weight he carries between his legs. All men, however they may face or fail to face it, however they may handle, or be handled by it, know something about each other, which is simply that a man without balls is not a man.

For these boys, then, "wilding in the park" and gang rape are simply resources for demonstrating essential "male nature" when more conventional means are unavailable. Participating in group rape—thereby securing group approval and praise—is a resource that enhances one's self-esteem as a "male," establishes one's masculine worth at the expense of someone else, and "extends the individual's own significance through negating that of another" (Plummer, 1984a: 44).

In this type of social context, it is not surprising to learn that during the Central Park rape the participants, reportedly, were happy and laughing; as one perpetrator stated, "It was fun" (Stone, 1989: 33). Moreover, after the rape the boys were "exuberant—laughing and acting stupid, leaping and cavorting in the air . . . they were twirling and flinging the victim's clothes" (p. 41).[11] This elated indifference to the consequences of violent acts demonstrates that their major concern throughout the wilding campaign was "impressing peers with acts of ever greater savagery" (p. 43). It was, quite simply, a specific collective masculine dynamic in the context of unequal race and class relations.

Although most lower–working-class, racial-minority boys do not commit rape, nor is this type of rape limited to the economically marginal,[12] still, the combined class and race social setting of these youth increases the incidence of this type of rape. As Dorie Klein (1982: 212) notes:

> Male physical power over women, or the illusion of power, is none the less a minimal compensation for the lack of power over the rest of one's life. Some men resort to rape and other personal violence against the only target accessible, the only ones with less autonomy. Thus sexual warfare often becomes a stand-in for class and racial conflict by transforming these resentments into misogyny.

Dunning, Murphy, and Williams (1988: 206) agree: "for a short, illusory moment," group rapists "are the masters; the downtrodden come out on top." And as Stone (1989: 43) concludes, "For a few horrific minutes, the boys who pummeled the jogger, unable to control their own lives, held the power of life and death over someone else's." Because the immediate sensation of masculine power was seductive for these boys, group rape became a resource for accomplishing gender and constructing a particular type of masculinity, a collective, publicly aggressive form of masculinity. And this helps explain why some men adopt a particular means—group physical violence—as opposed to other means (such as less violent forms of coercion discussed in Chapter 5) with which to assault women sexually and to accomplish gender. Consequently, analyzing masculinity as behavior situationally accomplished under specific structural constraints is crucial to understanding which men (e.g., by age, class, and race) are most likely to engage in which types of sexual assault (e.g., gang rape vs. wife rape).

Due to position in social divisions of labor and power, many young, marginalized, racial-minority men bond to form violent street-group formations. They adapt to their economic and racial powerlessness by competing with rivals of their own class, race and gender for personal power. For these young men, the personal power struggle with other young, marginalized, racial-minority men is a resource for constructing a specific type of masculinity—not masculinity in the context of a job or organizational dominance but in the context of "street elites" (Katz, 1988: 114–163) and, therefore, in the context of street group dominance. As Tolson (1977: 40–46) notes, these young men express themselves through a "collective toughness" that is observed and cheered by their buddies. And for "support and recognition, a sense of position and social status," young, marginalized, racial-minority men remain bound to the world of the street (p. 43). Throughout their adolescence, these young men are extremely "concerned with the physical presence" they are able to preserve "as a force to be reckoned with."

Marginalized, racial minority boys—as with white, middle- and working-class boys—produce specific configurations of behavior that can be seen by others within the same immediate social situation as "essentially male." As we have seen, these different masculinities emerge from practices that encompass different resources and that are simultaneously based on different collective trajectories. In this way, then, class and race relations structure the age-specific form of resources used to construct specific opposition masculinities. Young, middle-class, working-class, and lower–working-class men produce unique types of masculinity (situationally accomplished by drawing on different forms of youth crime) by acknowledging an already determined future and inhabiting distinct locations within the social structural divisions of labor and power. Collectively, young men experience their everyday world from a specific position in society and so they construct differently the cultural ideals of hegemonic masculinity.

Opposition masculinities, then, are based on a specific relation to school generated by the interaction of school authority with class, race, and gender dynamics. For white, middle-class boys, a nonviolent opposition masculinity occurs primarily outside school; for white, working-class and lower–working-class, racial-minority boys, specific types of opposition masculinities prevail both inside and outside school. Yet for each group of boys, a sense of masculinity is shaped by their specific relation to the school and by their specific position in the divisions of labor and power.

Social structures are constituted by social action and, in turn, provide resources for constructing masculinity. And the particular type of youth crime, as one such resource, ultimately is based on these social structures. Thus, social structures both constrain and enable social action and, therefore, masculinities and youth crime.

In Chapter 5 we analyze a different age category of men and thus different types of public and private masculinities and crimes.

Chapter 5

Varieties of "Real Men"

It was a theoretical breakthrough in social theory when the family came to be recognized generally as both gendered and political. Feminist work has now begun to reveal theoretically what we have known for some time in practice—that other social milieux, such as the street and workplace, are not only political but also gendered (Acker, 1990; Connell, 1987; Cockburn, 1983). Chapter 5 extends this theoretical insight through an analysis of how the social structures of labor, power, and sexuality constrain and enable social action within three specific social settings: the street, the workplace, and the family. I focus on how some men, within particular social situations, can make use of certain crimes to construct various public and private adult masculinities.

Research reveals that men construct masculinities in accord with their position in social structures and, therefore, their access to power and resources. Because men situationally accomplish masculinity in response to their socially structured circumstances, various forms of crime can serve as suitable resources for doing masculinity within the specific social contexts of the street, the workplace, and the family. Consequently, as in Chapter 4, I emphasize the significant differences among men and how men utilize different types of crimes to situationally construct distinct forms of masculinities. We begin with the street and an examination of pimping.

The Street

In Chapter 4, we examined how middle-class, working-class, and lower–working-class young men exhibit unique types of public masculinities that are situationally accomplished by drawing on different forms of youth crime. Moreover, class and race structure the age-specific form of resources employed to construct the cultural ideals of hegemonic masculinity. Such public arenas as the school and street are lush with gendered meanings and signals that evoke various styles of masculinity and femininity. Another type of public masculinity found in the social setting of the street is that of the adult pimp. This particularized form of masculinity is examined here within the context of "deviant street networks."

The Pimp and His Network

Eleanor Miller's (1986: 35–43) respected work *Street Woman* reports that in Milwaukee, Wisconsin, African American men in their mid to late twenties and early thirties dominate what she calls "deviant street networks." Deviant street networks are groups of men and women assembled to conduct such illegal profit-making ventures as prostitution, check and credit-card fraud, drug trafficking, burglary, and robbery. Although both men and women engage in various aspects of these "hustling activities," gender relations are unequal, reflecting the social structures of labor, power, and normative heterosexuality. Miller (p. 37) found that a major source of continuous income in these networks "derives from the hustling activity of women who turn their earnings over to the men in exchange for affection, an allowance, the status of their company, and some measure of protection." Commonly referred to as "pimps," the men act as agents and/or companions of these women, substantially profiting from their labor. Miller found that to work as street hustlers, it is essential that women have a "male" sponsor and protector. However, this "essential" has not always existed in the history of prostitution.

Throughout the 1800s, U.S. prostitution was condemned but not classified as a criminal offense, and was conducted primarily under the direction of a "madam" in brothels located in specific red-light districts (Rosen, 1982: 27–30). In an attempt to halt prostitution, state legislatures enacted laws in the early 1900s in order to close down these red-light districts and, contemporaneously, women-controlled brothels. Predictably, rather than halting prostitution, new forms of prostitution emerged from this attempt at legislating morality. As Rosen (p. 32) shows in *The Lost Sisterhood*, the closing of the brothels simply increased streetwalking for women; because prostitutes could no longer receive "johns" "in the semiprotected environment of the brothel or district, . . . they had to search for business in public places—hotels, restaurants, cabarets, or on the street." This search for customers in public places exposed prostitutes to violent clients and police harassment. Consequently, these women turned to men for help in warding off dangers, providing legal assistance, and offering some emotional support. Eventually, the overall prostitution business came to be dominated by individual pimp entrepreneurs or masculine-dominated syndicated crime.

In today's deviant street network, the pimp usually controls two to three women (labeled "wives-in-law") on the street (Miller, 1986: 37–38). The women turn over their earnings to the pimp and he decides how it will be spent. The disciplinarian of the network, the pimp also "decides upon and metes out the punishment" (Romenesko and Miller, 1989: 120). Indeed, as Romenesko and Miller (p. 117) show in their interviews with street hustlers, the pimp demands unquestioned respect:

> Showing respect for "men" means total obedience and complete dedication to them. Mary reports that in the company of "men" she had to "talk mainly to the women—try not to look at the men if possible at all—try not to have conversations with them." Rita, when asked about the rules of the street, said, "Just basic, obey. Do what he wants to do. Don't disrespect him. . . . I could not disrespect him in any verbal or physical way. I never attempted to hit him back. Never." And, in the same vein, Tina said that when her "man" had others over to socialize, the women of the family were relegated to the role of servant. "We couldn't speak to them when we wasn't spoken to, and we could not foul up on orders. And you cannot disrespect them."

This authority and control exercised by pimps over women is also clearly exemplified in biographies of pimp life (Malcolm X, 1965; Slim, 1967). Christina Milner and Richard Milner (1972: 52–53) reported a similar form of gendered power in their study of African American pimps in San Francisco:

> First and foremost, the pimp must be in complete control of his women; this control is made conspicuous to others by a series of little rituals which express symbolically his woman's attitude. When in the company of others she must take special pains to treat him with absolute deference and respect. She must light his cigarettes, respond to his every whim immediately, and never, never, contradict him. In fact, a ho [prostitute] is strictly not supposed to speak in the company of pimps unless spoken to.

Gender is a situated accomplishment in which we produce forms of behavior seen by others in the same immediate situation as masculine or feminine (see discussion in Chapter 3). Within the confines and social setting of the street, economically marginal men and women create street networks for economic survival, yet simultaneously "do gender" in the process of surviving. In this manner, deviant street networks become the condition that produces material survival as well as the social setting that reaffirms one's gender. The result is a gendered, deviant street network in which men and women do masculinity and femininity, albeit in a distinct manner.

In short, the division of street network labor is concerned both with rationally assigning specific tasks to network members and with the symbolic affirmation and assertion of specific forms of masculinity and femininity (discussed further below). Consequently, pimps simultaneously do pimping and masculinity. As marginalized men, street pimps choose pimping in preference to unemployment and routine labor for "the man." Lacking other avenues and opportunities for accomplishing gender, the pimp life-style is a survival strategy that is exciting and rewarding for them as men. The deviant street network provides the context within which to construct one's "essential nature" as a man and to survive as a human being.

The Cool Pose of the Badass

African American street pimps engage in specific practices (constrained by class and race) intended to construct a specific "cool pose" as an important aspect of their specific type of masculinity (Majors, 1986; Majors and Billson, 1992). In the absence of resources that signify other types of masculinity, sex category is held more accountable and physical presence, personal style, and expressiveness take on an increased importance (Messner, 1989: 82). Consequently, as Richard Majors (1986: 5) argues, many "black males have learned to make great use of 'poses' and 'postures' that connote control, toughness and detachment," adopting a specific carriage, that exemplifies an expressive and distinct assertion of masculinity.

The often flamboyant, loud, and ostentatious style of African American pimps signifies aspects of this cool pose. The exaggerated display of luxury (for example, in the form of flashy clothing) is also a specific aspect of the cool pose distinctively associated with African American pimps. Majors and Billson (1992: 81–84) argue that the "sharp" and "clean" look of pimps is intended to upstage other men in the highly competitive arena of the street where they earn street applause for their style, providing an "antidote to invisibility." Pimps literally prance above their immediate position in the class and race divisions of labor and power, thereby constructing a specific masculine street upper-crust demeanor.

Notwithstanding, this cool presence complements an intermittent and brutal comportment to construct masculinity and, in the process, show that the pimp means business. In other words, the African American pimp must always be prepared to employ violence both for utilitarian reasons and for constructing and maintaining a formidable, portentious profile (Katz, 1988: 97). The following account by Milner and Milner (1972: 232) illustrates this unpredictable use of violence:

One ho known as Birthday Cake said she worked for a pimp for four years, gave him a new Cadillac every year, and one night came home from work with her money "funny" and got the beating of her life. She walked in and handed over the money; he counted it and said, "That's all right, honey," drew her a bath, laid her down afterwards on the bed, went to the closet and got a tire iron and beat her senseless with it. She showed us the long scars which required hundreds of stitches and demonstrated her permanent slight limp.

This "badass" form of masculinity (Katz, 1988: 80–113) is also publicly displayed for, and supported by, other pimps. Milner and Milner (1972: 56) discuss how a pimp took one of "his" prostitutes (who was also a dancer) into the dancer's dressing room and "began to shout at her and slap her around" loud enough for everyone in the bar to hear. "The six pimps sitting at the back of the bar near the dressing room began to clap and whistle loudly," seemingly for the current dancer, "but in reality to cover the noise of the beating from the ears of the straight customers" (p. 56). Emerging from the dressing room and joining the others, the pimp exclaimed, "Well, I took care of that bitch." Then they all began to "joke around." In contrast, when the prostitute emerged, not "one of them (pimps) felt it proper to comfort her in any way" (p. 56). Such violence, neither out-of-control nor ungovernable, is situationally determined and regulated. Thus, pimp violence becomes a means of disciplining the prostitute and of constructing a badass public masculinity.

The combined cool pose and badass identity of African American pimps clearly represent a specialized means with which to transcend class and race domination. Yet, it also demonstrates the socially constrained nature of social action, and how African American pimps rework the ideals of hegemonic masculinity as a vehicle for achieving that transcendence. Pimping, then, is a resource for surmounting oppressive class and race conditions and for reasserting the social dominance of men. Moreover, like other men, pimps associate masculinity with work, with authority and control, and with explicit heterosexuality.

Within deviant street networks, the prostitute/pimp relationship represents a reworking of these hegemonic masculine ideals under specifically structured social possibilities/constraints. Through their authority and control within deviant street networks, pimps create a class- and race-specific type of masculine meaning and configuration, resulting in a remodeling of heterosexual monogamy in which the pimp provides love, money, and an accompanying sense of security for his "wives-in-law" (Romenesko and Miller, 1989: 123).

Normative heterosexuality is the major focus of activities: wives-in-law are expected to be sexually seductive to men, receptive to the sexual "drives" and special "needs" of men (including the pimp), and to work for men who "protect" them and negotiate the "rough spots."[1] Pimping, as a resource for demonstrating that one is a "real man," distinguishes pimps from prostitutes in a specific way. Within the social context of the deviant street network, this pimp type of masculinity is sustained by means of collective and gendered practices that subordinate women, manage the expression of violence against women, and exploit women's labor and sexuality. Indeed, the individual style of the pimp is somewhat meaningless outside the group (Connell, 1991: 157); it is the deviant street network that provides meaning and currency for this type of masculinity.[2] Pimping, in short, is a practice that facilitates a particular gender strategy.

In spite of the above, in attempting to transcend oppressive social structures, African American pimps ultimately reproduce them. Their masculine style is at once repugnant to "conventionality"—their source of wealth anathema to traditional morality (Katz, 1988: 97)— yet simultaneously reactionary and reproductive of the gendered social order. In other words, African American pimps respond in a gender-specific manner to race and class oppression, which in turn locks them into the very structured constraints they attempt to overcome. Thus, pimping becomes a form of social action that ultimately results in the reproduction of the gender divisions of labor and power as well as normative heterosexuality.

The following section examines two distinct types of masculinity constructed in the workplace.

The Workplace

The gender divisions of labor and power and normative heterosexuality structure gender relations in the workplace. The workplace not only produces goods and provides services but is the site of gendered control and authority. Because women historically have been excluded from paid work or segregated within it, today the gender division in the workplace is both horizontally and vertically segregated (Walby, 1986; Reskin and Roos, 1987; Game and Pringle, 1984).[3] The result is that women are concentrated overwhelmingly at the lower levels of the occupational hierarchy in terms of wages and salary, status, and authority. Indeed, a recent study of nearly four hundred firms revealed that the vast majority of women were either completely or nearly completely segregated by gender (Bielby and Baron, 1986). Consequently, gender relations throughout much of the paid-labor market—like gender relations in schools, youth groups, and deviant street networks—embody relations of power: the domination of men and the subordination of women. Moreover, the creation of "male" and "female" jobs helps to maintain and reproduce this power relationship. Accordingly, gender differences are maintained through gender segregation, and occupational segregation is born of practices ultimately based on conceptions of what constitutes the "essential" natures of men and women.

In addition, the concepts "worker" and "a job" are themselves gendered. As Joan Acker (1990) recently demonstrated, these concepts embody the gender divisions of labor and power. Historically, the idea of a job and who works it has assumed a specific gendered organization of public and private life: a man's life centers on full-time work at a job outside the household; a woman's life focuses on taking care of all his other needs. Consequently, as the abstract worker is masculinized (p. 152):

> it is the man's body, his sexuality, minimal responsibility in procreation, and conventional control of emotions that pervades work and organizational processes. Women's bodies—female sexuality, their ability to procreate and their pregnancy, breast feeding, childcare, menstruation, and mythic "emotionality"—are suspect, stigmatized, and used as grounds for control and exclusion.

Because organization and sexuality occur simultaneously, the workplace is sexualized and normative heterosexuality actually conditions work activities (Hearn and Parkin, 1987). As Rosemary Pringle (1989: 162) recently reported, heterosexuality in the workplace is actively perpetuated in a range of practices and interactions exemplified in "dress and self-presentation, in jokes and gossip, looks and flirtations, secret affairs and dalliances, in fantasy and in the range of coercive behaviors that we now call sexual harassment."

Within the social situation of gendered segregation, power, and normative heterosexuality, men and women in the paid-labor market actively construct specific types of masculinity and femininity, depending upon their position in the workplace. In other words, social action is patterned in the workplace in terms of a distinction between masculine and feminine. Regarding men specifically, a power hierarchy exists in the workplace among men and, not surprisingly, different forms of masculinity correspond to particular positions in this hierarchy.

Let us now look at two differing forms of masculinity in the workplace: (1) workers and their relation to shop-floor theft and a specific type of sexual harassment and (2) corporate executives and their involvement in corporate crime and a variant form of sexual harassment. In each case, I demonstrate how specific crimes are a resource for constructing particularized representations of private masculinity—those that are occluded from the vision, company, or intervention of outsiders.

Workers and Shop-Floor Theft

In Chapter 4, I discussed how white, working-class boys (the lads) associate manual labor with the social superiority of masculinity and mental labor with the social inferiority of femininity. These youths regard mental work as effeminate, "sissy-stuff," a type of work performed only by "wimps." Thus, work that is traditionally repetitive, unhealthy, demeaning, and mind numbing is turned into a virtue, because "real men" do it (Donaldson, 1987: 167).[4] A growing amount of research reveals that the meaningless work environment of the shop floor is given significance by associating manual work with a physically strong and active type of masculinity. After examining a good portion of this research, Paul Willis (1979: 196) concluded:

> The working situation is partially reinterpreted into a heroic exercise of manly confrontation with "the task." Difficult, uncomfortable, or dangerous conditions are seen, not for themselves, but for their appropriateness to a masculine readiness and hardness. They are understood more through the toughness required to survive them, than through the nature of the imposition which asks them to be faced in the first place.

Other evidence likewise indicates that masculinity on the shop floor stresses the presentation and celebration of physical prowess (Lippert, 1977; Cockburn, 1983; Clatterbaugh, 1990).

Furthermore, manual laborers construct this specific kind of masculinity in direct contrast to that of management. For manual laborers, the rough and tough masculinity of the shop floor is differentiated and superior to the politeness, cleanliness, and more restrained demeanor of management: the "true self" is expressed on the shop floor, not in an office (Collinson and Collinson, 1989: 97). Indeed, managers are dubbed "paper pushers" and "yes men," and consistently ridiculed on the shop floor as effeminate. In this way, within the social setting of the shop floor, manual laborers construct a specific type of collective masculinity that reflects a desire to deny their subordinate position within the hierarchical power relations among men in the firm.

Nevertheless, although the shop floor masculinizes, the workplace (like the school discussed in Chapter 4) simultaneously denies certain hegemonic masculine ideals: independence, control, and dominance. And the employer-employee implied contract sets the conditions for this masculine denial. Under contractual relations, workers exchange labor power for specified wages and fringe benefits. Management then translates their labor into productive ability by setting workplace standards, goals, rules, and regulations to which workers must adhere. In most cases, these commands are extremely inflexible, predictably despised, and thus opposed by a large proportion of workers.

Mike Donaldson (1987: 168), for example, demonstrates how workers experience the workplace as both masculinizing and "infantalizing." According to Donaldson, authoritarian workplace policies are perceived by men on the shop floor as "childish." Accordingly, the contradictory nature in the construction of shop-floor masculinity should be clear: masculinity is very much connected to the world of manual labor; yet, for working-class men this work experience is humiliating. They are subjected to work relations that threaten their conception of hegemonic masculinity (Game and Pringle, 1984: 22).

Thus, because of this authoritarian relationship between men, which is inherent in the job itself, contentious issues in the workplace focus on job control and enhancing autonomy. In short, a sense of independence develops on the shop floor that is expressed in thoughts and feelings of brotherhood. What is at stake is a fight for masculine status: "a dignity which is at least partially defined against the company and within a collective solidarity and brotherhood" (Donaldson,

1987: 171). Workers consistently attempt to wield control over shop-floor practices and in so doing, fashion a united masculine autonomy.

Because manual labor is collective labor, it is inexorably organized around the group. A collective masculinity arises that consists of a particular style—a way of asserting, within the constraints of the "contract," collective control of the shop floor. The manual workers' experiences at work, expressed through interaction with the group, create a compensating solidarity—shared masculinity that enables the manual worker to bond with his peers and to resist management authority (Clatterbaugh, 1990: 111). Tolson (1977: 59) describes this vividly:

> Manual labour is collective labour: it is necessarily organized around the work-group. In part, this is simply because conditions of work are made more manageable by keeping a "happy medium" with your mates. The individual contributes to a collective effort and the rhythms of working are reaffirmed by a collective culture—an "occupational culture" (of jokes, gestures, the exchange of favours) on the job itself. To be "one of the lads" is to be placed inside a group's informal boundary, to be a party to the symbolic play.

Major aspects of this solidarity and resistance to authority include the variety of practices employed to gain informal control of the work process. One such traditional practice is for workers to control the speed of production, thus limiting output. Another such practice is resource control, such as time at work and who performs what job (Mars, 1983: 93). This informal attempt at group control should not be minimized, however, inasmuch as it is here that "strategies for wresting control of symbolic and real space from official authority" emerge (Willis, 1979: 192). In addition, it is within the work group that extensive "fiddling" and shop-floor theft occurs. Because manual labor is often organized on the basis of informal masculine practices, workers either steal as a group or their individual theft is controlled by the group.

As Willis (p. 192) points out, theft of materials is widespread in working-class jobs and is "endorsed by implicit informal criteria. Ostracism is the punishment for not maintaining the integrity of this world against the persistent intrusions of the formal."[5] Shop-floor theft permits the worker to "symbolically liberate himself from the 'bullshit' by 'beating the system' " (Altheide, Adler, Adler, and Altheide, 1978: 105), and is thus symbolic of personal and collective control. Altheide et al. (pp. 106–107) provide numerous examples of shop-floor theft as a means of demonstrating "control of the situation." Shop-floor theft is not purely utilitarian in the economic sense; workers also steal on the job because of what it means to do so. In other words, men on the shop-floor simultaneously resist class oppression and construct a specific masculinity through the same ongoing practice of shop-floor theft. Shop-floor theft is a social practice that facilitates a particularized worker gender strategy.

In *Cheats at Work*, Gerald Mars's (1983) discussion of "Wolfpack Jobs" shows clearly that this type of employee theft cannot exist outside the context of the group. Indeed, survival of employee theft is linked to survival of the group. As Mars (1983: 96) emphasizes, "individual group members *must* cooperate" in such situations. On the shop floor, there exists a particular working-class sensibility and it is the ability to share this sensibility that admits the "insider" to an all-male work group (Tolson, 1977: 59). Moreover, group acceptance requires that the manual worker must also recognize and support group definitions of hierarchies based on such criteria as age and seniority. Mars (1983: 98–99) found that such hierarchies themselves structure shop-floor theft—for example, older men and men with more seniority have greater access to the "fiddles." Senior men always get the best "pickings" and newcomers get what remains. Mars (p. 102) states further that the group ranks and thus allocates jobs, which is crucial because "it gives both overall control of resources and specifically control of fiddles" to the group. Coworkers collectively determine, within a masculine power hierarchy, how and what to steal, and establish limits beyond which one must not go (Altheide et al., 1978: 111). Other research, as well, confirms that the shop-floor group determines what is acceptable and unacceptable behavior in employee theft (Henry, 1978; Ditton, 1977).

The presence of this informal group organization most clearly distinguishes shop-floor masculinity from corporate-executive masculinity. Moreover, this specific masculine articulation enables the group to control the shop floor. Accordingly, to be one of "the guys" at work—to avoid ostracism—most manual workers choose to participate in its functions. The group and its collective format are seductive, promising to fulfill the worker's search for strategic actions that permit him to accomplish gender in ways that capitalist relations deny. Nevertheless, the worker may engage in resistance only as part of the group. To enjoy solidarity with other workers, then, he participates in group activity and he does gender—he constructs his "essential na-

ture" in a specific way and within specific socially structured constraints. For to engage in group activities, including employee theft, is
to draw on and exhibit one's "essential nature" as a man. Consequently, what is produced and reproduced is manual labor, theft, and
a specific type of "maleness" that is sustained as a particular collective practice in a specific workplace milieu. By participating in this
collective effort, the manual worker simultaneously does gender (and
class) while he "does shop-floor theft." Indeed, shop-floor theft is a
principal resource for maintaining group solidarity and for constructing a specific type of masculinity that resolves the problem of masculine accountability at work.[6]

It is within the social setting of the shop floor that men experience
their daily lives from a particular position in society. In this specific
social setting, hegemonic masculinity is both reworked and constructed in a unique way. In other words, certain shop-floor practices
define and sustain specific conceptions of masculinity. And one such
practice is shop-floor theft that in the collective social situation of
manual labor, provides working-class men with an available resource
for "doing gender." For these men, their taken-for-granted "essential
nature" is undermined and threatened within the confines of the contract. Thus, faced with this predicament, one's sex category is particularly salient and masculinity is held more accountable. By joining the
work group and participating in shop-floor theft, working-class men
resolve the gender accountability problem and exhibit to others that
they are "real men." Participation in this group theft validates a man's
"essential nature" and is specifically chosen not only for "the
goods," but the capacity to impress other men. Shop-floor theft helps
workers shape a valued masculine identity by exhibiting those hegemonic masculine ideals the capitalist workplace denies—independence, dominance, daring, and control.[7]

Workers and Sexual Harassment

Studies also highlight the persistence and dominance of normative
heterosexuality on the shop floor—such practices as exhibiting men's
sexuality as biologically driven and perpetually incontinent, whereas
women are the objects of a sexuality that precipitates men's "natural
urges" (Willis, 1979; Cockburn, 1983; Hearn, 1985; Gray, 1987). This
macho sexual prowess, mediated through bravado and sexist joking, is
constructed and encouraged on the shop floor (Collinson and Collinson, 1989: 95–98). Moreover, failure to participate in this specific interaction raises serious questions about one's masculinity. In this way,

situationally specific notions of heterosexuality are reproduced through the construction of shop-floor masculinity and center on men's insistence on exercising power over women.

Under such conditions, when women enter the shop floor as co-workers, a threatening situation (for the men, that is), results. In this situation, some shop-floor men are likely to engage in forms of inter-action quite different from their interaction with women outside the workplace. Not surprising, sexual harassment is more prevalent in this type of social setting. For example, one study of a manufacturing firm (in which the vast majority of manual laborers were men) found (DiTomaso, 1989: 81):

> the men in the plant acted differently than they would if they interacted with these women in any other context. Their behavior, in other words, was very much related to the work context itself. It appeared to provide a license for offensive behavior and an occasion for attempting to take advantage of many of the women in the plant.

In DiTomaso's study, the younger women on the shop floor were perceived by the men as the most threatening because they were com-peting directly for the same kinds of jobs as were the men. Conse-quently, these women were more likely than other women to be sub-jected to demeaning forms of social interaction: the men's behavior was more likely to exceed simple flirtation and to involve specific forms of sexual harassment. The following are comments from several women in the plant (pp. 80–81):

> "The men are different here than on the street. It's like they have been locked up for years."

> "It's like a field day."

> "A majority of the men here go out of their way to make you feel uneasy about being inside the plant and being a female; nice guys are a minor-ity."

Research reveals that sexual harassment occurs at all levels in the workplace—from shop floor to management. However, sexual harass-ment by men on the shop floor generally is twice as serious and per-sistent, and is different from sexual harassment by managers (Hearn, 1985: 121). In the shop-floor setting (where men are the majority), sexual harassment is "a powerful form of economic protection and exclusion from men's territory. Women workers are perceived as a threat to solidarity between men" (pp. 121–122). Studies of shop-floor sexual harassment suggest that 36 to 53 percent of women workers report some type of sexual harassment (Gruber and Bjorn, 1982); furthermore, a recent study of workplace sexual assault suggests that manual workers (as opposed to other men in the firm) committed the overwhelming majority of both attempted and completed assaults within the entire firm (Schneider, 1991: 539).

Notwithstanding, the most common types of sexual harassment on the shop floor involve such demeaning acts as sexual slurs, pinches or grabs, and public displays of derogatory images of women (Schneider, 1991: 539; Carothers and Crull, 1984: 222). Perceptively, women shop-floor coworkers are more likely than women coworkers in other occupational settings to describe this sexual harassment as designed to label them as "outsiders." The "invasion" of women on the shop floor poses a threat to men's monopoly over these jobs, and one way to discourage women from attempting to compete in this domain is to remind them, through remarks and behavior, of their "female fragility" (Carothers and Crull, 1984: 224). In this way, then, shop-floor men attempt to secure the "maleness" of the job by emphasizing the "femaleness" of women coworkers (DiTomaso, 1989: 88).

Although most shop-floor workers clearly do not engage in sexual harassment, the unique social setting of the shop floor increases the likelihood that this particular type of sexual harassment will occur. Indeed, this specific shop-floor sexual harassment must be seen as a practice communicating anger against women for invading a "male" bastion and for threatening the economic and social status of men (Carothers and Crull, 1984: 224). In addition, however, the shop floor is an ideal arena for differentiating between masculinity and femininity—performing manual labor demonstrates to others that such workers are "real men." The presence of women on the shop floor dilutes this gender distinction: if women can do what "real men" do, the value of the practice for accomplishing masculinity is effectively challenged. Because "doing gender" means creating differences between men and women, by maintaining and emphasizing the "femaleness" of women coworkers, shop-floor men are attempting to distinquish clearly between women and men manual laborers, thus preserving the peculiar masculinity of the shop floor. This type of sexual harassment serves as an effective (albeit primitive) resource for solidifying, strengthening, and validating a specific type of heterosexual shop-floor masculinity, while simultaneously excluding, disparaging, and ridiculing women (Segal, 1990: 211).[8]

Moving from shop floor to boardroom, we will next consider how corporate crime and a different type of sexual harassment provide certain white corporate executives with resources for constructing a specific form of private masculinity.

White Corporate Executives and Corporate Crime

White corporate executives have major decision-making power in corporations. In terms of gender, it is critical to understand who become executives and how they obtain such positions. Concomitantly, the fact that men control the activities of management likewise is critical to understanding corporate crime.[9] As more and more women enter the paid-labor market, they find it organized not only for purposes of producing goods, services, and profits, but also for gender. In other words, the gender divisions of labor and power continue to operate within the labor market. This is especially so in the corporate setting.

Corporations are organized to ensure that men receive the greatest share of material benefits. Moreover, although women hold approximately 38 percent of all management, executive, and administrative positions in the United States, they are relegated to lower-status positions within these occupations (Blau and Winkler, 1989). In fact, women are relegated to such areas as personnel, research, affirmative action, and equal employment—management areas that do not lead to major decision-making positions within the corporation (Kaufman, 1989). Also, these "patronizing" positions are where women do the work to discern what is needed, make recommendations, and "then *men decide* what is to be done with regard to these recommendations" (Sokoloff, 1980: 243). This gendered segregation of corporate managerial positions perpetuates the gendered divisions of labor and power because women usually work for men (p. 243):

> at lower wages, with fewer resources, and with less power than male managers, thus allowing men the benefits of money, status, power, resources, and specialization in decision-making control and order—without directly competing with other male managers for their privileged positions.

In short, the gender (and race) division of labor, reproduced within the corporation today, ensures white men positions of power, where corporate crimes orginate.[10] Indeed, no more than 2 percent of top executive positions are held by women and there are no women who hold the position of chief executive officer in any *Fortune 500* U.S. corporation (Powell, 1988: 13; L. Brown, 1988: 267).

The old-boy network is crucial to maintaining the gender divisions of labor and power and for understanding corporate crime. The old-boy network basically is a sponsorship system that recruits junior executives to upper echelons of corporate managerial sectors. In other words, men recruit men who share similar norms, attitudes, values, and standards of behavior. Accordingly, junior executives who make decisions in the corporate interest are guaranteed career promotion. The hierarchy of senior and junior executives establishes "the allegiance of the former to the latter" (Sokoloff, 1980: 240). In other words, if junior executives do what they are expected to do, they are rewarded with wealth, authority, and corporate control. Maintaining business as usual—making profits—these men eventually are rewarded not only financially but also with power over men and women. Indeed, white-executive masculinity is constructed partially around competition with other men for status and prestige: junior executives must maneuver for position and negotiate their rank relative to other men (Cockburn, 1985: 178).

Men who are junior executives, hoping to make it to the top, learn quickly what is right and what is wrong from their sponsor: they learn to conduct themselves and perform practices in ways that exemplify executive conceptions of masculinity. Foremost among these is the ability to compromise personal principles in order to move up the ladder. In fact, junior executives frequently must sacrifice personal ethics for the "good" of the company simply to remain in business. A recent survey by the Columbia University Business School reports that 40 percent of a sample of 1,070 businessmen had been rewarded for engaging in conduct they considered "ethically troubling"; 31 percent of men who refused to commit an ethically troubling act had been penalized (*Wall Street Journal*, 1990: B1).

A study by Edward Gross (1978) sheds some light on this situation. Gross analyzed a substantial body of research on corporate mobility to discern what qualities corporate positions demand and what sort of junior executives are most likely to be promoted. He found that men who are promoted to top corporate positions are ambitious, shrewd, and nearly amoral. Their ambition, however, is not merely personal—they soon discover their personal goals are best attained by assisting the corporation in attaining its goal—profit. As Gross (p. 71) states, these men "believe in the organization, they want it to attain its goals, they profit personally from such goal attainment. So they will try hard to help the organization attain those goals."

The gendered promotion system within the corporation, however, promotes not exclusively men who strongly identify with the goals of the corporation, but also (as Gross found) men who possess the personal characteristics necessary to commit, if needed, corporate crime. Given that the corporation "must engage in illegal activities to attain its goals, men with a nondemanding moral code have the least compunctions about engaging in such behavior" (p. 71). Men with nondemanding moral codes are more likely to be promoted to the top, a characteristic that frees them to engage (when necessary) in corporate crime. For corporate executives face both "pressure for profits" and "pressure for promotion." Most often remedied by legal means, when legitimate approaches fail, corporate executives are positioned to engage in specific illegitimate practices that seek to ensure not only their own, but corporate success as well. For example, executives involved in the production of the exploding Pintos operated under an ideology that "safety doesn't sell." As Cullen, Maakestad, and Cavender (1987: 161) point out, "When asked whether anyone had gone to Lee Iacocca and informed him of the Pinto's problems, a high-ranking company engineer responded, 'Hell no. That person would have been fired.' "

Another executive who worked at Ford for thirty years exemplified the nondemanding moral code of many Ford engineers by stating (p. 166): "Engineers who spoke out about safety didn't 'get that promotion' or 'salary increase.' " In short, "safety doesn't sell" became a defining feature of corporate executive masculinity and social practice. This type of masculinity was sustained as a collective practice within the context of the corporate boardroom.

Essentially, corporate crime simply assists the corporation and young upwardly mobile men reach their goals. In other words, corporate crime is a practice with which men gain corporate power through maintaining profit margins. Moreover, as corporate executives do corporate crime, they simultaneously do masculinity—construct a masculinity specific to their position in the gender, race, and occupational divisions of labor and power.

Tolson (1977: 81–82) points out that this type of masculinity differs from that found on the shop floor in two important ways. First, the corporate executive "does not do a 'job,' he pursues a 'career,' he is paid not a 'wage,' but a 'salary'; he works not by the 'clock,' but by 'appointment.' His career is a long-term investment, a ladder of individual achievement, finally rewarded by the 'golden handshake' " (p. 81). Highly committed to the future, the corporate executive cultivates a strategic expertise and fuels an inner desire to achieve. Second, because career is a long-term commitment, a man's undivided identification and a sense of duty are required. The discipline of corporate executive effort "is not the impersonal discipline of factory production, but *self*-discipline, an internalized desire to work" (p. 82). This desire is sustained by one's faith in a higher authority, the corporation. Corporate-executive masculinity, then, entails calculation and rationality as well as struggle for success, reward, and corporate recognition. The corporate executive perceives work as "a series of stages, leading finally to recognition by the community of individual achievement" (p. 83). Such men struggle with other men and measure masculinity by their success in the corporate world. Corporate crime is a practice that facilitates this particular gendered strategy of action.

Nevertheless, this type of white masculinity—devotion to achievement and success measured by promotion and profit making—can be threatened by certain obstacles that interfere with executive ability to realize profitmaking easily and without violating regulations. Stuart Hills (1987: 190) notes the following:

> In a capitalist economy, profit-seeking firms must often compete in an uncertain and unpredictable environment. Competitive market pressures, fluctuating sales, increasing costs for safety and health measures, consumer and environmental concerns, government regulations, and other constraints may limit the ability of the business firm to achieve its profit goals through legitimate opportunities. Thus, some corporations may evade and violate the law or engage in practices that many Americans would consider unethical, endangering the well-being of workers, consumers, and citizens.

Because threats to profitmaking are threats concurrently to masculine accomplishment, corporate crime is a means of overcoming both problems: corporate crime is a resource for accomplishing profit and gender. If profitmaking is undermined, an important resource for corporate executive masculinity is threatened. In such a predicament, sex category is particularly salient and doing masculinity necessitates extra effort. Thus, corporate crime may be invoked as a practice when corporate executives lack other resources for profitmaking and, therefore, to accomplish gender.

Moreover, social action is often designed with an eye to one's gender accountability both situationally and in the future (see discussion in Chapter 3). Crime can provide a resource for doing masculinity in specific social settings, such as the corporate boardroom, as well as for some future time when gender accountability may be at risk. The following statement by a B.F. Goodrich executive who conspired with others to cover up falsified test data on aircraft braking systems shows his concern for maintaining a "good provider" masculinity then, and in the future (Vandivier, 1987: 155):

> At forty-two, with seven children, I had decided that the Goodrich Company would probably be my "home" for the rest of my working life. The job paid well, it was pleasant and challenging, and the future looked reasonably bright. My wife and I had bought a home and were ready to settle down into a comfortable, middle-age, middle-class rut. If I refused to take part in the fraud, I would have to either resign or be fired. . . . But bills aren't paid with personal satisfaction, nor house payments with ethical principles.

The fraud was viewed by this executive as contributing not only to corporate profits, but also maintaining an income with which he could continue to provide for his family. Thus, in this case, corporate crime is a resource for being both a successful executive and an effective father/husband. Corporate crime helped solve the "male" accountability problem at work and home.

Consequently, within the corporation a specific masculinity is created among men at the top. This masculinity centers on practices reflecting not only the nondemanding moral code identified by Gross and the struggle for success, reward, and recognition identified by Tolson, but also "a tough-minded approach to problems" and "a capacity to set aside personal, emotional considerations in the interests of task accomplishments" (Kanter, 1977: 22). By setting aside such emotional reflections, white corporate executives are better prepared to handle the problems of profitmaking and are less inclined to question the corporate theft and violence they may generate. "Tough decisions" often involve making people suffer; not everyone can make the "necessary" decisions that simultaneously inflict pain upon others. It is the gendered corporate process that ensures that those who reach the top are sufficiently unemotional to make the tough decisions. Indeed, John McMullan (1992: 77) reviewed several studies on gender and the corporation, concluding that the studies "strongly suggest that the hallmark of modern corporate bureaucratic organization is a type of

heartless masculinist rationality that undervalues collective nurturance
and responsibility." For McMullan (pp. 77–78), it is a cold and abstract masculine calculus that underlies corporate crime.[11]

White corporate executives construct an accommodating corporate
masculinity that reflects their wholehearted obligation to the corporation and its overall enterprise. Thus, because masculinity is a behavioral response to the particular conditions and situations in which men
participate, corporate executives do masculinity when they do corporate crime. Moreover, their corporate position both constrains and enables certain forms of social action, and they monitor their actions
accordingly. And when profitmaking is threatened through environmental uncertainties, sex category is particularly salient, and therefore,
doing masculinity necessitates extra effort.

Corporate crime serves as a resource, then, for masculine accomplishment and facilitates profitmaking. Consequently, executives who
reach the top of the corporate ladder enjoy positions of nonaccounta-
ble and unconstrained power, and are "in a high state of preparedness
to commit corporate crime should they perceive it as being necessary
'for the good of the company' " (Box, 1983: 41).

Choosing corporate profit over people is made easier by gender relations that demand emotional insensitivity in executive men. In short,
the desire to "get to the top" and to maintain profit margins often
entails illegal and socially harmful behavior. Doing promotion, doing
profitmaking, and doing masculinity involve essentially the same ongoing practices—and corporate crime is a resource for accomplishing
all three. As McMullan (1992: 78) points out, this callous and insen-
sitive masculinity of the corporate boardroom silences opposition and
discourages "all but the most aggressive and competitive from engaging in business." Moreover, (p. 78):

> It lends support to law evasion, law avoidance and law-breaking. Against
> a backdrop of instrumental rationality and a dichotomized social world,
> corporate men stride and stumble into their illegal and criminal enter-
> prises, loudly proclaiming their virtue and respectability from the bureau-
> cratic shadows in the name of profits.

Corporate crime, then, can be understood as a practice for maintaining or reestablishing a masculine identity that has, or is about to be,
damaged. Corporate executive masculinity—accountable to other executives in identical situations and accomplishing gender by engaging

in corporate crime—provides a masculine resolution to the spectacle of environmental uncertainties.[12]

White Corporate Executives and Sexual Harassment

Sexual harassment is yet another resource available to corporate executives for constructing a specific type of masculinity. Because of their subordinate position in the corporation, women "are vulnerable to the whim and fancy of male employers or organizational superiors, who are in a position to reward or punish their female subordinate economically" (Box, 1983: 152). In other words, corporate-executive men are in a unique position to sexually exploit, if they desire, women subordinates. Executive exploitation of sexuality is often a means of reinforcing men's power at the same time as making profits. For example, secretaries frequently are treated as conspicuous "possessions"; therefore, by hiring the "best looking" instead of the most competent secretary, managers exploit secretarial sexuality to "excite the envy of colleagues, disarm the opposition and obtain favors from other departments" (Hearn, 1985: 118). Thus, as Jeff Hearn (p. 118) points out, exploitation of secretarial sexuality is not only a matter of directly objectifying women but also of using their sexuality for the eyes of other men. Economic and gender relations are produced simultaneously through the same ongoing sexual practices.

In addition to this direct exploitation of secretarial sexuality, corporate executives sometimes engage in specific types of sexual harassment. While shop-floor men who engage in sexual harassment are more likely to undertake practices that create a sexually demeaning work environment characterized by slurs, pictures, pinches, and grabs, white corporate-executive men are more likely to threaten women workers and lower-level managers who refuse to comply with demands for sexual favors with the loss of their jobs (Carothers and Crull, 1984: 222). One secretary described this type of sexual harassment from a corporate executive as follows (cited in Carothers and Crull, 1984: 222):

> He always complimented me on what I wore. I thought he was just being nice. It got to the place that every time he buzzed for me to come into his office for dictation, my stomach turned. He had a way of looking at me as if he were undressing me. This time as his eyes searched up and down my body and landed on my breast, he said, "Why should your boyfriend have all the fun. You could have fun with me *and* it could pay off for you. *Good* jobs are really scarce these days."

The harassment of women in subordinate positions by an executive man more likely involves hints and requests for dates or sexual favors, which, when rejected, are likely followed by work retaliation (p. 224). Essentially, this particular type of sexual harassment involves economic threats by white, corporate-executive men such that if a woman employee or would-be employee refuses to submit, she will, on the one hand, not be hired, retained, or promoted or, on the other hand, will be fired, demoted, or transferred to a less-pleasant work assignment. Assuming that the woman employee or potential employee does not desire a sexual relationship with the executive, such threats are extremely coercive. Given the economic position of many of these women, termination, demotion, or not being hired is economically devastating. When women depend on men for their economic well-being, some men take advantage of their economic vulnerability and engage in this particular practice of sexual harassment.

Although the imbalance of corporate gender power can be exercised coercively, sexual harassment is by no means automatic. Women often enter into genuine and humane relationships with men in the workplace, notwithstanding the fact that these men may be in supervisory positions vis-à-vis the woman.[13] Nevertheless, the general power imbalance within the corporation often creates conditions such that men in supervisory positions may exercise economic coercion to gain sexual access without genuine overt consent. Indeed, the corporate structural position of white executive men ensures that such exploitation will more likely be manipulative than violent.

One recent study of workplace assaults found that shop-floor workers utilized physical force more often than other forms of coercion because they lack the institutionalized economic means with which to force compliance. Corporate executives are much more likely to use economic coercion than physical force as a means with which to obtain sexual access to women subordinates (Schneider, 1991). Two women who experienced this type of sexual assault stated in part (cited in MacKinnon, 1979: 32):

"If I wasn't going to sleep with him, I wasn't going to get my promotion."

"I was fired because I refused to give at the office."

When women refuse to "give at the office," some corporate executives retaliate by exercising their power over women's careers. In one case, an executive, "following rejection of his elaborate sexual advances, barraged the woman with unwarranted reprimands about her job performance, refused routine supervision or task direction, which made it impossible for her to do her job, and then fired her for poor work performance" (MacKinnon, 1979: 35).

The social construction of masculinity/femininity in the executive/secretary relationship shows clearly how this specific type of sexual harassment comes about. A secretary is often expected to nurture the executive by stroking his ego, making his coffee, cleaning the office, and ensuring he is presentable (Sokoloff, 1980: 220). Secretaries are often symbolically hired as "office wives." In one case, an executive had his secretary do all his grocery shopping and even go to his home and take his washing off the line! (Pringle, 1989: 169–170).

Rosabeth Moss Kanter (1977: 88) noted some time ago that a "tone of emotional intensity" pervades the relationship between secretary and executive. The secretary comes to "feel for" the executive, "to care deeply about what happens to him and to do his feeling for him." In fact, according to Kanter (p. 88), secretaries are rewarded for their willingness "to take care of bosses' personal needs." In other words, women subordinates construct a specific type of femininity by performing an extensive nurturing service for the executive.[14] Women do in the workplace what they traditionally have done in the home. It should come as no surprise that some executives come to expect such nurturance from women subordinates, just as they do from their wives, and that some take this nurturance further to include sexual nuturing. The result is that some women are coerced to exchange sexual services for material survival. As Carothers and Crull (1984: 223) observe in their important study of sexual harassment:

> The male boss can use his power over women within the organizational structure to impose sexual attentions on a woman, just as he can coerce her into getting his coffee. They both know that if she does not go along, she is the one who will lose in terms of job benefits.

Corporate-executive harassment and sexual coercion are practices that simultaneously construct a specific form of masculinity. This type of sexual harassment arrogantly celebrates hegemonic masculinity, its presumed heterosexual urgency, and the "normality" of pursuing women aggressively. In an attempt to "score" with his secretary, the corporate-executive sexual harasser strengthens gender hierarchy, thereby "affirming in men a shared sense of themselves as the dominant, assertive and active sex'' (Segal, 1990: 244). The corporate executive enjoys an immediate sensation of power derived from this practice, power that strengthens his masculine self-esteem.

In this way, in addition to normative heterosexuality, white, corporate-executive sexual harassers attempt to reproduce their gender power. Through the practice of corporate sexual harassment, executives exhibit, as MacKinnon (1979: 162) argues, "that they can go this far any time they wish and get away with it." White, corporate-executive sexual harassment, constructed differently than by shop-floor men, provides a resource for constructing this specific type of heterosexual masculinity that centers on the "driven" nature of "male" sexuality and "male" power.

Although clearly most corporate executives do not engage in sexual harassment, the social setting of the executive/secretary relationship increases the probability that this specific form of sexual harassment will occur. Corporate executives engage in sexual harassment to reinforce their power by sexualizing women subordinates, creating "essential" differences between women and men by constructing this particular type of masculinity.

The Family

In addition to the street and the workplace, the divisions of labor and power frame social interactions and practices in the contemporary nuclear family where, for example, women remain responsible primarily for unpaid housework and child care while men remain responsible primarily for paid labor. Indeed, the gender division of household labor defines not only who does most of the unpaid household labor but also the kind of household labor assigned to men and women. Moreover, the sociological evidence indicates clearly that in Western industrialized societies gender asymmetry in the performance of household labor continues to exist (Andersen, 1988: 141–145; Messerschmidt, 1986: 74; Hartmann, 1981; Berk, 1985; Hochschild, 1989, 1992) and women share less in the consumption of household goods (from food to leisure time) than do men (Walby, 1989: 221).

It is true that barely 10 percent of all U.S. heterosexual households consist of a husband and wife with two children living at home, where the husband is the sole breadwinner (Messerschmidt, 1986: 74). Further, as fertility is delayed or declines, and with more and more women working during pregnancy and child-rearing years, active motherhood is shrinking as a component of most women's lives (Petchesky, 1984: 246). Nevertheless, evidence indicates that women continue to perform most of the household labor, even as these demographic changes occur and women's participation in the paid-labor market increases dramatically. Indeed, Arlie Hochschild (1992: 512) concluded in her study of fifty-two heterosexual couples over an eight-year period that just as "there is a wage gap between men and women in the work place, there is a 'leisure gap' between them in the home. Most women work one shift at the office or factory and a 'second shift' at home."

This gender division of labor embodies the husband's power to define the household setting in his terms. While conscious efforts are being made in many households to dismantle familial power relations (Connell, 1987: 124), especially in the middle class (Ehrenreich, 1983), for most couples the capacity of each spouse to determine the course of their shared life is unequal: men alone make the "very important" decisions in the household; women alone make few "important" decisions (Komter, 1989). In many dual-career families, men's power is deemed authentic and an acceptable part of social relations. This legitimized power in the family provides men with considerably greater authority (Kompter, 1989; Pahl, 1992; Bernard, 1982). Concomitantly, the marital sexual relationship, as with other aspects of marriage, likely embodies power, unless consciously dismantled, and "in most cases it is the husband who holds the initiative in defining sexual practice" (Connell, 1987: 123).

Chapter 2 argued that the concept of patriarchy has lost its strength and usefulness as a theoretical starting point for comprehending gender inequality in Western industrialized societies. Nevertheless, the concept is helpful to describe a certain type of masculinity that persists today: some men are simply *patriarchs* in the traditional sense. Patriarchs fashion configurations of behavior and pursue a gender strategy within the family setting that control women's labor and/or sexuality. Moreover, these men will most likely use violence against women in the family. In this final section of Chapter 5, the discussion focuses on two forms of violence against women in the family—wife beating and wife rape—and analyzes how these crimes serve as a resource for the construction of specific types of patriarchal masculinities.

Wife Beating and Battering Rape

Victimization surveys indicate that in the home, wives are assaulted much more often by their husbands than husbands are by their wives (less than 5 percent of domestic violence involves attacks on husbands by their wives) and women are much more likely than men to suffer injury from these assaults (Dobash, Dobash, Wilson, and Daly, 1992).[15] Wife beating also develops within a setting of prolonged and persistent intimidation, domination, and control over women (Dobash et al., 1992; Dobash and Dobash, 1984; Pagelow, 1984). Accordingly, wife beating is the "chronic battering of a person of inferior power who for that reason cannot effectively resist" (Gordon, 1988: 251).

Violence by men in the household derives from the domestic authority of men and is intimately linked to the traditional patriarchal expectation (1) that men are the credible figures within monogamous relationships and (2) that men possess the inherent right to control those relationships. As Susan Schechter (1982: 222) argues, "a man beats to remind a woman that the relationship will proceed in the way he wants or that ultimately he holds the power."

Katz's (1988: 18–31) discussion of "righteous slaughter"—killing among family members, friends, and acquaintances—by men aids in understanding how this focus on household authority and control results in wife beating as a resource for masculine construction. Katz argues that for the typical killer, murder achieves *Good* by obliterating *Bad*. Moreover, the killer has no capacity to "ignore a fundamental challenge" to his self-worth and identity. From the killer's perspective, the victim teases, dares, defies, or pursues the killer. Accordingly, the killer sees himself as simply "defending his rights." In other words, the killer's identity and self-worth have been taken away—by an insult, losing an argument, an act of infidelity—and such events attack an "eternal human value" that calls for a "last stand in defense of his basic worth." The "eternally humiliating situation" is transformed into a blinding rage and the compulsion to wipe away the stigmatizing stain through the act of murder. And the rage is not random and chaotic but, rather, "coherent, disciplined action, cunning in its moral structure" (p. 30). The killer "does not kill until and unless he can fashion violence to convey the situational meaning of defending his rights" (p. 31).

Investigations of wife beating indicate further the application of the notion "defending his rights." Violence is regarded by the husband as achieving *Good* by pulverizing *Bad*; such men engage in a coherent and disciplined rage to defend what they consider to be their rights. According to interviews with wife beaters, their wife is perceived as not "performing well," not accomplishing what her "essential nature" enjoins and stipulates. Women are beaten for not cooking "up to standards," for not being obeisant and deferential, and for not completing or performing housework sufficiently—for not being a "good wife" (Ptacek, 1988: 147). According to the offender, the "privileges of male entitlement have been unjustly denied" because the wife is not submissive and, therefore, not conforming to his standards of "essential femininity" (p. 148). Irene Frieze's (1983: 553) interviews with wife beaters found that they believe "it is their right as men to batter wives who disobey them."

Dobash and Dobash (1984: 274) similarly found that most wife beating is precipitated by verbal confrontations centering on possessiveness and jealousy on the part of the husband and a husband's demand concerning domestic labor and services. During an argument over such issues, "the men were most likely to become physically violent at the point when the woman could be perceived to be questioning his authority or challenging the legitimacy of his behavior or at points when she asserted herself in some way" (p. 274). In other words, wife beating arises not solely from gendered subordination but also from women actively contesting that subordination (Gordon, 1988: 286). In such situations, the wife beater is punishing "his wife" for her failure to fulfill adequately her "essential" obligations in the gender division of labor and power and for her challenge to his dominance. The wife beater perceives that he has an inherent patriarchal right to punish "his woman" for her alleged wrongdoing.

Wife beaters are piously sure of their righteousness, and thus fashion their violence to communicate the situational meaning of defending their patriarchal rights. Indeed, the more traditional the gender division of labor (regardless of class and race position) the greater the likelihood of wife beating (Edleson, Eisikovits, and Guttman, 1986; Messerschmidt, 1986; Smith, 1990). In such traditional patriarchal households, both husband and wife tend to perceive the lopsided gender division of labor and power as "fair" (Berk, 1985). Linda Gordon's (1988: 260–261) historical study of family violence found that in households where wife beating is prevalent:

> Women as well as men professed allegiance to male-supremacist understandings of what relations between the sexes should be like. These shared assumptions, however, by no means prevented conflict. Women's assumptions of male dominance did not mean that they quit trying to improve their situations.

The wife beater attempts to resolve in *his* way what he regards as a conflict over this "fair" arrangement, even when the wife is not actively or consciously contesting that "fair" household organization.[16] Accordingly, as West and Zimmerman (1987: 144) argue, "It is not simply that household labor is designated as 'women's work,' but that a woman to engage in it and a man not to engage in it is to draw on and exhibit the 'essential nature' of each." By engaging in practices that maintain gender divisions of labor and power, husbands and wives do not simply produce household goods and services, but also produce gender. Indeed, husbands and wives develop gendered rationalizations and justifications for this asymmetrical household labor. What follows are selected but representative examples (Komter, 1989: 209):

By wives:
"He has no feeling for it."
"He is not born to it."
"It does not fit his character."

By husbands:
"She has more talent for it."
"It is a woman's natural duty."

When this asymmetry is questioned (whether consciously or not), the wife beater assumes that his "essential rights" are being denied— an injustice has occurred, a violation of the "natural" order of things. The "essential nature" of wife beaters is that they control familial decision making and thus dominate the family division of labor and power. When wives "question" this decision making, through words or actions, they threaten their husband's control of the gender division of labor and power. In other words, the husband interprets such behavior as a threat to his "essential nature"—control and domination of the household. Because spousal domestic labor is a symbolic affirmation of a patriarch's masculinity and his wife's femininity, such men are extremely vulnerable to disappointment when that labor is not performed as they expect (Gordon, 1988: 268).

According to the wife beater, it is his duty to determine, for example, what constitutes a satisfactory meal, how children are cared for, when and how often sexual relations occur, and the nature of leisure activities (Ferraro, 1988: 134). Women are beaten for some of the most insignificant conduct imaginable: for example, preparing a casserole instead of a meat dish for dinner, wearing their hair in a ponytail, or remarking that they do not like the pattern on the wallpaper. Kathleen Ferraro (p. 135) discusses a case in which even the issue of wearing a particular piece of clothing was perceived by the husband as a threat to his control:

> On her birthday, she received a blouse from her mother that she put on to wear to a meeting she was attending without Steven. He told her she could not wear the blouse, and after insisting that she would, Steven beat her. It was not only her insistence on wearing the blouse that evening that triggered Steven's abuse. It was the history of his symbolic control, through determining her appearance that was questioned by wearing the new blouse.

Wife beaters (regardless of class and race position) presume they have the patriarchal right—because it is part of their "essential nature"—to dominate and control their wives, and wife beating serves both to ensure continued compliance with their commands and as a resource for constructing a "damaged" patriarchal masculinity. Thus, wife beating increases (or is intended to do so) their control over women and, therefore, over housework, child care, and sexual activity.

Yet wife beating is related not only to the husband's control over familial decision making, but also develops from another form of control, possessiveness. For some wife beaters, spousal demonstration of loyalty is a focal concern and is closely monitored. For instance, time spent with friends may be interpreted by a wife beater simply as disloyalty. Indeed, sexual jealousy of friends is a common theme in the literature on wife beating (Dobash and Dobash, 1979, 1984; Ferraro, 1988; Frieze, 1983), and indicates the importance of the social structure of normative heterosexuality to understanding wife beating. The wife's uncommitted wrong is the potential to be unfaithful, which to her husband is not only a serious challenge to his patriarchal ideology, but his very real fear that his wife will choose another man and, thereby, judge him less "manly" than his "competitor." Thus, because time spent with friends endangers his ongoing interest in heterosexual performance, wife beating reassures him that his wife is his to possess sexually.

Moreover, not only potential sexual competitors can threaten a patriarchal husband, but relatives may also pose threats to a wife's loyalty. Pregnancy, for example, is closely associated with wife beating, and reflects the husband's resentment of the fetal intruder (Ferraro, 1988). Walker (1979: 83–84) offers an example of a husband and wife who planned to spend the day together, but the wife broke off the plans, choosing instead to baby-sit her three-year-old granddaughter.

Her husband (Ed) seems to have interpreted this choice as disloyal behavior and a challenge to his ultimate control:

> Ed became enraged. He began to scream and yell that I didn't love him, that I only loved my children and grandchildren. I protested and said, "Maybe you would like to come with me," thinking that if he came, he might feel more a part of the family. He just became further enraged. I couldn't understand it. . . . He began to scream and yell and pound me with his fists. He threw me against the wall and shouted that he would never let me leave, that I had to stay with him and could not go. I became hysterical and told him that I would do as I saw fit. . . . Ed then became even further enraged and began beating me even harder.

Thus, under conditions where labor services are "lacking" and possesiveness is "challenged," a wife beater's masculinity is threatened. In such a scenario, predictably, the wife beater attempts to reestablish control by reconstructing his patriarchal masculinity through the practice of wife beating.

Approximately 30 to 40 percent of battered women are also victims of wife rape (Walker, 1979; Russell, 1982; Frieze, 1983). These "battering rapes," as Finkelhor and Yllö (1985) describe them, do not result from marital conflicts over sex; rather, the rape is an extension of other violence perpetrated on the victim. The wife beating/rape represents punishment and degradation for challenging his authority and, thus, the traditional division of labor and power. In fact, although wife beating and battering rapes extend across all classes and races (for the reasons discussed above), they occur most frequently in working-class and lower–working-class households wherein the traditional patriarchal gender division of labor and power—husband decision maker and wife caretaker—is strongest (Straus, Gelles, and Steinmetz, 1980; Finkelhor and Yllö, 1985; Smith, 1990a; Walker, 1977–78; Messerschmidt, 1986: 144). Research consistently shows that class conditions are associated with wife beating: for example, low-income (Straus et al., 1980; DeKeseredy and Hinch, 1991) and working-class wives are approximately twice as likely as middle-class wives to experience wife beating (Smith, 1990; Stets and Straus, 1989). Moreover, among couples in which the husband is unemployed or employed part-time, the level of husband-to-wife violence is three times as high as the level among couples in which the husband is fully employed (Straus et al., 1980; DeKeseredy and Hinch, 1991).

Finally, Michael Smith's (1990a: 49) study of risk factors in wife beating found that "the lower the income, the higher the probability of abuse." This same study went on to report that the chances of a low-income woman being severely battered during marriage exceed those of a middle-class woman by a factor of ten. Smith's (1990: 267) data reveals that "men with relatively low incomes, less educated men, and men in low-status jobs were significantly more likely than their more privileged counterparts to subscribe to an ideology of familial patriarchy. These men were also more likely to have beaten their wives."

Although at work he is individually powerless, at home the working-class battering rapist is a patriarch endowed with individual authority. His ability to earn money (if available) "authorizes" his patriarchal power as husband/father. But his masculine identity depends on the demarcation of public and private responsibility; consequently, any challenge to the status quo in the home is taken personally as a confrontation (Tolson, 1977: 70). In seeking to sustain this specific type of patriarchal masculinity, working-class men develop an intense emotional dependency on the family/household (Donaldson, 1987), demanding nurturance, services, and comfort on their terms when at home. As Lynne Segal (1990: 28) points out, "the sole site of authority" for such men is in the home. And when their power and authority are threatened or perceived to be threatened at home, working-class men are more likely than other men to employ battering rapes to accomplish gender and reestablish their control. As Harris and Bologh (1985: 246) point out in their examination of "blue collar battering," "If he can establish an aura of aggression and violence, then he may be able to pass as a 'real man,' for surely it is admirable to use violence in the service of one's honor."

Battering in this sense is a resource for affirming "maleness." Because of their structural position in the class division of labor, working-class men—in particular, lower–working-class men—lack traditional resources for constructing their masculinity and, as a result, are more likely than are middle-class men to forge a particular type of masculinity that centers on ultimate control of the domestic setting through the use of violence. Moreover, unemployment and low occupational status undermine the patriarchal breadwinner/good provider masculinity: he cannot provide for his wife and children. Such men are more likely than are economically advantaged husbands to engage in wife beating and battering rapes to reestablish their masculinity. As Kathleen Ferraro (1988: 127) puts it, "for men who lack any control in the civil realm, dominance within the private realm of the home becomes their sole avenue for establishing a sense of self in control of others."[17]

In sum, most working- and lower–working-class husbands do not abuse their wives, nor is this particular type of abuse limited to this class of men. Nevertheless, the peculiar social conditions prevalent in working- and lower–working-class families increase the incidence of this type of abuse. For these men, power is exercised in the home in ways that hegemonic masculinity approves: men are allowed to be aggressive and sexual. Lacking dominance over others at work or the ability to act out a breadwinner (or even economic contributor) masculinity, sex category is particularly important, and working- and lower–working-class men are more likely to express their masculinity as patriarchs, attempting to control the labor and sexuality of "their women." Consequently, when patriarchal relations are "challenged," their taken-for-granted "essential nature" is undermined and, accordingly, doing masculinity requires extra effort. Wife beating/rape is a specific practice designed with an eye to one's accountability as a "real man" and, therefore, serves as a suitable resource for simultaneously accomplishing gender and affirming patriarchal masculinity.

Force-only Rape

However, wife rape is not limited to the victims of wife beating. Indeed, in Finkelhor and Yllö's (1985) study, 40 percent of their sample were "force-only rapes"—situations in which husbands use only the force necessary to coerce their wives into submission. The perpetrators and victims of force-only rapes were significantly more educated than those of battering rapes, more often middle-class, and almost half held business- or professional-level jobs.[18] Moreover, the perpetrators and victims of force-only rapes were much less likely to have been in a relationship based on the traditional gender divisions of labor and power. Sex was usually the issue in force-only rapes, and the offenders were "acting on some specifically sexual complaint," such as how often to have sex or what were acceptable sexual activities (p. 46).

In some sectors of the "progressive" middle class, there have been serious attempts to become truly equal marriage partners, where the wife has a career and where the husband participates equally in child care and housework. However, the greater the income differential between husbands and wives, the less involved some husbands are in parenting and housework, and there exists greater equality in dual-career families than in dual-income families (Segal, 1990: 38). Consequently, as Barbara Ehrenreich (1989: 218–220; see also 1983, 1984) argues, a new heterosexual masculinity on the part of certain progressive, middle-class men has emerged, consisting of choosing a mate who can "pull her own weight" economically and who is truly committed to sharing household labor equally.

Notwithstanding, this progressive "dual-career" relationship is not supplemented, in many cases, by a progressive sexual relationship. As Andrew Tolson (1977: 121) argued as early as 1977, for many progressive, middle-class men, sexual passion is "still acted out in familial terms of masculine 'conquest'—to which women could only 're-spond.' " Although many progressive, middle-class men seriously seek "free women" who live for themselves and their careers (Ehrenreich, 1984), in bed they continue to demand submission and the affirmation of masculinity through heterosexual performance (Tolson, 1977: 121). That is, many progressive, middle-class men continue to adhere to the hegemonic masculine ideology that "entitles" them to sex with their wives whenever they want it. For example, Finkelhor and Yllö (1985: 62–70) discuss the case of Ross, a middle-class businessman who somewhat represents this progressive middle class, yet who frequently raped his wife. Ross describes below how one such rape occurred during an argument over sex that his wife was winning (p. 66):

She was standing there in her nightie. The whole thing got me somewhat sexually stimulated, and I guess subconsciously I felt she was getting the better of me. It dawned on me to just throw her down and have at her . . . which I did. I must have reached out and grabbed at her breast. She slapped my hand away. So I said, "Lay down. You're going to get it." She replied, "Oh, no, you don't," so I grabbed her by the arms and she put up resistance for literally fifteen seconds and then just resigned herself to it. There were no blows or anything like that. It was weird. I felt very animalistic, and I felt very powerful. I had the best erection I'd had in years. It was very stimulating. . . . I walked around with a smile on my face for three days.

Ross believed his wife not only controlled the sexuality in their lives, but that she had "completely and totally emasculated" him (p. 68). The rape was both a way to overcome that loss of power in his life and a means to construct a specific type of patriarchal masculinity centering on heterosexual performance and the domination and control of women's sexuality.

Another businessman, Jack, stated to Finkelhor and Yllö (p. 72), "When she would not give it freely, I would take it." He felt that his wife did not have the right to deny sex, he had the right to sex when he pleased, and it was her duty to satisfy his sexual needs. Similarly, in Irene Frieze's (1983: 544, 553) study of wife rape, the vast majority of wife rapists engaged in this form of violence in order to prove their "manhood," believing "that their wives were obligated to service them sexually in whatever ways they desired."

Thus, in force-only rapes, the assaults are practices of masculine control based on expectations that sex is a right. Both battering and force-only rapists consciously choose such violent action to facilitate a patriarchal gender strategy and to protect what they view as their "essential" privileges. The resulting masculine construction is not only an exhibition of their "essential nature," but also illustrates the seductive quality of violence for displaying that "essential nature." For these men, masculine authority is quite simply expressed through the violent control of women.

Nevertheless, such personal choices become enigmatic when detached from social structures. In battering rapes, because the traditional division of labor and power is prevalent and the struggle is over authority and control of that division, these men construct a patriarchal form of masculinity that punishes and degrades the wife for deviating from her "essential" duties. In force-only rapes, however, the gender division of labor is not the issue: this is the classic, middle-class, dual-career family in which both partners participate in decision making and household tasks, and in which the husband accepts, in a general way, his wife's autonomous right to develop her own interests. However, the force-only rapist feels specifically wronged, cheated, and deprived in the sexual realm. Some progressive, middle-class men simply adhere to the hegemonic masculine ideology that entitles them to sex whenever they want it. Sex is considered a marriage right by which gender is accomplished through effective performance in the sexual realm. Like sexual harassment, a similar type of crime, wife rape can be a resource for accomplishing masculinity differently. And as the social setting within the nuclear family changes, so does the conceptualization of what is normative masculine behavior. Different social settings generate different masculinities, even when the particular resource (crime) is similar.

In sum, the structure of the gender division of labor and power and normative heterosexuality impinges on the construction of masculinity. These structural features both preclude and permit certain forms of crime as resources that men may use to pursue a gender strategy and construct their masculinity. Although both battering and force-only rapists try to control their wives, they do so in qualitatively different ways. The social relations extant within their respective gender divisions of labor and power are different, and different options exist for maintaining their control. The choices made by each type of rapist, and the resources available to carry out those choices, develop in response to the specific social circumstances in which they live. For these reasons, then, these men employ different forms of violence to construct different types of private masculinities.

This chapter has attempted to demonstrate that men produce specific configurations of behavior that can be seen by others within the same immediate social setting as "essentially male." These different masculinities emerge from practices that utilize different resources, and class and race relations structure the resources available to construct specific masculinities. Pimps, workers, executives, and patriarchs generate situationally accomplished, unique masculinities by drawing on different types of crime indigenous to their distinct positions within the structural divisions of labor and power. Because men experience their everyday world from a uniquely individualistic position in society, they construct the cultural ideals of hegemonic masculinity in different ways.

Social structures are framed through social action and, in turn, provide resources for constructing masculinity. As one such resource, specific types of crime ultimately are based on these social structures. Thus, social structures both enable and constrain social action and, therefore, masculinities and crime. In Chapter 6, we address the question of how the social construction of masculinities shapes the state and gender politics.

Chapter 6

The State and Gender Politics

The state and its plurality of agencies is rarely seen as a gendered milieu. Yet feminist research over the past decade demonstrates that gender is a major characteristic of the state and a principal domain of its operations (Burstyn, 1983; Ursel, 1986; MacKinnon, 1989; Smart, 1989; Franzway, Court, and Connell, 1989; Connell, 1990). Indeed, in terms of personnel, style, and function, the state is a masculine-dominated institution. For example, in the United States there has never been a woman president or vice-president; only nine women have served in presidential administrations; and even after the Year of the Woman in U.S. politics, only 48 of the 435 representatives in Congress and 6 of the 100 senators in 1993 were women. Elite state-governmental positions are dominated by men, and the coercive apparatus of the state—the criminal justice system and the military—is likewise masculinized in terms of physical work force and social practice.[1]

Concurrently, the state embodies gender relations of power: both decision making and enforcement of such decisions are substantially in the hands of men (Franzway et al., 1989: 8–9). Because it is centrally and distinctively the institutionalization of gendered power relations, the state possesses considerable resources for *regulating* gender relations in society as a whole (Connell, 1990: 527). This institutionalization is not, however, omnipotent; the state is clearly the focus for the mobilization of special interests, including feminist interests. As such, the state provides a site in which a variety of social forces struggle to influence policy.

This does not mean that the state is simply an empty vessel into which any collection of special interests can be poured. On the contrary, the state is an apparatus with an institutionalized bias toward protecting the gendered status quo (Burstyn, 1983). In other words, although the state is a site for mobilization of special interests, this mobilization is lopsided. Men rarely mobilize as a group in an effort to gain access to the state, for, as Franzway et al. (1989: 39) point out, such access is institutionalized in the state itself:

> This is a major difference from the pattern of class politics, since capi-
> talist parties have not only emerged in response to labour mobilizations
> but have been highly successful. The absence of this kind of mobilization
> "from above" in gender politics raises crucial questions about the way
> men's power is institutionalized, and about the connections between dif-
> ferent sites of power. The key point is that masculine domination is so
> firmly entrenched in existing political institutions . . . that they can nor-
> mally be expected to do the job as they stand.

In gender relations, therefore, the state is both an actor in social struggle and what is at stake in social struggle (p. 40).

The goal of the following discussion is to contribute to the expanding literature on the gendered nature of the state by focusing particularly on its role in regulating gender relations in society as a whole.
Because of this role, the state has been used effectively as an instrument for enacting feminist demands ranging from the suffrage movement of the late 1800s and early 1900s, to law reform campaigns on
violence by men against women (such as rape law reform) in the
1970s and 1980s (Hinch, 1991; Los, 1990; Carringella-MacDonald,
1988; Snider, 1985). Jeff Hearn (1992: 95–115) has shown how
changes in nineteenth-century western industrialized societies increasingly have brought the "private powers of men" (e.g., as individual
fathers) into such public domains as the state. The result has been that
for the first time, the private and public powers of men were exposed
in public discourse, rather than hidden away in the private realm of
the family, which made it easier for women to challenge such powers.
Thus, increasingly throughout the late nineteenth and early twentieth
centuries (pp. 118–119):

> the state (that is, men in the state) was subjected to demands and pres-
> sures from women, not just in terms of the formal obtaining of suffrage,
> but also in all manner of other social and political services. State men,
> especially middle-class state men, were located as *receivers* of the de-
> mands and opinions of women, especially middle-class women.

Feminism has been a major force in gender politics since at least the
late 1800s.

We begin with an in-depth examination of the late nineteenth- and
early twentieth-century feminist mobilization against prostitution (as

one example) and analyze how certain feminists (whom historians of the Progressive Era have termed "social feminists") of this period entered a coalition with the conservative social purity movement to increase the age of sexual consent in an effort to protect young girls from allegedly being forced into prostitution through so-called "white-slave traffic."[2] As we shall see, however, this feminist effort did little to decrease the sexual exploitation of young girls; rather, the prohibition of working-class girls' right to engage in heterosexual activity when they pleased created a new class of girl offenders—teenage sex "delinquents." This historical example raises salient questions not only about the gendered nature of the state and its role in regulating gender relations, but also about the state as a site for feminist mobilization and what strategies might be employed during such mobilization.

The Rise of the "Girl Sex Delinquent"

In the 1860s and the 1870s, U.S. feminists organized a campaign against state regulation of prostitution. Susan B. Anthony, one of the leaders of the feminist movement, lectured across the country on the danger of legalized prostitution (Pivar, 1973: 51). A countergroup, "regulationists," favored medical control, claiming this would contribute to the preservation of public health. As one of their proponents expounded, "Given man's nature and the laws of health . . . prostitution was a social requisite" (p. 56). As noted throughout this book, nineteenth-century, white, hegemonic masculinity emphasized, in part, the existence of an excessive sexual drive in men and a white femininity constructed, in part, on the alleged *a*sexuality of women.[3]

According to regulationists, for men who could not control their excessive sexual drive, regulated prostitution would serve as an "outlet" that would protect "their women" and, thus, their family. As Ruth Rosen (1982: 5) points out:

> If men were not to unleash their passions on "young ladies of their acquaintance," or wives too delicate and asexual to cope with their sexual demands, they had to exert heroic self-control; if they failed in these efforts, they could still protect women in their own milieu by going to prostitutes.

Consequently, police regulation and medical supervision were seen by regulationists as in the best interests of both family and prostitute (Pivar, 1973: 56–57). Moreover, regulationists favored compulsory medical examinations for prostitutes rather than complete suppression of prostitution, the latter being too costly and not serving overall societal interests (Degler, 1980: 284–285).

Feminists, on the other hand, argued that regulation forced alleged prostitutes into vaginal examinations and licensing, allowing men the freedom to engage in sex with prostitutes without incurring the risk of venereal disease (Dubois and Gordon, 1984: 38). Moreover, they demonstrated that regulation did not really protect anyone, since men, who were not similarly examined, oftentimes were carriers of venereal disease who contacted prostitutes not yet infected. For feminists, then, regulation was masculine-defined in that it served exclusively the interests of men (customers) rather than of women (prostitutes). As Ellen Dubois and Linda Gordon (1984: 38) further point out, feminist opposition drew "not only on their anger at men who bought female flesh, but also reaffirmed their identification with prostitutes' victimization. Feminists asserted that all women, even prostitutes, had a right to the integrity of their own bodies."

Regulation of prostitution, feminists argued, simply allowed clients, physicians, and criminal justice personnel (inevitably men) access to and control over women's bodies. Thus, the intent of regulation was not to protect society, feminists asserted, but rather to blame and punish women prostitutes for the spread of venereal disease and grant men the arbitrary control of women's bodies. In the end, the U.S. movement against regulation, already in place in England and other parts of Europe (Walkowitz, 1980), proved so strong and successful that only one city ever tried it (St. Louis) and the experiment lasted but four years (Degler, 1980: 285). This particular example of gender politics demonstrates that state institutionalization of masculine power is not invincible, and that mobilizations "from below" are, at times, successful.

Yet, in the process of defeating regulation, certain feminists—"social feminists"—coalesced with the emerging conservative social purity movement (Pivar, 1973). The social purity movement was composed of a variety of individuals from different groups (men and women) who shared the goal of changing social attitudes toward sex. Their intent was to achieve a single standard of sexual morality for men and women. In short, the publicly avowed aim was that men conform to the standards of chastity enjoined on white women in nineteenth-century U.S. society.

Social purity was the logical reality in a society dominated by the ideology of conservative Darwinism. U.S. citizens, especially in the middle and upper classes, were exposed to the writings of the architect of conservative Darwinism, Herbert Spencer, who extrapolated Charles Darwin's evolutionary theory into a social philosophy. For Spencer, the so-called natural abilities of the more "fit" or adaptable members of society would select them out to take control of a society. This "natural selection" allowed society to progress, as long as the "detriments" to social progress were efficiently curtailed. Only the moral could attain progress; it was the immoral who had to be controlled "to make possible the conditions necessary for general welfare" (Boostrom, 1973: 156). In other words, evolutionary progress required a curb on what was termed "immorality." It was within this ideological setting that social purity flourished.[4]

Many feminists coalesced with the social purity movement, and as such, prostitution eventually became subsumed under the rubric of purification. As David J. Pivar (1973: 63) shows in his work, *Purity Crusade: Sexual Morality and Social Control, 1868–1900*:

> In the process of active participation, purity reform, at first lacking clear contours, rapidly took shape, with the woman's and purity movements converging ideologically in a common drive for social transformation. . . . Prostitution, as an issue, was subsumed by the larger concern for social purification, and the feminist leadership willingly participated in its suppression.

After defeating regulation, many feminists joined with the conservative social purity movement to press for the total abolition of prostitution. They began consolidating and expanding their initial victory against regulation into an abolitionist movement containing a program of social purity measures (Vertinsky, 1976: 68–69). Between 1885 and 1895, the feminist movement against legalized prostitution changed from a defensive action against regulation to an aggressive campaign for abolitionism.

The alleged white-slave traffic (the idea that prostitutes were physically forced into the business, rather than entering it voluntarily) greatly influenced many feminists. Prostitutes were seen as the sexually innocent, passive victims of evil men, a view that "allowed feminists to see themselves as rescuers of slaves" (Dubois and Gordon, 1984: 38). As Kathleen Daly (1988: 177) points out, these feminists "attributed women's 'fall' to men's deceit and sexual desire." The white-slave ideology encouraged white middle- and upper-class feminists to challenge the sexual double standard through other women's lives (not their own), in this way focusing their anger on men other than their husbands (Dubois and Gordon, 1984: 38). These feminists believed that abolition of prostitution would help raise men to the purity level of women—because it would allegedly reform "male sexuality"—and, therefore, contribute both to social progress and to the creation of a gender-equal society.

The Coalition and the Age of Consent

These issues—the white-slave ideology, the view of prostitutes as sexually innocent and passive victims of evil men, and the concept that men were possessed of excessive sexual essence (drive)—coalesced feminists and social purists to seek to raise the age of sexual consent: the age at which a girl is considered legally competent to consent to sexual intercourse. Consider Helen H. Gardner's (1895: 196) comments in the *Arena*, where she wrote on the alleged sexual innocence of young women and the biological lechery of all men:

> There is not, there has never been, there never can be any fact of nature that is not a protest in letters of flame against the infamy of legal enactments which place the innocence and ignorance of childhood at the mercy of licensed lechery. . . . No being who is not too degraded or too utterly, mentally and morally diseased to be a safe person to be at large, could wish that a little child, a baby girl fourteen, twelve, aye, ten years of age should be made, as is the case in many of our states, the legal and rightful prey of grown men.

Gardner (p. 196) argued further that the then current age of sexual consent laws (mandating the age of consent as low as ten in some states) were "in the interest of the brothel, in the interest of the grade of men who prey upon the ignorance and helplessness of childhood." Vie H. Campbell (1895: 286), president of the Wisconsin Women's Christian Temperance Union, added:

> It is time for plain-speaking to reveal to innocent, unsuspecting girlhood the snares that are set to entangle her feet. This long-continued silence is the tribute which unbridled lust has demanded of us; and that we have, without remonstrance, paid it too long, the increasing army of unwarned, unfortunate, helpless victims will bear witness.

Feminists and social purists argued that by raising the age of sexual consent, sexually innocent girls would be protected and men would be forced to control their sexual "drive" to conform to nineteenth-century, U.S. standards of abstinence demanded of white women. According to conservative Darwinist ideology, this result would contribute to social progress. In this way, the feminist/purity coalition demanded reform of "male sexuality" by means of coercive state policy.

In 1886, many states had set the age of sexual consent for girls at ten. Frances Willard, the feminist and social purist who "made the Womens Christian Temperance Union (WCTU) the largest women's organization in the nation" (Degler, 1980: 286), stated, "we at once declared ourselves determined to 'clean house' in a governmental sense, until this record of defilement should be washed away" (Willard, 1895: 198). The WCTU representatives from every state petitioned state legislatures to raise the age of sexual consent (p. 199). The WCTU campaign was, of course, part of a larger feminist agenda, and Willard (p. 204) noted how fighting for higher age-of-sexual-consent laws was but part of a broader program challenging masculine dominance:

> The husband of the modern woman will not have the right to will away her unborn child; to control her property; to make the laws under which she is to live; to fix her penalties; to try her before juries of men; to cast the ballot for her and, in general, to hold her in the estate of a perpetual minor.

Continuing this line of reasoning, Willard (p. 204) stated further, "it will not do to let the modern man determine the 'age of consent.' "

In response to this concerted feminist effort, and in coalition with social purists, state after state in the 1890s raised the age of sexual consent (Degler, 1980: 288). For example, in Colorado, the age of sexual consent sharply increased from ten in 1893 to eighteen only two years later. In 1889, Idaho's age of sexual consent was twelve; by 1895 it was raised to eighteen. Wyoming's began at ten in 1886, rose to fourteen in 1889, and reached eighteen in 1893 (Pivar, 1973: 141–43). By 1900, only two states or territories maintained the age of sexual consent below fourteen, whereas twelve had raised it to eighteen (Degler, 1980: 288). Dubois and Gordon (1984: 38) point out that like most nineteenth-century feminist causes, "this one had a radical moment: it communicated an accurate critique of the limitations of 'consent' by women in a male-dominated society." In other words, feminists rightly pointed to U.S. societal gender relations of power, and how such power relationships can limit, in certain situations, women's ability to actually "consent" (e.g., adult/child, husband/wife, employer/employee).

This concentration, however, on the alleged passivity and sexual innocence of young girls as the victims of white slavers, blinded many feminists from understanding the limited choices available to working-class girls in U.S. society. To be sure, the root causes of nineteenth-century juvenile prostitution are not found in alleged white-slave traffic, in the sexual innocence of girls, or in an alleged excessive sexual essence (drive) of men— but rather in a gendered and class-stratified social order.

Realistically, the white-slave traffic was more myth than reality. True, some women were physically forced into prostitution; nevertheless, history suggests that white-slavery was experienced by less than 10 percent of the U.S. prostitute population (Rosen, 1982: 133). Because it served their interests, the extent of forced prostitution was exaggerated by feminists and social purists; simply put, the white slavery ideology emphasized women's alleged passivity. According to feminists, women would never choose prostitution, they could only be forced to enter it. However, most young women who became prostitutes chose to do so because of their gendered position in society. Consider now what that gendered position entailed.

In the late 1800s, there began to appear a surplus of youthful labor throughout the United States. Prior to 1880, children had traditionally formed an integral part of the labor force in agriculture, manufacturing, and mining. In the nineteenth century, labor scarcity in the United States increased demand for inexpensive youthful labor—the earliest U.S. cotton mill employed only youthful labor. Visiting this cotton mill early in the nineteenth century, a journalist stated (cited in Lebergott, 1964: 50):

> All processes of turning cotton from its rough into every variety of marketable thread state . . . are here performed by machinery operating by waterwheels, assited only by children from four to ten years old, and one superintendent.

In 1820, 43 percent of all textile workers in Massachusetts, 47 percent in Connecticut, and 55 percent in Rhode Island were children (p. 50). As the factory system grew, it "reached out" for youthful labor.

Since the 1840s, the percentage of child labor in manufacturing and mining continuously and prominently declined; there was even a mild decline reported in agriculture from 1880 to 1910. Further, the overall percentage of child labor for all occupations plunged by two-thirds between 1910 and 1930. Historically, the long-run, permanent decline of youthful employment and labor force participation increased most rapidly in the latter part of the nineteenth century and during the early years of the twentieth century. Even though the gainfully employed population quadrupled from 1870 to 1930, the number of gainfully employed workers in the ten- to fifteen-year-old age bracket declined drastically (Greenberg, 1977: 196). Curiously, there appears to be no nexus between fertility changes and adolescent worker rates during this time period (Lebergott, 1964: 54–56).

This decline in child labor since the 1840s reflected the economic changes in capitalism (and the institution of the family wage system as discussed in Chapter 3). The market for child labor decreased as these newly formed monopolistic industries underwent rapid technological change. The declining employment of children in factories, mines, and agriculture (the result of monopolization) contributed substantially to a youthful surplus labor problem. As a further result, many young U.S. women arguably chose to reject unemployment by turning to prostitution.

In the nineteenth century, because it was expected that working-class girls would go to work as early as possible in order to contribute to family income, it seems reasonable to conclude that upon losing their jobs, marginalization meant, for many, turning to prostitution to keep from sliding into poverty. Linda Gordon (1986: 263) argues that because wage labor was not available:

> Children were encouraged to contribute through casual bits of paid labor, "gleaning," begging, or stealing. In some cases, as soon as the word got out that some man was willing to pay for sexual favors, the number of girls involved would snowball, so eager were they for the coins or treats they might receive. Some parents alleged that they did not know the sources of contributions. Some evidently knew the sources and raised no objections; a few may have participated in the prostitution arrangements.

In addition to unemployment reasons, many working-class girls turned to prostitution because it paid more than employment available in the legitimate wage labor force. The average wage paid girls in the legitimate labor force was between four and six dollars a week. Prostitutes, however, could earn that amount in one evening. Moreover, many girls expressed disdain for the work available to working-class girls and, therefore, chose prostitution (Rosen, 1982: Chapter 8). The feminist and social-purist concentration on prostitution resulting from force and passivity, however, obscured the social conditions that working-class girls faced. Given such conditions, prostitution presented a rational choice—a social practice in the overall construction of a specific type of femininity.[5]

For white, middle-class feminists, however, social conditions were not the problem; rather, the "impurity" of men was the root cause of social decay. Changing men, then, was crucial both for women's advancement and for evolutionary progress (Mort, 1985). In other words, because teenage prostitution resulted from "male sexuality," state intervention was required both to protect women and girls, and to teach men sexual self-restraint.

The Concern with Flappers

Once the age of sexual consent was raised, social purists and feminists grew deeply concerned over "illicit" sex practiced by adolescent girls—girls who were now below the newly raised age of sexual consent. Social purists and feminists were highly disturbed by the perceptible increase in "flappers"—adolescent girls openly rebellious against rigid Victorian sexual standards (Walkowitz, 1980: 133). These girls directly challenged the self-image of social purists and feminists (who assumed that stereotypical femininity was natural); in spite of the fact that they were under the new age of sexual consent, they freely engaged in sexual exploration.

The sexual habits of this small vanguard was symptomatic of a larger sexual revolution that occurred at the beginning of the twentieth century within certain segments of society: it was a movement toward free, rather than restrictive, sexuality. As Gordon (1976: 190) argues:

> Unmarried people spent nights together, even lived together; unmarried women took lovers whom they were not even engaged to, often many consecutively, sometimes more than one at a time; a few experimented with drugs such as peyote, and many women drank and smoked with men; sex was discussed in mixed groups; and all these things were done without disguise, even with bravado.

A small group of "sex radicals"—feminists such as Emma Goldman, Margaret Sanger, and Elizabeth Gurley Flynn—asserted their right to be sexual, to recognize their own sexuality. As Inez Milholland wrote in 1913, "we are learning to be frank about sex. And through all this frankness runs a definite tendency toward an assault on the dual standard of morality and an assertion of sex rights on the part of women" (cited in Banner, 1974: 116).

Although most were not feminists, and for the most part their goal was marriage, flappers were clearly exerting some degree of control over their own sexuality. As Mark Connelly (1980: 39) points out, these girls (flappers) "had achieved a degree of autonomy outside the context of a male-controlled or domestic setting," consequently leading "lives markedly different from their mothers." "Flappers" were legitimately challenging their gender subordination; their sexual behavior, however unconscious, was a protest against conventional femininity.

For social purists and social feminists this was a developing crisis, and a sense of emergency pervaded their lives (Foster, 1914). After all, it was supposed to be men who changed their sexual habits to become "purer." Girls were not expected to alter their behavior in the direction of "free sex." Highly suspicious of sensuality, especially the sensuality of girls under the age of consent, social purists and feminists believed it their duty to now protect the morals of girls. Young women under the age of sexual consent who engaged in any type of sexual exploration were now seen simply as "immoral." As Leslie Fishbein (1980: 29) found in her examination of evolving feminist views on sexuality in the Progressive Era, "most feminists were convinced that increasing rather than releasing the taboos on extramarital sex would enhance their position, and they fervently supported social purity campaigns." For these feminists, men's essential excessive sex drive could be resisted only with the help of women. Thus, the particular evil of flappers was attracting and enticing men, which helped reinforce rather than reduce "male sexuality." Social purists and feminists urgently called for creative programs designed to recognize and reaffirm traditional femininity—thereby creating a new type of masculinity—by controlling the behavior of flappers.

Establishment of Vice Commissions

In response to the aforementioned call in the early part of the twentieth century, major U.S. cities and several smaller ones established vice commissions to investigate and publicize (within their respective cities) the nature and extent of prostitution and "sexual immorality" of girls (Connelly, 1980: 92). Many of these commissions reported that sexual flapperism was a major problem. For example, the Newark Vice Commission reported that there were in their city a "large number of girls and young women who sin sexually in return only for the pleasures given or the company of the men with whom they consort" (Newark, 1914: 11–12). The Commission went on to point out that these girls (p. 12):

> have no ethical standards and believe that they have as good a right, as it is generally supposed men have, to lead a double life; that they have the right to the pleasure they can gain from their bodies if they can do so without exposure.

The Commission concluded that "this spirit is growing with alarming rapidity" (p. 12). The Syracuse Vice Commission reported that "girls, many in number, go out with men for an evening of pleasure" and then engage in "intercourse where no money is asked or offered" (Syracuse, 1913: 67). According to this commission (p. 67), these girls pick up men and boys on the streets:

> and then go to the bed houses, especially to those where they do not have to register. Often this class of girls will go freely with men entirely for pleasure with no economic pressure responsible for driving them to the life.

The Vice Commission of Minneapolis (Minneapolis, 1911: 76–77) reported that one of "the most disturbing phases of the present situation in Minneapolis . . . is the large number of young girls in the streets at night in the downtown sections." The Commission (p. 77) pointed out that these girls were:

> found in numbers loitering about the fruit stores, drug stores and other popular locations, haunting hotel lobbies, crowding into the dance halls, the theaters and other amusement resorts; also in the saloon restaurants and the chop suey places and parading the streets and touring out in automobiles with men.

The Commission (p. 77) concluded that the "situation is unmistakeably sinister" although some of these girls were involved in prostitution, many were not, but were simply on the road of "immorality."

An analysis of Boston reached similar conclusions. Girls hung out at night, hoping to pick up boys or men, in such notorious places as the Sullivan Square Station, Scollay Square in the old West End, the Charlestown Navy Yard, and Revere Beach. The girls "travelled in groups and covered and solicited for each other. They were truant from school, sought out men in bars (and on ships), and generally engaged in provocative behavior'' (Gordon, 1986: 262).

The vice commissions, with the active support of feminists and social purists, called for novel means of moral control as the solution to this new age of sexual flapperism.

The State Moves In

Stanley Cohen (1985: 13) has shown that four major transformations occurred during the aforementioned time period in the social control of "deviants":

1. The increasing involvement of the state in the business of deviancy control—the eventual development of a centralized, rationalized, and bureaucratic apparatus for the control and punishment of crime and delinquency and the care or cure of other types of deviants.
2. The increasing differentiation and classification of deviant and dependent groups into separate types and categories, each with its own body of "scientific" knowledge and its own recognized and accredited experts—professionals who eventually acquire specialized monopolies.
3. The increased segregation of deviants into "asylums"—penetentiaries, prisons, mental hospitals, reformatories and other closed, purpose-built institutions. The prison emerges as a dominant instrument for changing undesirable behavior and as the favored form of punishment.
4. The decline of punishment involving the public infliction of pain. The mind replaces the body as the object of penal repression, and positivist theories emerge to justify concentrating on the individual offender and not the general offense.

State regulation of gender relations was part of this general transformation of the vicissitudes of social control. The state answered the vice commission's call by implementing special treatment for youth in general, but girls in particular. For example, special "morals" and "girls" courts were established for the sole purpose of adjudicating prostitutes and sexually recalcitrant girls. Many reformers argued that special courts should be established for girls, with a woman acting as judge. A woman judge was crucial because (Rippey, 1914: 254):

to oblige a girl to tell the story of her downfall (most girl delinquents are offenders against sex) to a man, however wise or sympathetic he might be, could only help to destroy such modesty as her experience might have left her.

Although the idea of a woman judge represented a reasonable feminist demand, a special girls court presided over by a woman judge would also teach "such delinquents that there are some matters which are not to be discussed with or before men, or even to be spoken at all, save in hushed whispers of shame" (p. 254). Thus, the public was "rigidly excluded" from the courtroom, as the court did not want to further destroy "her chances of a useful womanhood" (p. 254). These unique and special courts were established in such cities as New York, Philadelphia, and Chicago (Rosen, 1982: 19).

These special courts, as well as the Juvenile Court, established in both Chicago and Denver in 1899, became the forum for controlling the sexuality of working-class girls. It is clear that the vast majority of children brought before these courts were poor, lower- and working-class, and usually racial/ethnic minorities and recent immigrants (Platt, 1969; Schlossman and Wallach, 1978; Wiley, 1915; Shelden, 1981). Moreover, girls, as opposed to boys, were brought to court for either real or alleged sexuality. For example, in Chicago, between 1899 and 1909, 80.9 percent of girls (only 1.6 percent of the boys) were brought to court for alleged "immorality" (Breckinridge and Abbott, 1912: 28–40). Immorality meant not only having sexual intercourse, but also "attending tough dances," "staying out until two or three o'clock in the morning," and masturbating (pp. 35–36). Immorality, therefore, involved admitting or being caught in the act of intercourse, or demonstrating through their action that they had engaged in intercourse in the past or probably would in the future.

Frequently the courts even went to the extent of subjecting girls to vaginal examinations to determine whether or not they had engaged in intercourse. For example, Schlossman and Wallach (1978: 73) cite a case of a girl in Milwaukee named Annagret, who:

> like every girl who appeared in court, was subjected to a vaginal examination. The only proof of virginity was an intact hymen. To his own surprise the examining doctor concluded that Annagret was still a virgin, but he informed the court that irritation in her clitoral area indicated that she was a regular masturbator. . . . Thus, according to the court, Annagret's masturbatory habits explained her penchant for fantasy and justified labeling her a delinquent.

This same pattern—charging girls, but not boys, with immorality—was implemented in other parts of the country. For example, between 1907 and 1913 in New Haven, Connecticut, approximately 65 percent of the girls brought to court were charged with immorality (Wiley, 1915: 8–9, 15). And in Memphis, Tennessee, between 1910 and 1917, over 30 percent of the girls were charged with immorality but only 0.6 percent of the boys (Shelden, 1981: 61–63).

In Chicago, the case of Angeline exemplifies who, and what type of behavior, was subjected to such vigilant control by the state (Rippey, 1914: 252–256). Angeline, at fourteen—because of sordid poverty, family drunkeness, and physical and sexual abuse from her father— left home and obtained a five dollar a week job in a candy factory. However, because of the costs of rent and food, "she was no better off than she had been at home." But, "one dream bade fair to come true—a 'fella' rose on Angeline's horizon." The advances of the "fella" represented to her "the opening of a door to hitherto untasted delights," and Angeline eventually engaged in intercourse with the "strapping young blond teamster." Her mother, interested in Angeline's income, eventually had her arrested and brought before the woman judge in the Chicago "Girls Court." The following transpired between Angeline and the judge (cited in Rippey, 1914: 253):

> "Did no one tell you these things you are doing are wrong, Angeline?" asked the judge.
>
> "No," sobbed Angeline, burying her face in her handkerchief.
>
> "Little girls who run away from home so they can keep the money their mothers need, and live in roominghouses, and go about with strange men always get into trouble sooner or later," the judge went on.
>
> Angeline threw back her head defiantly. "I wanted to have some fun," she flashed out. "I *never* had any fun!"
>
> "Yes, I know," sympathized the judge. "Every girl needs to have fun, but it must be the right kind. There's fun that's good, you know, Angeline, and fun that's bad."
>
> "And now, Angeline," the judge concluded, "would you like to go back home and try again?"
>
> All the wretchedness of Angeline's fourteen dreary, unloved, drudgery-filled years was compressed into her quick, panic stricken cry: "Oh, I don't *want* to go home! I don't *want* to go home!"

Angeline was sent to a reformatory for girls.

The case of Angeline is significant because it illustrates the multiple victimization of some girls. Not only were they victimized by reformers of another class, they were also, at times, victimized by men of their own class, even men of their own families. In addition, as these girls roamed the streets, they were extremely vulnerable to sexual victimization—not only by rape, but also by being tricked, pressured, or bribed into sexual submission to men (Gordon, 1986: 261). For some girls their "immorality" was indeed forced. However, many girls were, like Angeline, victims of sexual abuse by their fathers. Of all the sex delinquent cases reported in Boston in 1920, 40 percent of the girls alleged incest and another 20 percent alleged nonincestuous rape (p. 262). When these girls were unable to prevent their victimization at home, they attempted to escape—as did Angeline—their families altogether. As Gordon (p. 262) points out, "in their flight from home, incest victims may have been successfully preserving an autonomy vital to their survival." Yet such resistance was not sanctioned, as evidenced by a new form of victimization: state repression of their own sexuality.[6]

Reformatories for Flappers

Feminists and social-purity activists advocated special reformatories for girls and women: feminists were concerned with protecting youth from moral weaknesses; social-purity activitists encouraged criminal justice reformers to focus on "loose women." As Nicole Rafter (1985: 47) points out, the "social purifiers found an outlet for their program of moral education, and their concern with protecting women, in the women's prison movement." Reformatories—for both boys and girls, it was argued—should be run by women, as women were perceived as especially suited to working with children, particularly those on the "verge of ruin" (Platt, 1969: Chapter 4). Through architecture and available programs, youth reformatories were to reflect "the good home life"—nurturing, caring, and above all, morality. In particular, girl reformatories were to implement programs centering on general housework: sewing, cooking, laundering, dressmaking, training in the care of young children, and beauty culture (Reeves, 1929: 299). In addition to training young incarcerated women for their predetermined place in society—the home—it was essential that each girl complete an extensive program in sex education. As Margaret Reeves (1929: 215) points out in her study of the history of girl juvenile reformatories:

> The true purpose of sex education with these delinquent girls is not so much a matter of giving detailed information (though misinformation must be corrected), as of creating the proper attitude toward sex. Most of these girls have had considerable experience in life which they need to forget. With some the sex impulse has been permitted so free an expres-

sion that it overshadows all other impulses. Such girls need to be given a different perspective in relation to the whole question.

In short, the "immoral flapper," threatened by her sexuality, had to be controlled through rehabilitation: her oppositional femininity had to be redirected to conventional femininity. In fact, in the reformatory, rehabilitation became the order of the day for the "immoral" girl, whereas boys who engaged in criminal acts were placed on probation, not institutionalized. For example, in the Chicago Juvenile Court (again between 1899 and 1909), 59 percent of boys were placed on probation, but only 37 percent of girls. Even more striking, 21 percent of boys were committed to institutions, but 51 percent of girls were committed (Breckinridge and Abbott, 1912: 40). In Memphis, girls were almost twice as likely as boys to be committed, primarily for immorality (Shelden, 1981: 67–69). In Milwaukee, twice as many girls were committed to reformatories as boys (Schlossman and Wallach, 1978: 72). And although in New Haven only 31 percent of girls were committed to reformatories between 1907 and 1913, according to Mabel Wiley (1915: 18), this was because the courts "are still far from putting into practice the newer ideas of penology. To a large extent it is still the crime that is punished, rather than the individual reformed."

In short, although girls were charged with immorality and boys with crimes (such as theft and violence), the severest sanctions were reserved for girls—incarceration in a reformatory. Feminists and social purists believed they were helping girls by providing special reformatory care; yet their good intentions did not alter the fact that in attempting to help, they underwrote a double standard that punished girls more severely than boys (Rafter, 1985: 36).

Feminists and social-purity activists supported reformatories for girl sexual "delinquents" as a means for removing flappers—a source of sexual temptation for boys, from society. In addition, reformatories were advocated because they allegedly protected girls from white-slave traffic and provided a means for rehabilitating "fallen" girls. However, rather than becoming a program of moral uplift, the feminist/social-purity plan simply became a means for controlling working-class, girl sexuality.[7] As many young women attempted to control their sexuality (Schlossman and Wallach, 1978: 91):

> Reformatories offered a warning that society would still not tolerate girls who showed the same interest in sex as boys and reinforced the traditional belief that "normal" girls were sexually impassive.

However, court cases and statements by working-class girls in re- formatories clearly reflect that they were not the sexually innocent and passive "little girls" they were alleged to be. What feminists and so- cial purists ignored was that those whom they sought to protect— working-class girls—did not behave as if they were sexually inert, or for that matter, concerned about the dangers of white slavery. In fact, it is fair to conclude that most girls brought into court and sent to reformatories engaged in sexuality out of personal inclination. By first raising the age of sexual consent and then advocating state-sponsored social control of sexually recalcitrant "girls," feminists in coalition with social purists denied teenage, working-class, white and racial/eth- nic-minority girls the power to control their sexuality. Flappers called into question the prevailing dominant feminist ideology: a woman must be the sexual partner of only one man. Thus, social control of flappers rested upon and reinforced state control of girl sexuality and continuance of traditional femininity.

By the early part of the twentieth century, the state had invested heavily in the custody and "treatment" of the new girl sex "delin- quent." Between 1860 and 1900, on average, approximately five new state-operated girl reformatories were created each decade (a total of 22). However, between 1900 and 1920, 27 new state-operated refor- matories opened in the United States (Reeves, 1929: 39). Moreover, between 1910 and 1920, girl reformatories were expanded in size, staff, and clientele, and several states began taking over private girls' reformatories (Schlossman and Wallach, 1978: 70).

What is the significance of this historical case study? Whereas ini- tially feminists organized against legalized prostitution to challenge masculine dominance (and won that struggle), they eventually aligned themselves with a conservative social force, the social purity move- ment, in an effort to reform "male sexuality" by abolishing prostitu- tion and, in particular, by raising the age of sexual consent. It was the success of this latter effort that set the stage for working-class white and racial/ethnic-minority girl sexual repression.

By the early part of the twentieth century, when some women and girls began to threaten the sexual status quo through their attempt to reject traditional femininity and control their own sexuality, a discur- sive alignment between the masculine-dominated state and the femi- nist/social-purity coalition occurred. The plan to redistribute power among men and women was abandoned, and the focus changed to re- habilitating the "immoral flapper." Gender relations of power and normative heterosexuality were buttressed by the creation of a new type of working-class girl offender: the teenage sex "delinquent." Through the reformatory movement the state contributed to the control of a surplus population of redundant, working-class, and racial/ethnic-minority girls.

Quite simply, the feminist/purity strategy was part of the overall effort to regulate behavior of working-class and racial/ethnic minorities. In addition, the state and its newly created juvenile justice system regulated girl sexuality by attempting to "teach" young working-class and racial/ethnic-minority women early on that their sexuality was not their own—indeed, that certain types of heterosexuality were taboo. By incarcerating young "flappers," the state provided a mechanism for reproducing traditional, white, middle-class notions of femininity and, therefore, maintaining social structures of gender—labor, power, and normative heterosexuality. In short, the desire of feminists and social purists to protect young working-class girls masked a coercive aspiration to control voluntary sexuality. In this way, reformist feminist energies eventually were channeled, through a coalition with social purists, into a conservative and sexually repressive movement. As state agencies for social control were expanded, the causes of women's economic and sexual exploitation remained unchanged.

The state, then, became a vehicle for advancing the interests of white, middle-class women and men, which generated unintended consequences for other women and girls: widening class and race divisions among women and expanding state powers of sexual surveillance. Feminists were not simply coopted by purists, as some historians suggest (Pivar, 1973); rather, as with white middle-class feminists in England, the emphasis on morality (Mort, 1985: 211):

> provided women, quite literally, with a means of representation in the male-defined world of public political debate and with a language which enabled them to develop a feminist critique of male power and domination. This ethical approach often led women to endorse coercive moral regulation.

The lesson in this case study is that since the state regulates gender relations in society as a whole, it is not simply a vessel into which any group can pour content and meaning. As Franzway et al. (1989: 35) point out, the shape of the state reflects specific social struggles; therefore, "what kind of state we have depends on who was mobilized in social struggle, what strategies were deployed, and who won." The state is an apparatus with an institutionalized bias toward protecting the gendered status quo; aligning themselves with non- and antifeminist forces, whose goals and values resonate with those of the state, is clearly a dangerous feminist strategy and practice (Burstyn, 1985).

Additionally, what the above suggests is that state process itself is composed of gendered practices. That is, the state's overall procedures, dispositions, established standards, and cardinal assumptions are the result of gender structured action. Indeed, the ongoing social construction of gender practiced by state personnel institutionalizes varieties of masculinity (and femininity)—and therefore masculine dominance—in state agencies. In the next section, we examine this structured gender practice in a contemporary state agency, the police.

Structured Action, Masculinities, and the Police

As argued throughout this book, three specific social structures—gender division of labor, gender relations of power, and sexuality—underly relations between women and men. Moreover, these structures are not external to social actors nor simply and solely constraining. Rather, structure is realized only through social action and social action requires structure as its condition. Women and men effect gender in specific social situations; in so doing, they reproduce and sometimes change social structures. And this not only occurs in the school, the peer group, the street, the workplace, and the family, but also takes place in the state.

As primary agents of the state, men experience the daily world "at work" from their particular position in society, thereby constructing specific cultural ideals of hegemonic masculinity. Different social settings within the state reflect such patterned representations of masculinity. Depending upon the state agency, institutionalized practices define and sustain specific conceptions of masculinity that express and reproduce social divisions of labor and power as well as of normative heterosexuality. In this way, state agents do gender in response to the socially structured circumstances in which they perform their work. Gender, then, is a behavioral response to the particular conditions and situations in which we participate: we do gender according to the social setting in which we find ourselves. Consider one such social setting within the state—the police—and how gender, specifically masculinity, is socially constructed and resultingly institutionalized.

First, within the overall criminal justice system, the gender division of labor is obvious: "judges, lawyers, police and prison officers are in the main, male. Women are employed primarily as secretaries or perform stereotypical tasks" (Morris, 1987: 134). Regarding the police in particular, until the 1970s, women officers engaged in such "feminine" functions as working primarily with juveniles, women offenders, women victims, vice-squad assignments, and community relations (Weisheit and Mahan, 1988: 146). Although by the 1970s women were increasingly assigned to routine patrol duty, today less than 10 percent of all police officers are women (Martin, 1989: 4). Moreover, not only are women considerably less likely than men to be police officers, within police departments themselves "women are virtually excluded from upper level management . . . just as they are in corporate boardrooms and law partnerships" (p. 6). In short, policing remains, in the 1990s, a masculine-dominated workplace.

This gender division of labor in police work simultaneously embodies gender relations of power. Gender relations of power are thus reproduced within the police force, and its police officers help regulate gendered relations of power in society. These dual virtues of police work impact the situational construction of masculinity by policemen.

Within police agencies, men's power is deemed an authentic and acceptable part of social relations. This legitimacy of the power by men in police work adorns them with greater authority. Indeed, gender relations of power promote and constrain the social action of men and women police officers. For example, the traditional policemen's opposition to women officers (amply documented elsewhere) does not bear repeating (Martin, 1980, 1989; Remmington, 1981). Police work is defined culturally as an activity only "masculine men" can accomplish. As Allison Morris (1987: 144) shows, police work is viewed by the police and public as a masculine pursuit: the imagery is "of the armed man of action fighting crime and criminals," the Clint Eastwood model. Moreover, the informal world of the street, where rank-and-file officers spend most of their workday, is perceived by police*men* as a masculine domain that excludes "moral" women, and is, therefore, "for men only" (Hunt, 1984: 286). However, it is not simply that police work is culturally designated to be men's work. From the perspective of a theory of structured action, for a man to engage in police work and for a woman not to engage in police work simply labels the "essential nature" of each. Police work is, in essence, a resource for masculine construction.

Not surprisingly, the presence of women officers tarnishes this masculine association with police work—if women can do it, the value of the practice as a means for exhibiting masculinity is cast into question. Consequently, where police agencies are gender integrated, specific forms of masculinity and femininity are accomplished through the actual practice of policing. For example, when men and women officers are partners, men tend to dominate the partnership: they are more likely to drive the police automobile, to dictate the activities of the shift, and to conduct interviews of suspects and victims. Women officers routinely do the paperwork and often "merely record the responses to questions posed by the male partner" (Remmington, 1981: 196). Moreover, Remmington (p. 117) found that women officers not partnered with men:

> were frequently backed up on calls by males. The latter often usurped the female officer's role and dominated the encounter. . . . Some males even arrived on a female's routine call, stood around for awhile as if assessing the possibility of trouble, and then left. . . . The men's frequent presence and domination of the females' calls undoubtedly does affect the latter's style of policing. In any case, it is difficult to assess females' performance since they are seldom permitted to act alone.

In short, while policemen exercise their gendered power to control the social settings of police work by engaging in practices that maintain the gender divisions of labor and power, both policemen and policewomen are not simply doing policing, but also "doing gender." Within the social setting of policing, then, men and women officers actively construct specific types of masculinity and femininity in interaction.[8]

As argued earlier, in addition to the social construction of gendered power within police agencies, the police have the capacity to regulate gendered power relations in society as a whole, while in the process constructing gender themselves. The "social control" of wife beating is an obvious example. The police have a long history of nonintervention in wife beating cases, and not until police legitimacy itself became an issue did the police formally change this policy.

A study by Sherman and Berk (1984) found that arresting wife beaters was a more effective deterrent to future battering than separation and/or mediation. This study coincided with increasing pressure from feminists for a stricter application of the law and more intensive policing of men who batter women (Edwards, 1990: 146). In time, police agencies across the United States began to institute "presumptive arrest policies," wherein police officers were required to arrest wife beaters (when probable cause existed) even if the victim did not wish to press charges. Such a policy would more effectively control wife beating, it was argued, and, in turn, would help the police gain legitimacy in the eyes of feminists who would view the policy as sympathetic to victims, not to batterers (Stanko, 1989: 64).

Notwithstanding, research shows that discretionary decision making in police work, which entails the social construction of masculinity, preempts such a policy in several ways. First, most rank-and-file police officers view their mandate as preserving public, not private, order and peace. As Ferraro (1989) shows, "domestic disturbance calls," as the police term them, are consistent with this mandate only insofar as such violence impinges on public order and peace. Many rank-and-file policemen view the family as a private realm in which men and women freely choose to participate, therefore, private problems are outside the legitimate expertise and scope of police work. For these officers, "domestics" are cause for police concern only when public order and peace are affected. Ironically, this masculine public/private split is built into the policing of battering, all of which tends to negate the spirit of the proarrest policy.

Second, many policemen dichotomize a community into normal and deviant populations, in which lower–working-class, racial minorities are more likely than working- and middle-class whites to fall into the deviant category. Thus, wife beating among lower–working-class, racial minorities generally is taken less seriously than is wife beating in white, working-class and middle-class homes (Ferraro, 1989). Indeed, the police have a long history of lesser response to complaints made by lower–working-class racial minorities, especially African American women (Young, 1986; MacLean and Milovanovic, 1991a). Consequently, presumptive arrest policies are mediated by class and race police bias.

Third, the perceived demeanor of the battered woman affects police decision making. For example, when a victim is ambivalent over spousal arrest, is intoxicated, disorderly, or states a preference for nonarrest, police officers infrequently make arrests of batterers (Ferraro, 1989).

Fourth, arrests in "domestics" are afforded scant prestige in police work; it is not seen in many police circles as real crime (Stanko, 1989: 51). Policemen continue to "judge each other's competence on the basis of performing crime fighting tasks such as the apprehension of acknowledged criminals" (Buzawa and Buzawa, 1990: 28). Because officers derive dubious masculine recognition from handling a "domestic," many policemen do not treat these cases seriously and practice avoiding them: the cases have little value as a resource for constructing masculinity. Research on rank-and-file police-occupational culture shows that certain of their images of wife beating often include assumptions about "male rights" and "female blame" (Stanko, 1989). Consequently, when the police do investigate a battering situation, initially they are hesitant over criminalizing wife beaters, "dutifully" scrutinizing the woman's behavior versus the behavior of her assailant, with both parties assumed to have contributed to the onset of the violence (pp. 55, 52). Indeed, when arrests are made, victims are often charged. In *Domestic Violence: The Criminal Justice Response*, Eve Buzawa and Carl Buzawa (1990: 99) report that since the emergence of "mandatory arrest policies," there has been "an unprecedented increase in 'dual arrests,' " in which both spouses are arrested. In the State of Washington, for example, in 50 percent of cases where an arrest was actually made, the woman was charged (p. 104). As Buzawa and Buzawa (p. 99) correctly point out, this is "hardly the result hoped for by advocates of change."

This focus on lower–working-class street crime rather than on men's domestic violence against women not only reflects working-class conceptions of law-and-order (police officers are recruited overwhelmingly from the working class), as Kinsey, Lea, and Young (1986: 172) declare, but also street-cop conceptions of masculinity. *Steering clear of "domestics" is a basic practice in the overall social construction of "street cop"—as opposed to "office cop"—masculinity.* Reuss-Ianni and Ianni (1983) showed how police officers are dichotomized into street-cop and office-cop occupational cultures. Basic to these cultures is the social construction of gender. Jennifer Hunt's (1984: 287) research demonstrates, for example, that New York street cops perceive that office cops:

> engaged in "feminine labor" such as public relations and secretarial work. These "pencil-pushing bureaucrats" were not involved in the "masculine" physical labor which characterized "real police work" on the street. High-ranking administrators were also viewed as "inside tit men," "asskissers" and "whores" who gained their positions through political patronage rather than through superior performance in the rescue and crime-fighting activities associated with "real police work."

Moreover, police-agency power hierarchies exist among men, and (not surprising) different forms of masculinity correspond to specific positions in the hierarchy. Street-cop masculinity predictably stresses presentation and celebration of physical prowess. In other words, a street cop is a "brave and aggressive soldier who has mastered the art of violence" and, while the office cop is naive and caring, the "real cop" is "suspicious, cynical and maintains an emotional distance from the people he polices" (p. 288). Only "feminine men" work "inside units"—as opposed to "outside units"—such as juvenile law, research and planning, administration, and police academy administration. Thus, street cops construct a specific masculine type diametrically opposed to that of management.

Street-cop masculinity—differentiated from and elevated above the demeanor of management—reflects, in part, street-cop desire to deny a subordinate position within hierarchical departmental power relations among men. Concomitantly, policing wife beating is not a valued resource for constructing street-cop masculinity. This relationship of "policing domestic violence" to the social construction of street cop masculinity explains Buzawa and Buzawa's (1990: 28–29) conclusion that:

> the response to a domestic violence call has little occupational value to an officer. It does not give him a chance to protect his compatriots, and most officers don't view the crime as serious. Arrests have typically been infrequent, and since the offender is known and it is a "minor" crime, any arrest that results from the intervention would be considered a "garbage arrest," not worthy of recognition.

Consequently, and for all of the aforementioned reasons, police officer decision making is not eliminated by the adoption of a presumptive arrest policy. Indeed, because the social construction of street-cop masculinity effectively deregulates wife beating, it comes as no surprise, as Ferraro (1989: 179) demonstrates, that "the vast majority of family fight calls do not result in arrest." In short, the state limits, through police*men's* gendered practices, the extent to which men may be violent in the home and, thus, regulates gendered power through the construction of street-cop masculinity. Moreover, focusing solely on increased policing to "solve" wife beating actually diverts attention from the sources of violence (discussed in Chapter 5). Wife beating, as constructed by police practice, attaches to a "deviant" minority of violent husbands, and criticisms of masculine power, which generates the violence in marriage, are effectively deflected (Connell, 1990: 527).[9]

Normative heterosexuality is also constructed within police agencies and regulated by police in society at large. Remmington's (1981:

122–125) study of a southern police department reveals a variety of on-duty forms of sexuality in police work. Single policemen in this department seem to have a considerable "feminine following" of single women who "pass from officer to officer" (p. 122). Remmington also found that a number of married policemen do not "place a high value upon fidelity," many openly bragging about their "affairs." As for detectives, Remmington (p. 123) reports the following:

> Frequently, one detective partner drops the other at his mistress's home and spends almost the entire watch handling any calls alone. This act of generosity is reciprocated in kind by offering the other officer opportunities to visit his woman friend or his wife on another shift.

Thus, in addition to having affairs, some policemen spend time with women friends, fiances, and wives during working hours. Finally, Remmington found that men and women police officers frequently form sexual relationships that are often initiated and developed during working hours.

Reuss-Ianni and Ianni (1983: 272) discuss how street cops demonstrate opposition to management by "foot dragging, sabotage, and stealing department time." Heterosexual dalliances illustrate this, especially "stealing" time by engaging in "on-duty" affairs. Whereas hegemonic masculinity involves practices characterized by dominance, control, and independence, the relative social position of street cops discourages such practices—it is management who has control and independence. Thus, street cops construct behavior patterns, such as "stealing department time," that help restore the very hegemonic masculine ideals being discouraged. In turn, such behaviors demonstrate one's "essential nature" as a man.

As discussed earlier, heterosexual performance is one of the foremost hallmarks of one's identity as a man; making this public both impresses other cops and helps confirm masculinity. Street cop practices are often designed with an eye to their gender accountability and, as such, they draw on available resources to construct a specific type of masculinity. In this way, the police department is sexualized, and normative heterosexuality actually conditions police work. Quite obviously, heterosexuality is actively produced by policemen through a wide range of practices and interactions.

In spite of the fact that men and women police officers often engage reciprocally in genuine and humane relationships at work, sexual harassment continues. Women police officers are questioned frequently about their sexual orientation; witness certain comments by police-women recorded by Wexler and Logan (1983: 48–49):

"The majority will make a pass to see if you are a lesbian."

"Sometimes I feel I'll have to get up on the table and screw right in front of them in the squad room."

"If you are sleeping with someone, you are a slut; if you are not, you are a dyke."

This same study concluded that the most common source of stress for policewomen derives from their being women. As a result, police-women frequently experience a work situation wherein they are "ignored, harassed, watched, gossiped about and viewed as sexual objects" (p. 52).

Remmington (1981: 71) similarly reports that "sexual joking and innuendos towards . . . female officers were commonplace." Indeed, a recent study reports that various types of demeaning sexual harassment were the form most commonly experienced by women officers; for example, men officers would (Martin and Levine, 1991: 28):

• view "pornography" while women officers were present
• physically touch women officers in ways the women found offensive
• make jokes about the way women officers look
• try to force women officers to have sexual intercourse.

Although most policemen do not engage in sexual harassment, the specific social situation of these officers increases the likelihood of such sexual harassment occurring. I discussed earlier how shared masculinity enables street cops to feel a solidarity with their peers and thus resist managerial authority. Similarly, for some policemen, sexual harassment acts as a form of masculine protection against women officers perceived as threats to the solidarity among men. Additionally, the strident concerns so many policemen express about women officers reveals how the perceived threat establishes a masculine construction—if women are fully integrated into police work, policemen must then redefine themselves as "men."

Although the presence of women makes men more aware of what they have in common, their presence simultaneously threatens that commonality. Predictably, men exaggerate both their commonality and women's difference (Kanter, 1977a). Police work becomes a means whereby these men differentiate masculinity from femininity—a resource for constructing oneself as a "real man." Obviously, the presence of women police officers weakens this gender separation: if a woman can do what "real cops" do, the value of the practice for accomplishing masculinity is effectively contested.

"Doing gender" means creating differences between men and women (see discussion in Chapter 3). By maintaining and emphasizing the "femaleness" of women officers, policemen attempt to create a clear distinction between women cops and men cops, thus preserving the peculiar masculinity of street cops. And differential treatment and harassment of policewomen by policemen consistently create and maintain gender differences that reproduce the gender division of labor, gendered power, and normative heterosexuality. In time, this situation militates against acceptance of women as "true officers."[10]

In addition to the foregoing, police agencies also help regulate sexuality in society generally, thereby reproducing normative heterosexuality. A prime example is repression of homosexuality. Remmington (1981: 94), for example, observed the following in her examination of a southern police department:

> A disproportionate amount of time is spent by both uniformed officers and detectives cruising the city parks looking for homosexual solicitors. Flashlights are used to illuminate couples in cars, searching for two homosexuals. Apparently the ideal object of the search is to locate two men in the process of solicitation or sexual activity. The outcome involves much police "man" handling—referred to by the police as "jacking up queers." The police rationale is to rid the city streets of homosexual perversion.

This example indicates that policing gay men may actually be central to routine police procedures and practices. Indeed, Smith (1988) examined Canadian policing of gay steambaths, specifically how certain police practices transform scenes of sexual pleasure into sites of "crime." This tranformation, Smith showed, does not depend on homophobic cops (although homophobic cops exist), but rather forms a procedure essential to controlling sexuality as reflected in the criminal code. Canadian law-enforcement procedures require investigation of gay steambaths to verify compliance with standards mandated for "bawdy-houses": places "kept, occupied, or resorted to . . . by one or more persons . . . for the purpose . . . of indecent acts" (cited in Smith, 1988: 175). Under Canadian law, an "indecent act" is any sexual act not focused on procreation; yet even procreational sex is "indecent" if it occurs in public.

The code, then, is designed to enforce and perpetuate normative heterosexuality as occurring privately within "the home." Further, the very definitions of "bawdy-house" and "indecent acts," as found in the Canadian Criminal Code, mandate a specific course of action by the police. Because any place individuals might frequent for acts of "indecency" is an illegal place, such legal precepts shape and determine policing practices. As Smith (pp. 177-178) states:

> It is in this sense that the conceptual formulation of the Criminal Code intends a form of society that the work of the police accomplish (i.e., a heterosexual society where legitimate sexuality is focused on procreative sex within private, familial settings). The bawdy-house law, in this sense, "crystallizes" a form of life which is both the social organization of the Code's construction and the social organization which its application brings into being in local settings, such as a steambath. The internal relations here are recursive.

Thus, although law-enforcement practices appear objective, they are in fact gendered. That is, Canadian police procedure itself, regardless of how individual police officers view homosexuality, enforces normative heterosexuality by ensuring that human sexual activity takes place in private-home settings.

The police are also expected to protect lesbians and gay men from anti-homosexual crimes, in spite of the fact that police are not immune from viewing such crimes as "harmless pranks or as an acceptable form of behavior" (Berrill, 1992: 31). Moreover, many police officers themselves engage in such acts. Research reveals that police have engaged in verbal and physical abuse, entrapment, blackmail, selective law enforcement, and intentional mishandling of anti-gay violence cases (Berrill, 1992). Furthermore, approximately 10 percent of reported anti-gay violence—between 60 and 90 percent are never reported—involves physical assault by police officers and police officers regularly conduct raids on homosexual bars and bathhouses, during which time violence is perpetrated (Comstock, 1991: 152; Adam, 1987).

To policemen who engage in such acts, homosexuality is simply "unnatural" and "effeminate" sex. As one street cop put it (cited in Comstock, 1991: 153):

Now in my own cases when I catch a guy like that I just pick him up
and take him into the woods and beat him until he can't crawl. I have
had seventeen cases like that in the last couple of years. I tell that guy if
I catch him doing that again I will take him out to the woods and I will
shoot him. I tell him that I carry a second gun on me just in case I find
guys like him and that I will plant it in his hand and say that he tried to
kill me and that no jury will convict me.

Gay-bashing by police officers serves as a resource for constructing
a specific form of masculinity: physical violence against gay men wit-
nessed by other heterosexual street cops reaffirm's one's commitment
to what is "for them" natural and masculine sex—heterosexuality.
Thus, the victim of police gay-bashing serves symbolically as an instrument for confirming one's heterosexual status among street cops.

Repression of gay men reveals another critical gendered aspect of
law enforcement—the primary focus of police and criminal justice action is men (evident from arrest and incarceration statistics) (Mauer,
1990). This focus of police repression—primarily lower- and working-
class, racial minority men—parallels the status of gay men, in the
sense that such men represent subordinated masculinities. In this way,
then, the police construct a white, heterosexual form of hegemonic
masculinity through the authorized practice of controlling "deviant"
behavior of "inferior" men.[11]

This repression of African American men should not be minimized.
While white, corporate criminals essentially receive a "slap on the
wrist" (if that) for their extensive social harms (Coleman, 1989; Frank
and Lynch, 1992), African American men are far more likely to be
controlled repressively by the criminal justice system (Mauer, 1990).
Indeed, on any given day, approximately one in four African American men (ages twenty to twenty-nine) is either in jail, in prison, on
probation, or on parole, while for white men of the same age, approximately one in sixteen is under such state control (p. 3). More to this
point, the number of young African American men under the control
of the criminal justice system is greater than the total number of African American men of all ages enrolled in college (p. 3), and as Mark
Mauer (1992: 1) more recently reported, "Black males in the U.S. are
now incarcerated at a rate almost five times that of black males in
South Africa. The U.S. rate for black males is now 3,370 per 100,000,
compared to 681 per 100,000 in South Africa." In short, the "get
tough" approach to crime control of the Reagan/Bush era has contributed significantly to the reproduction of class, race, and gender relations.

What I hope to have demonstrated here is that although the state clearly institutionalizes masculinities and, therefore, masculine dominance, it is not omnipotent. That is, masculine dominance in the state is neither fixed nor inevitable, but results from social struggles—who was mobilized, what strategies were utilized, and who prevailed—as well as from the social construction of gender in daily interaction. Indeed, there is a demonstratively active gendered (as well as class and race) process occurring in the state—as in the school, peer group, street, workplace, and family—wherein gender is inextricably a part of state procedures. It is in this not-so-subtle way that gender structures are regulated and reproduced by state agents through daily practices.

Consequently, in pursuing a more egalitarian society, it is axiomatic that feminists and pro-feminist men must critically and sensitively select appropriate strategies. There are limits and oftentimes disadvantages to relying on the state for social change. If, indeed, our goal is to *empower women* and, thereby, alter the actual conditions of women's and men's lives, we cannot simply abdicate more power to the state. We must develop strategies that bring about institutional and interactional change, and struggles involving the state inevitably are part of such a program for change. But how much a part is in question.

The Reagan/Bush "get tough" approach to crime control through increased arrest, prosecution, and incarceration has had no effect on the street crime rate. As Steffensmeier and Harer (1991: 347) recently showed:

> Imprisonment rates rose far more sharply in the eighties than in any previous decade in the nation's history. In spite of their record-setting pace, there was no discernible drop in either the nation's crime rate as a whole or in the "serious" street crime rate.

As these authors go on to point out, this failure of the law-and-order approach to reduce street crime "suggests that the criminal justice system does not contain the solution to the nation's crime problem, and that no law enforcement strategy can be confidently recommended to remedy it" (p. 348).

It should be clear, then, that to curb crime we do not need to expand repressive state measures, but we do need to reduce gender (as well as class and race) inequalities. This requires that we pursue social change at both the institutional and interactional levels (West and Zimmerman, 1987). Bob Connell's (1992: 36) proposed "practical politics of gender for heterosexual men" is a starting point, and I close this book by quoting him directly:

1. Share the care of babies and young children equally between women and men. Change hours of work and politics of promotion to make this practical.
2. Work for equal opportunity, affirmative action, and the election of women, until women occupy at least 50 percent of decision-making positions in both public and private organizations.
3. Support women's control over their own bodies, and contest the assertion of men's ownership of "their" women. Actively challenge misogyny and homophobia in the media and popular culture, as well as sexual harassment in the workplace.
4. Work for pay equity and women's employment rights, until women's earnings are at least equal to men's.
5. Support the redistribution of wealth and the creation of a universal social security system.
6. Talk among men to make domestic violence, gay bashing, and sexual assault discreditable. Work positively to create a culture that is safe for women and for gays and lesbians.
7. Organize political and economic support for battered women's shelters, rape crisis centers, and domestic violence intervention.

Notes

Chapter 1

1. Indeed, because of the masculinist nature of criminology, feminist criminologists have been, as Maureen Cain (1990: 6) puts it, "forced to transgress criminology, to break out of it."

2. A variant of control theory, "power-control theory" attempts to do this and is discussed below.

3. Feminism is considered a critical criminology and has now begun, as part of its program, to study men and masculinity. See Cain (1990).

4. To be fair to Bonger, social scientists still, in the 1990s, have difficulty determining women's social class position.

5. Chesney-Lind and Shelden (1992: 96–97) also add that power-control theory has important methodological problems, and that the theory ignores how girls are affected by class and race.

6. During this period, considerable attention was also devoted by feminists to men's violence against women. See Chapter 2.

7. Not all feminist criminologists support the idea of a special theory for understanding women's and girls' crime. For example, Daly and Chesney-Lind (1988: 518) cautiously argue that feminists should use "domesticated feminism to modify previous theory."

8. This is not to imply that a relationship between the body and social practice is nonexistent. As Connell (1987: 78) rightly points out, social practice "deals with" the characteristics of human bodies and gives them a social determination: "the connection between social and natural structures is one of *practical relevance*, not of causation." Although I do not attempt such a theoretical connection in this book, the important piece by Judith Allen (1989) has begun the process. Nevertheless, Allen's assumptions seem to be grounded in the strict gender dichotomy criticized earlier. Moreover, while Allen (pp. 34–35) argues strongly against a sex/gender distinction, she makes no sugges-

tion how we may apply to crime her idea that "subjectivities are formed in persons with male bodies."

Chapter 2

1. The first wave of the U.S. feminist movement grew out of the abolitionist movement of the 1830s. In 1848, the first women's rights convention was held in Seneca Falls, New York, and in 1920, women were guaranteed the right to vote when Congress adopted, after approximately fifty years of suffrage struggle, the Nineteenth Amendment. Although many women continued to pursue feminist goals following passage of the Nineteenth Amendment, a full-fledged movement did not reappear in the United States until the late 1960s.

2. I agree, however, with David Morgan (1992: 6) that although feminism remains the major influence on men examining masculinity, "the experiences and writings of gay men in particular contributed to the exploration of inequalities and relationships between men and the need to pluralize 'masculinities.' "

3. Max Weber (1978; 1924) was the first sociologist to use the term "patriarchy," arguing that patriarchy was found only in the domestic economy of agricultural societies. Patriarchy, for Weber, embodies the personal domination of the husband/father over the wife/mother within the domestic household. Once the household ceases to be the political and economic unit of society—that is, when legal-rational authority and capitalism materialize— patriarchal domination begins to disintegrate. With the rise of individualism, which permits one to "enjoy the fruits of his own abilities and labor as he himself wishes"—and as the "domestic" increasingly separates from the "public," legal-rational norms replace tradition, and patriarchal domination crumbles (p. 375).

4. Curiously, as with MacKinnon discussed earlier, these contemporary radical feminists do not provide an historical analysis of "heteropatriarchy," which tends to make their sociological view fundamentally indistinquishable from essentialism. That is, if heteropatriarchy is unchangeable, it is inescapably biologically determined.

5. This is not to deny that many men may be similar in some respects (e.g., cherish hegemonic masculine ideals). Indeed, a major contribution of radical feminism is its emphasis upon what many men share in common among themselves as well as with the institutions of society. This concentration on what men share most likely followed radical feminist research efforts on women's experiences of men's vi-

olence. In a personal communication (February 22, 1993), Betsy Stanko stated that "according to women's accounts any man *could* be a rapist." Thus, from the point of view of women, the differences among men may be less significant than are the similarities, especially when it comes to violence. This seems evident from the personal actions women take for their own, and others', safety. As Stanko (personal communication, February 24, 1993) points out:

> The work of radical feminists who have challenged traditional viewpoints of criminology's characterisation of violence against women (Kelly, Stanko, MacKinnon to name a few) has meant to document women's experiences first. Documenting how women—of many classes, races, economic positions—take measures for their sexual safety, guard against the potential for sexual violation, provides evidence of how women "accommodate" themselves to the reality of sexual violence. Many studies have illustrated the pervasiveness of violence in women's lives.

Moreover, we must acknowledge that the battered woman shelters, rape crisis centers, and child abuse programs now in place all over North America, Australia, and much of Europe are products, in the first instance, of the work of grass-roots feminist activists, radical feminists in the lead. Not only have radical feminists given hundreds of thousands of women help, they have raised awareness of these issues in society and shown women they need not be eternally victimized. We must therefore be sensitive to the effects this work has taken on radical feminist theorizing. Stanko (personal communication, February 24, 1993) points to:

> the toll it has taken for those of us working in this field to "put violence against women" on the agenda. I myself have been working in this area for 15 years. Frankly, I do not have the energy to find the most appropriate "theoretical" niche for describing what I know about women's coping skills in terms of men's violence. But *all* the evidence suggests that coping with men's violence is part of women's skills in contemporary life, and I suspect, in the past as well. I have no doubt that the anger, the frustration, and the stress caused by hearing the stories about men's abusive and threatening behavior has had profound effects on all of us who work in this field. If that has obscured my ability to develop the theoretical alacrity and cool detachment to the subject, then so be it.

According to Stanko (personal communication, February 22, 1993), the result of the above has been, at "this stage of development of social thought and attempt to theorize, a failure to see men as multi-dimensional.'' In other words, the unintended consequence of this sole emphasis on the similarities has been to collapse the differences among men into one version of masculinity—"the typical male.'' To gain deeper theoretical insight into the mysteries of masculinity (why men commit differing amounts and types of crimes among themselves; why some men engage in crime and some men do not), the differences among men must fundamentally be addressed. Some radical feminists, such as Stanko, now agree with this argument. As Stanko states (Stanko and Hobdell, 1993: 15):

> Men are not a homogenous group to be referred to simplistically as think-ing, experiencing or behaving in *a* particular way. Rather their social and psychological worlds are mediated by their age, ethnic origin, sexual ori-entation, religion, employment and so on. Indeed, their understanding of, and playing out of, their masculinity is also affected in just such ways.

6. According to Bob Connell, "wife burning" in India usually oc-curs in the course of disputes over dowries and is commonly per-formed by the husband's kinship group (which may include women) not the husband as an individual (Personal communication, October 11, 1992).

7. The idea of "sexual passionlessness" was applied primarily to white, middle-class women. Working-class and African American women continued to be identified as sexually passionate and, thus, sexually available (D'Emilio and Freedman, 1988: 46).

8. This concentration on women as nurturing might explain why radical and cultural feminists have eschewed an examination of women and crime. It should be noted that radical and cultural femi-nists have attempted to explain no types of crimes—by men or women—other than violence against women by men.

Chapter 3

1. Bob Connell's (1987) book *Gender and Power* is clearly a landmark text in the development of feminist theory and has influ-enced my theoretical underpinnings enormously. However, readers fa-miliar with this work will note that I draw qualifiedly upon his frame-work while adding my own specific and particular theoretical proclivities.

2. Criminology not only has failed to perceive men as gendered,

it has likewise failed to see white people as having a "race." Ignoring its social construction, criminology has naturalized whiteness. However, what constitutes a race is based on historical practices; consequently, the meaning of race is always undergoing change. After about 1680, the racial category "black" emerged, and for the first time, colonial Europeans began to identify themselves as "white." In terms of a racial division of labor analysis, the consequence of this has been that "the definition of labor ('slave' versus 'free'), the allocation of workers of distinct places in dual/segmented/split labor markets, and the composition of the 'underclass' have all been dependent on race as organizing principles or 'rules of the game' " (Omi and Winant, 1986: 67).

3. Smart (1989: 38) is not arguing that intercourse may not be pleasurable at times for women but that the "focus on phallic pleasure does not inevitably coincide with the potential of female sexuality."

4. Nevertheless, we cannot lose sight of other relations in the social construction of sexuality. As Jeffrey Weeks (1986: 41) shows, there are class and race sexualities and, therefore, sexuality "is a continuing process in which we are simultaneously acted upon and actors, objects of change, and its subjects."

5. Hochschild (1989: 15–18) also points out that frequently individuals experience a contradiction between their gender ideals and actual practice. That is, some men may actually reject the ideals of hegemonic masculinity yet because the resources are not available to support that rejection, they engage in a pragmatic use of the resources accessible and reproduction of hegemonic masculinity is the result.

Chapter 4

1. Research in this section concentrated on the white middle class. Although it is conceivable that middle-class African American boys, for example, may emphasize similar masculine patterns discussed here, there is no reason to *assume* that this specific type of masculinity speaks for all racial and ethnic groups of men, even though they may be from the same class. In the same vein, the type of masculinity discussed here is not the only version of masculinity within a given population of young white, middle-class men.

2. The English boarding school study referred to earlier evidenced that "school failures" were the most likely to be the "rebellious pranksters," whose pranks occurred primarily outside the school and were nonviolent in nature (Heward, 1988: 54, 139–140). See also

Cookson and Persell (1985) for similar evidence in a U.S. boarding school.

3. Within the same working-class school, the lads and the ear'oles construct different types of white masculinity. The latter comply with school rules and do well academically, constructing an accommodating in-school white masculinity similar to white, middle-class boys. That is, the ear'oles are constructing a different gendered strategy of action than are the lads. The working-class school itself fosters this differentiation among boys and masculinities through such institutionalized processes as tracking and grading systems. In other words, the ear'oles are the white, working-class high achievers and do well academically, while the lads are the opposite. The result is a *"contest of hegemony* between rival versions of masculinity" (Connell, 1989: 295) and those who adopt the accommodating form—as school status evidence shows (see Messerschmidt, 1979)—are the least likely to engage in youth crime both inside and outside school. Since academic achievement is unattractive to the lads, they search out other resources for masculine accomplishment, such as youth crime. Notwithstanding, the focus in this chapter is on boys who engage in youth crime and how these boys, by reason of their social structural position (race and class), view the school differently and primarily (but not always) make use of different forms of youth crime with which to construct different types of masculinities. And although adversarial masculinities clearly develop within the specific setting of the school (e.g., accommodating vs. opposition), among youth who specifically engage in youth crime we can observe (by class and race, for example) distinct types of opposition masculinities. For excellent work on the construction of different masculinities by working-class boys originating from the same class and race position, see Connell (1989; 1991).

4. Many working-class girls also oppose school. Although opposition among boys, in the manner of the lads, can be understood as a practice that attempts to confirm specific notions of hegemonic masculinity, similar behavior among girls actually violates stereotypical femininity. Because convention maintains that girls are to engage in practices that express courtesy, docility, and refinement, contradictory practices are seen as part of a project protesting conventional femininity and, as Kessler, Asheden, Connell, and Dowsett (1985: 38) note, "a genuine challenge to their subordination as women." Yet these young women are by no means masculine in style or outlook. As in other avenues of everyday life, they reproduce conventional notions of femininity. Similarly, McRobbie's (1991: 45–51) sample of white,

working-class girls opposed the school in specific ways (e.g., smoking in the lavatory), yet accepted unquestioningly conventional femininity within the school. Thus, considerable evidence suggests that white, working-class girls—like white, working-class boys—construct specific styles of gender (femininity) within the confines of the school and draw on forms of youth crime as a resource for that femininity.

5. Clearly, most white, working-class boys do not engage in such behaviors and boys from other class backgrounds may indeed engage in such behaviors. My argument is simply that the combined class and race social setting of these youth increases the likelihood of this type of violent behavior.

6. I do not suggest that "reproduction" is simply automatic. Reproduction of class, race, and gender relations must constantly be realized through social action that depends upon the collective efforts of the specific participants.

7. I refer here only to those youth who engage in youth crime. Just as in middle- and working-class schools, in lower—working-class schools the majority of boys construct some type of accommodating masculinity and, thus, rival versions of masculinity develop.

8. Nevertheless, hooks (1992: 87) is quick to point out that although this is the most esteemed version of "maleness," it is not the only version; both hooks and her brother violated stereotypical gender identities—"I was tough, he was not. I was strong willed, he was easy going. We were both a disappointment."

9. I do not imply that only young men are involved in street violence. As Campbell (1991: 271) reports: "though girls may be less likely to become involved in gang-related violence, those that do are as involved as the males." Nevertheless, such violence by young women in the street group should not be interpreted as masculine behavior. Rather, violence is but one practice in the overall process of constructing a specific type of femininity. A young woman in a street gang remains "subject to evaluation in terms of normative conceptions of appropriate attitudes and activities for her sex category and under pressure to prove that she is an 'essentially' feminine being, despite appearances to the contrary" (West and Zimmerman, 1987: 139–140). Consequently, violent women in street groups are simultaneously and decisively heterosexual, monogamous, do most, if not all, of the cooking and child care, prepare the food and drink for parties, and are "very fussy" over gender display (clothes, hair, and makeup) being clearly feminine (Campbell, 1984: Chapter 4). Accordingly, their fem-

ininity consists of a combination of conventional and unorthodox practices (such as participating in gang violence).

10. Again, this is not the most common version of masculinity constructed by lower–working-class, racial-minority boys, but the class and race setting increases the probability of it occurring relative to other race and class settings.

11. In September 1990, the Central Park youths were convicted of rape. At the time of writing, however, their conviction has been appealed, and some argue that although a rape clearly occurred, the young men convicted of the crime may not be the actual rapists. See Hornung (1990) and James (1992) for details.

12. Gang rape seems to be much more prevalent in college fraternities than previously thought; yet within this particular social setting it occurs quite differently than on the street. For example, alcohol rather than physical violence is commonly used to "work a yes out" of the victim (Sanday, 1990: 113–134). Thus, in this way, the specific setting determines how, as a resource for masculine construction, gang rape is acted out.

Chapter 5

1. Prostitutes, or "wives-in-law," are constructing a femininity that both confirms and violates stereotypical "female" behavior. In addition to the conventional aspects of femininity just mentioned, prostitute femininity also ridicules conventional morality by advocating sex outside of marriage, sex for pleasure, anonymous sex, and sex that is not limited to reproduction and the domesticated couple. This construction of a specific type of femininity clearly challenges, in certain respects, stereotypical femininity. Nevertheless, the vast majority of prostitutes do not consider themselves feminists: they know very little about the feminist movement, do not share its assumptions, and believe men and women are "naturally" suited for different types of work (Miller, 1986: 160).

2. The masculinity constructed by African American pimps is fittingly comparable to the masculinity associated with men (usually from working-class backgrounds) who are members of white motorcycle gangs. The men in such groups act extremely racist and similarly exploit the sexuality and labor of "biker women." However, biker men do not display a "cool pose" with an accompanying show of luxury in the form of flashy clothing and exotic hairstyles. On the contrary, a biker usually has long unkempt hair, a "rough" beard, and

his "colors" consist of black motorcycle boots, soiled jeans, and a simple sleeveless denim jacket with attached insignia (see Hopper and Moore, 1990 and Willis, 1978).

3. Horizontal segregation allocates men and women to different types of jobs; vertical segregation concentrates men and women in different occupations at different steps in an occupational hierarchy.

4. Approximately 45 percent of all men in the active labor force hold these types of proletarian jobs (Harris, 1992: 221). Moreover, although the proportion of African American men holding these jobs is almost twice as high as that of white men (Farley, 1989), because the research utilized here does not distinguish by race, my discussion concentrates solely on class and masculinity.

5. This is not to say that employee theft is insignificant at the managerial level; on the contrary, it is quite widespread (Beirne and Messerschmidt, 1991: 174–175).

6. Dock pilferage by longshoremen provides a good example of this type of theft. In dock work, cargo is winched from the ship onto the dock, stacked, and checked. A work group of twelve to twenty men "work a boat" with the group deciding who will have which responsibilities. Thus it allocates available jobs to its members (Mars, 1983: 101). Moreover, the group orchestrates employee theft. As Mars (p. 104) points out, to steal cargo, "holdsmen need the support of the winchman and signaller, while stowers need the support of the fork-lift truck drivers and acquiescence of the hatch-checker." Group members are judged as "men" by how well they work within the group and by how consistently, not to what extent, they steal goods.

7. This specific masculine meaning attached to group employee theft most likely explains women's lesser involvement in this type of occupational crime. Moreover, Box (1983: 181–182) adds that employment is not as criminogenic for women as it is for men because "the aggregation of male workers and their collectivist responses has a longer history and a greater impact" for men than women. The result is, as Kathleen Daly (1989: 772) points out, "that work place social bonds are stronger for men than for women, and thus occupational crime as a group activity is more likely for men."

8. Nevertheless, it should be pointed out that increasing numbers of men are attempting to counter sexism on the shop floor and, therefore, reconstruct shop-floor masculinity. For an excellent example see Gray, 1987.

9. Corporate crime is defined as "illegal and/or socially injurious acts of intent or indifference, that occur for the purpose of furthering

the goals of a corporation, and that physically and/or economically abuse individuals in the U.S. and/or abroad" (Beirne and Messerschmidt, 1991: 184; see pp. 185–198 of this work for a wide range of examples).

10. It has been determined that 5.2 percent of executive, administrative, and managerial positions and 6.7 percent of professional positions are held by African Americans (Beirne and Messerschmidt, 1991: 566). As Anthony R. Harris (1991: 118) concludes after examining the relationship among class, race, and corporate crime: "the advantages of race exist *over and above* those of class. The opportunity to commit suite crime is still greater for a class-advantaged white than for a class-advantaged black."

11. The deregulation policies of the Reagan administration in the 1980s ushered in a new form of corporate crime, what Calavita and Pontell (1990: 321) call, "collective embezzlement," or "the siphoning off of funds from savings and loan institutions for personal gain at the expense of the institution itself *and with the implicit or explicit sanction of its management*." This type of corporate crime is quite different from manufacturing and industrial corporate crime. In the latter, corporate crime helps the corporation reach its goal of profit maximization and continued financial stability. Indeed, corporate executives have an individual and gendered interest in the continued survival of the corporation. In contrast, perpetrators of collective embezzlement in the savings and loan industry "have little to lose by their reckless behavior" and their "main concern is to get in and out of the 'house' with as much of the pot as possible" (p. 336). This crime against the corporation by those who run it clearly represents not only a new crime, but a new type of white corporate masculinity as well.

12. Kathleen Daly's (1989: 788) important study, "Gender and Varieties of White-Collar Crime," found that women's involvement in corporate crime was negligible, and this rare presence of women who are corporate criminals can be explained in the sense that women "may be more averse than men to abusing positions of organizational power, or they may be excluded from men's corporate crime groups, or perhaps both." The latter explanation is clearly the most plausible. Yet a woman who does engage in corporate crime is not simply doing masculinity. Although her very position is a protest against conventional femininity, she is still gender accountable and under pressure to show that she is an "essentially" feminine being, despite appearances to the contrary (West and Zimmerman, 1987: 140). In other avenues

of everyday life, she most likely engages in stereotypical femininity. Thus, as with girls in street gangs who engage in violence, women who participate in corporate crime are constructing a specific type of femininity that consists of a combination of conventional and unorthodox gendered practices.

13. Indeed, office romances seem to be flourishing because women more routinely work beside men in professional and occupational jobs (Ehrenreich, 1989: 219).

14. This particular type of femininity has been explored by Pringle (1988).

15. Despite devastating criticisms of the Conflict Tactics Scale as a methodological tool (Dobash, Dobash, Wilson, and Daly, 1992), some researchers (remarkably) continue to use it to guide their work, concluding that women are about as violent as men in the home (Straus and Gelles, 1990), or even in some cases, that more men are victimized in the home than are women (McNeely and Mann, 1990).

16. Unfortunately, there is scant research on wife beating in racial-minority households. Nevertheless, what evidence there is on African American households suggests that when violence does occur, both husband and wife are likely to accept the traditional patriarchal division of labor and power as natural and that complete responsibility for the battering, when questioned, "lies with white society" (Richie, 1985: 42; see also Asbury, 1987). Consequently, I am forced to concentrate solely on class and wife beating.

17. This is not to deny that many middle-class men engage in wife beating for the reasons discussed earlier in this section. What I suggest, following Segal (1990: 255) and others, is that it is clearly less common in middle-class households because such men have access to other resources, possibly more effective resources, through which they exert control over women without employing violence.

18. Because Finkelhor and Yllö (1985: 9) found no significantly higher rate of marital rape among African Americans than among whites, I do not distinguish by race.

Chapter 6

1. Similarly, there has never been an African American president or vice-president, and only 5 percent of House members, and only one senator, are currently African American. Moreover, the highest governmental positions in the United States historically have derived from the capitalist and professional-managerial classes (Beirne and Mes-

serschmidt, 1991: 546, 566). Thus, the state is dominated by white-capitalist and professional-managerial men.

2. "Social feminism" and "social feminist" refer primarily to nineteenth- and twentieth-century feminists who maintained conservative views on sexuality and attempted to reform society within existing gender relations, not to more militant feminists critical of the entire social order. However, this does not mean the two groups never advocated the same causes; in fact, many times they did. Indeed, it is difficult to characterize some feminists one way or the other. For example, Charlotte Perkins Gillman was very critical of women's passivity and "maleness," yet as a social feminist she spoke out on the alleged dangers of "excessive sex indulgence."

3. During this period, both African American men and women were characterized as uncontrollably lustful and chronically promiscuous, which "legitimated" sexual violence against African American women (rape) and African American men (lynching) (Collins, 1990).

4. Indeed, in the *Descent of Man*, Charles Darwin (1871) emphasized the development of "morality" as essential to evolutionary progress.

5. Some feminists writing during this period argued that prostitution resulted primarily from the economic and social status of women. For example, Emma Goldman (1910: 20–21) showed how the focus on an alleged "traffic in women" obscured the economic and social subordination of women as the real cause of prostitution.

6. These girls were also oppressed by women of their own class and from their own families. Many girls had mothers who intensely attempted to control their daughters, and used moral purity authority against them. Numerous girls, as with Angeline, were sent to state authorities for prosecution by their mothers. In short, oppression and victimization of these girls crossed many boundaries.

7. However, social feminists and other reformers were not always repressive. In many instances, young women sought to be noticed and helped, and occasionally middle-class feminists and reformers did help. See the important work on this issue by Linda Gordon (1988).

8. Indeed, policewomen, challenging stereotypical femininity, are constructing a new type of femininity—the "woman cop." Further, women cops are not simply masculine in style and outlook. On the contrary, they accept unquestioningly their femininity but specifically construct it to suit their perception of the social setting of police work (Remmington, 1981; Hunt, 1984).

9. Nevertheless, law enforcement remains the only option for

many victims in need of swift and short-term protection. As Ferraro (1989: 180) states, "arrest is a statement of wrongdoing, and provides symbolic support to women seeking to escape violent relationships." We must be aware, however, of the contradictions inherent in this solution and the limits of police response to wife beating.

10. Similar processes occur in other areas of the criminal justice system. For example, Nancy Jurik's (1985) important study of women employed as correctional officers in men's prisons found that women officers threatened the masculinity of men officers, resulting in extensive gendered segregation and sexual harassment.

11. Moreover, this implies a relationship between situational accomplishment of masculinities within the state and crimes committed by the state. Consider, for example, the calculative and rational decision making attendant to the conduct of Oliver North, contrasted with the physically aggressive and violent behavior of the Los Angeles street cops who beat Rodney King. Two different types of masculinities are being constructed through two different practices associated with these events.

References

Acker, Joan. (1990). "Hierarchies, Jobs, Bodies: A Theory of Gendered Organization." *Gender and Society* 4 (2): 139–58.

Acker, Joan. (1989). "The Problem with Patriarchy." *Sociology* 23 (2): 235–40.

Acker, Joan. (1988). "Class, Gender and Relations of Distribution." *Signs* 13 (3): 473–97.

Adam, Barry. (1987). *The Rise of a Gay and Lesbian Movement.* Boston: Twayne Publishers.

Allen, John. (1978). *Assault with a Deadly Weapon.* New York: McGraw-Hill.

Allen, Judith. (1989). "Men, Crime and Criminology: Recasting the Questions." *International Journal of the Sociology of Law* 17 (1): 19–39.

Altheide, David L., Patricia A. Adler, Peter Adler, and Duane A. Altheide. (1978). "The Social Meanings of Employee Theft." In *Crime at the Top*, ed. John Johnson and Jack Douglas, 90–124. New York: Lippincott.

Andersen, Margaret. (1988). *Thinking About Women.* New York: Macmillan.

Asbury, Jo-Ellen. (1987). "African-American Women in Violent Relationships: An Exploration of Cultural Differences." In *Violence in the Black Family*, ed. Robert L. Hampton, 89–105. Lexington, MA: Lexington Books.

Banner, Lois W. (1974). *Women in Modern America.* New York: Harcourt Brace Jovanovich.

Barrett, Michele, and Mary McIntosh. (1985). "Ethnocentrism and Socialist Feminist Theory." *Feminist Review* 20 (1): 23–47.

201

Barry, Kathleen. (1979). *Female Sexual Slavery.* Englewood Cliffs, NJ: Prentice-Hall.

Beechy, Veronica. (1978). "Women and Production: A Critical Analysis of Some Sociological Theories of Women's Work." In *Feminism and Materialism*, ed. Annette Kuhn and Ann Marie Wolpe, 155–97. Boston: Routledge & Kegan Paul.

Beechy, Veronica. (1987). *Unequal Work.* London: Verso.

Beirne, Piers. (1988). "Heredity Versus Environment: A Reconsideration of Charles Goring's *The English Convict* (1913)." *British Journal of Criminology* 28 (3): 315–39.

Beirne, Piers, and James W. Messerschmidt. (1991). *Criminology.* San Diego, CA: Harcourt Brace Jovanovich.

Benston, Margaret. (1969). "The Political Economy of Women's Liberation." *Monthly Review* 21 (4): 13–27.

Berk, Sarah Fenstermaker. (1985). *The Gender Factory: The Apportionment of Work in American Households.* New York: Plenum Press.

Bernard, Jessie. (1992). "The Good-Provider Role: Its Rise and Fall." In *Men's Lives*, ed. Michael S. Kimmel and Michael A. Messner, 203–21. New York: Macmillan.

Bernard, Jessie. (1982). *The Future of Marriage.* New Haven, CT: Yale University Press.

Berrill, Kevin T. (1992). "Anti-Gay Violence and Victimization in the United States: An Overview." In *Hate Crimes: Confronting Violence Against Lesbians and Gay Men*, ed. Gregory M. Herek and Kevin T. Berrill, 19–45. Newbury Park, CA: Sage.

Bielby, William, and James N. Baron. (1986). "A Woman's Place Is with Other Women: Sex Segregation within Organizations." In *Sex Segregation in the Workplace: Trends, Explanations, Remedies*, ed. Barbara Reskin, 27–55. Washington, DC: National Academy Press.

Blau, Francine D., and Anne E. Winkler. (1989). "Women in the Labor Force: An Overview." In *Women: A Feminist Perspective*, ed. Jo Freeman, 265–86. Palo Alto, CA: Mayfield.

Bonger, Willem. (1916). *Criminality and Economic Conditions.* New York: Little, Brown.

Boostrom, Ronald. (1973). "The Personalization of Evil: The Emergence of American Criminology, 1865–1910." Unpublished Ph.D. dissertation, University of California, Berkeley.

Boston, Sarah. (1987). *Women Workers and the Trade Unions*. London: Lawrence and Wishart.

Bowker, Lee H., ed. (1981). *Women and Crime in America*. New York: Macmillan.

Bowker, Lee H., ed. (1978). *Women, Crime, and the Criminal Justice System*. Lexington, MA: Lexington Books.

Bowles, Samuel, and Herbert Gintis. (1976). *Schooling in Capitalist America*. New York: Basic Books.

Box, Steven. (1983). *Power, Crime and Mystification*. New York: Tavistock.

Breckinridge, Sophonisba, and Edith Abbott. (1912). *The Delinquent Child and the Home*. New York: Russell Sage.

Brittan, Arthur. (1989). *Masculinity and Power*. New York: Basil Blackwell.

Brown, Beverly. (1988). "Review of *Capitalism, Patriarchy and Crime.*" *International Journal of the Sociology of Law* 16 (3): 408–12.

Brown, Linda Keller. (1988). "Female Managers in the U.S. and in Europe." In *Women in Management Worldwide*, ed. Nancy J. Adler and Dafna N. Izraeli, 265–74. Armonk, NY: M.E. Sharpe.

Browning, Frank. (1981). "Life on the Margin: Atlanta Is Not the Only City Where Black Children Are Dying." *The Progressive* 45 (1): 34–37.

Brownmiller, Susan. (1975). *Against Our Will: Men, Women and Rape*. New York: Simon and Schuster.

Burstyn, Varda. (1985). "Political Precedents and Moral Crusades: Women, Sex and the State." In *Women Against Censorship*, ed. Varda Burstyn, 4–31. Vancouver, B.C.: Douglas & McIntyre.

Burstyn, Varda. (1983). "Masculine Dominance and the State." In *The Socialist Reader*, ed. Ralph Miliband and John Saville, 45–89. London: Merlin Press.

Buzawa, Eve Schlesinger, and Carl G. Buzawa. (1990). *Domestic Violence: The Criminal Justice Response*. Newbury Park, CA: Sage.

Cain, Maureen. (1990). "Towards Transgression: New Directions in

Feminist Criminology." *International Journal of the Sociology of Law* 18 (1): 1–18.

Calavita, Kitty, and Henry N. Pontell. (1990). "Heads I Win, Tails You Lose: Deregulation, Crime and Crisis in the Savings and Loan Industry." *Crime and Delinquency* 36 (3): 309–41.

Campbell, Anne. (1991). *The Girls in the Gang*. Second edition. Cambridge, MA: Basil Blackwell.

Campbell, Anne. (1990). "Female Participation in Gangs." In *Gangs in America*, ed. C. Ronald Huff, 163–82. Newbury Park, CA: Sage.

Campbell, Anne. (1984). *The Girls in the Gang*. Cambridge, MA: Basil Blackwell.

Campbell, Vie H. (1895). "Why an Age of Consent?" *Arena* 12 (July): 285–88.

Caputi, Jane. (1989). "The Sexual Politics of Murder." *Gender and Society* 3 (4): 437–56.

Caputi, Jane. (1987). *The Age of Sex Crime*. Bowling Green, OH: Bowling Green State University Press.

Carothers, Suzanne C., and Peggy Crull. (1984). "Contrasting Sexual Harassment in Female- and Male-Dominated Occupations." In *My Troubles Are Going to Have Trouble with Me*, ed. Karen Brodkin Sacks and Dorothy Remy, 219–28. New Brunswick, NJ: Rutgers University Press.

Carrigan, Tim, Bob Connell, and John Lee. (1987). "Hard and Heavy: Toward a New Sociology of Masculinity." In *Beyond Patriarchy: Essays by Men on Pleasure, Power and Change*, ed. Michael Kaufman, 139–92. New York: Oxford University Press.

Carringella-MacDonald, Susan. (1988). "Marxist and Feminist Interpretations on the Aftermath of Rape Reforms." *Contemporary Crises* 12 (2): 125–43.

Cernkovich, Stephen A., and Peggy C. Giordano. (1992). "School Bonding, Race and Delinquency." *Criminology* 30 (2): 261–91.

Chambliss, William J. (1973). "The Saints and the Roughnecks." *Society* 11 (1): 24–31.

Chesney-Lind, Meda. (1989). "Girl's Crime and Woman's Place: Toward a Feminist Model of Female Delinquency." *Crime and Delinquency* 35 (1): 5–29.

Chesney-Lind, Meda, and Randall G. Shelden. (1992). *Girls, Delinquency and Juvenile Justice*. Pacific Grove, CA: Brooks/Cole.

Clark, Lorenne M. G., and Debra J. Lewis. (1977). *Rape: The Price of Coercive Sexuality*. Toronto: Canadian Women's Educational Press.

Clatterbaugh, Kenneth. (1990). *Contemporary Perspectives on Masculinity*. Boulder: Westview Press.

Cloward, Richard A., and Lloyd E. Ohlin. (1960). *Delinquency and Opportunity*. New York: Free Press.

Cockburn, Cynthia. (1985). *Machinery of Dominance: Women, Men and Technical Know-How*. London: Pluto Press.

Cockburn, Cynthia. (1983). *Brothers: Male Dominance and Technological Change*. London: Pluto Press.

Cohen, Albert. (1955). *Delinquent Boys: The Culture of the Gang*. New York: Free Press.

Cohen, Stanley. (1985). *Visions of Social Control*. Cambridge: Polity Press.

Coleman, James. (1989). *The Criminal Elite: The Sociology of White Collar Crime*. New York: St. Martin's Press.

Coleman, Wil. (1990). "Doing Masculinity/Doing Theory." In *Men, Masculinities, and Social Theory*, ed. Jeff Hearn and David H. J. Morgan, 186–202. Cambridge, MA: Unwin Hyman.

Collins, Patricia. (1990). *Black Feminist Thought*. Boston: Unwin Hyman.

Collinson, David L., and Margaret Collinson. (1989). "Sexuality in the Workplace: The Domination of Men's Sexuality." In *The Sexuality of Organization*, ed. Jeff Hearn, Deborah L. Sheppard, Peta Tancred-Sheriff, and Gibson Burrell, 91–109. Newbury Park, CA: Sage.

Comstock, Gary David. (1991). *Violence against Lesbians and Gay Men*. New York: Columbia University Press.

Conklin, John. (1972). *Robbery and the Criminal Justice System*. New York: Lippincott.

Connell, R. W. (1992). "The Big Picture: Masculinities in Recent World History." Unpublished paper.

Connell, R. W. (1992). "Drumming up the Wrong Tree." *Tikkun* 7 (1): 31–36.

Connell, R. W. (1991). "Live Fast and Die Young: The Construction of Masculinity among Young Working-Class Men on the Margin of the Labour Market." *Australian and New Zealand Journal of Sociology* 27 (2): 141–71.

Connell, R. W. (1990). "The State, Gender, and Sexual Politics: Theory and Appraisal." *Theory and Society* 19 (4): 507–44.

Connell, R. W. (1989). "Cool Guys, Swots and Wimps: The Interplay of Masculinity and Education." *Oxford Review of Education* 15 (3): 291–303.

Connell, R. W. (1987). *Gender and Power.* Stanford, CA: Stanford University Press.

Connelly, Mark. (1980). *The Response to Prostitution in the Progressive Era.* Chapel Hill: University of North Carolina Press.

Cookson, Peter W., and Caroline Hodges Persell. (1985). *Preparing for Power: America's Elite Boarding Schools.* New York: Basic Books.

Cott, Nancy F. (1979). "Passionlessness: An Interpretation of Victorian Sexual Ideology, 1790–1850." In *A Heritage of Her Own* ed. Nancy F. Cott and Elizabeth H. Pleck, 162–81. New York: Simon and Schuster.

Crites, Laura. (1976). *The Female Offender.* Lexington, MA: Lexington Books.

Crompton, Rosemary, and Kay Sanderson. (1990). *Gendered Jobs and Social Change.* Boston: Unwin Hyman.

Cullen, Francis, William J. Maakestad, and Gray Cavender. (1987). *Corporate Crime Under Attack.* Cincinnati: Anderson.

Daly, Kathleen. (1989). "Gender and Varieties of White-Collar Crime." *Criminology* 27 (4): 769–93.

Daly, Kathleen. (1988). "The Social Control of Sexuality: A Case Study of the Criminalization of Prostitution in the Progressive Era." In *Research in Law, Deviance and Social Control,* Vol. 9, ed. Steven Spitzer, 171–206. Greenwich, CT: JAI Press.

Daly, Kathleen, and Meda Chesney-Lind. (1988). "Feminism and Criminology." *Justice Quarterly* 5 (4): 497–538.

Daly, Mary. (1978). *Gyn/Ecology: The Metaethics of Radical Feminism.* Boston: Beacon Press.

Daly, Mary. (1975). "the qualitative leap beyond patriarchal religion." *Quest* 1 (4): 28–40.

Darwin, Charles. (1871, 1936). *Descent of Man*. New York: The Modern Library.

Datesman, Susan K., and Frank R. Scarpitti, eds. (1980). *Women, Crime, and Justice*. New York: Oxford University Press.

Davidoff, Lenore, and Catherine Hall. (1987). *Family Fortunes: Men and Women of the English Middle Class, 1780–1850*. London: Hutchison.

Degler, Carl. (1980). *At Odds: Women and the Family from the Revolution to the Present*. New York: Oxford University Press.

DeKeseredy, Walter, and Ronald Hinch. (1991). *Woman Abuse: Sociological Perspectives*. Lewiston, NY: Thompson Educational Pub., Inc.

D'Emilio, John, and Estelle B. Freedman. (1988). *Intimate Matters: A History of Sexuality in America*. New York: Harper and Row.

DiTomaso, Nancy. (1989). "Sexuality in the Workplace: Discrimination and Harassment." In *The Sexuality of Organization*, eds. Jeff Hearn, Deborah L. Sheppard, Peta Tancred-Sheriff, and Gibson Burrell, 71–90. Newbury Park, CA: Sage.

Ditton, Jason. (1977). *Part-Time Crime*. New York: Macmillan.

Dobash, R. Emerson, and Russell P. Dobash. (1984). "The Nature and Antecedents of Violent Events." *British Journal of Criminology* 24 (3): 269–88.

Dobash, R. Emerson, and Russell P. Dobash. (1979). *Violence Against Wives*. New York: Free Press.

Dobash, Russell P., R. Emerson Dobash, Margo Wilson, and Martin Daly. (1992). "The Myth of Sexual Symmetry in Marital Violence." *Social Problems* 39 (1): 71–91.

Donaldson, Mike. (1987). "Labouring Men: Love, Sex and Strife." *Australian and New Zealand Journal of Sociology* 23 (2): 165–84.

Draper, Patricia. (1975). "!Kung Women: Contrasts in Sexual Egalitarianism in Foraging and Sedentary Contexts." In *Toward an Anthropology of Women*, ed. Rayna R. Reiter, 77–109. New York: Monthly Review Press.

Dubois, Ellen C., and Linda Gordon. (1984). "Seeking Ecstasy on the Battlefield: Danger and Pleasure in Nineteenth Century Feminist Thought." In *Pleasure and Danger: Exploring Female Sexuality*, ed. Carol S. Vance, 31–49. Boston: Routledge & Kegan Paul.

Dunning, Eric, Patrick Murphy, and John Williams. (1988). *The Roots of Football Hooliganism*. New York: Routledge & Kegan Paul.

Dworkin, Andrea. (1987). *Intercourse*. New York: Free Press.

Dworkin, Andrea. (1980). "Pornography and Grief." In *Take Back the Night*, ed. Laura Lederer, 286–91. New York: William Morrow.

Dworkin, Andrea. (1980a). "Why So-Called Radical Men Love and Need Pornography." In *Take Back the Night*, ed. Laura Lederer, 148–54. New York: William Morrow.

Dworkin, Andrea. (1979). *Pornography: Men Possessing Women*. New York: Plume.

Dyck, Noel. (1980). "Booze, Barrooms and Scrapping: Masculinity and Violence in a Western Canadian Town." *Canadian Journal of Anthropology* 1 (2): 191–98.

Echols, Alice. (1989). *Daring to Be Bad: Radical Feminism in America, 1967–1975*. Minneapolis: University of Minnesota Press.

Edleson, Jeffrey L., Zvi Eisikovits, and Edna Guttman. (1986). "Men Who Batter Women: A Critical Review of the Evidence." *Journal of Family Issues* 6 (2): 229–47.

Edwards, Anne. (1987). "Male Violence in Feminist Theory: An Analysis of the Changing Conceptions of Sex/Gender Violence and Male Dominance." In *Women, Violence and Social Change*, ed. Jalna Hanmer and Mary Maynard, 13–29. Atlantic Highlands, NJ: Humanities Press International.

Edwards, Anne. (1983). "Sex Roles: A Problem for Sociology and for Women." *Australian and New Zealand Journal of Sociology* 19 (3): 385–412.

Edwards, Susan. (1990). "Violence against Women: Feminism and the Law." In *Feminist Perspectives in Criminology*, ed. Loraine Gelsthorpe and Allison Morris, 145–59. Philadelphia: Open University Press.

Ehrenreich, Barbara. (1989). *Fear of Falling*. New York: Pantheon.

Ehrenreich, Barbara. (1984). "A Feminist's View of the New Man." *New York Times Magazine*, May 20, 1984: 36–48.

Ehrenreich, Barbara. (1983). *The Hearts of Men*. New York: Doubleday.

Ehrenreich, Barbara, and Deidre English. (1978). *For Her Own Good*. Garden City, NY: Anchor Press.

Eisenstein, Hester. (1983). *Contemporary Feminist Thought*. Boston: G.K. Hall.

Eisenstein, Zillah. (1979). "Developing a Theory of Capitalist Patriarchy and Socialist Feminism." In *Capitalist Patriarchy and the Case for Socialist Feminism*, ed. Zillah Eisenstein, 5–40. New York: Monthly Review Press.

Elliott, Delbert S., and David Huizinga. (1983). "Social Class and Delinquent Behavior in a National Youth Panel." *Criminology* 21 (2): 149–77.

Elliott, Delbert S., and Harold L. Voss. (1974). *Delinquency and Dropout*. Lexington, MA: Lexington Books.

Farley, Reynolds. (1989). "Three Steps Forward and Two Back? Recent Changes in the Social and Economic Status of Blacks." In *Ethnicity and Race in the USA: Toward the Twenty-first Century*, ed. Richard D. Alba, 4–28. New York: Methuen.

Fenstermaker, Sarah, Candace West, and Don H. Zimmerman. (1991). "Gender Inequality: New Conceptual Terrain." In *Gender, Family and Economy*, ed. Rae Lesser Blumberg, 289–307. Newbury Park, CA: Sage.

Ferguson, Ann. (1991). *Sexual Democracy: Women, Oppression and Revolution*. Boulder: Westview Press.

Ferraro, Kathleen J. (1989). "The Legal Response to Woman Battering in the United States." In *Women, Policing and Male Violence*, ed. Jalna Hanmer, Jill Radford, and Elizabeth A. Stanko, 155–84. New York: Routledge.

Ferraro, Kathleen J. (1988). "An Existential Approach to Battering." In *Family Abuse and its Consequences*, ed. Gerald T. Hotaling, David Finkelhor, John T. Kirkpatrick, and Murray Straus, 126–38. Newbury Park, CA: Sage.

Finkelhor, David, and Kristi Yllö. (1985). *License to Rape: Sexual Abuse of Wives*. New York: Holt, Rinehart and Winston.

Firestone, Shulamith. (1970). *The Dialectic of Sex*. New York: William Morrow.

Fishbein, Leslie. (1980). "Harlot or Heroine? Changing Views of Prostitution, 1870–1920." *The Historian* 43 (1): 23–35.

Fishman, Laura T. (1988). "The Vice Queens: An Ethnographic Study of Black Female Gang Behavior." Paper presented at the annual meeting of the American Society of Criminology.

Folbre, Nancy. (1982). "Exploitation Comes Home: A Critique of the Marxian Theory of Family Labour." *Cambridge Journal of Economics* 6 (4): 317–29.

Foster, William T. (1914). *The Social Emergency*. New York: Houghton-Mifflin.

Foucault, Michel. (1978). *The History of Sexuality*. New York: Pantheon.

Frank, Blye. (1987). "Hegemonic Heterosexual Masculinity." *Studies in Political Economy* 24 (Autumn): 159–70.

Frank, Nancy K., and Michael J. Lynch. (1992). *Corporate Crime, Corporate Violence*. New York: Harrow and Heston.

Franzway, Suzanne, Dianne Court, and R. W. Connell. (1989). *Staking a Claim: Feminism, Bureacracy, and the State*. Boston: Allen and Unwin.

Frieze, Irene H. (1983). "Investigating the Causes and Consequences of Marital Rape." *Signs* 8 (3): 532–53.

Game, Ann, and Rosemary Pringle. (1984). *Gender at Work*. Boston: Allen and Unwin.

Gardner, Helen H. (1895). "What Shall the Age of Consent Be?" *Arena* 11 (January): 196–98.

Garfinkel, Harold. (1967). *Studies in Ethnomethodology*. Englewood Cliffs, NJ: Prentice-Hall.

Giddens, Anthony. (1989). "A Reply to My Critics." In *Social Theory of Modern Societies: Anthony Giddens and His Critics*, ed. David Held and John B. Thompson, 249–301. New York: Cambridge University Press.

Giddens, Anthony. (1981). "Agency, Institution, and Time-Space Analysis." In *Advances in Social Theory and Methodology: Toward an Integration of Micro- and Macro-Sociologies*, ed. K. Knorr-Cetina and A. V. Cicourel, 161–74. Boston: Routledge & Kegan Paul.

Giddens, Anthony. (1976). *New Rules of Sociological Method*. London: Hutchison.

Gilmore, David D. (1990). *Manhood in the Making*. New Haven: Yale University Press.

Glenn, Evelyn Nakano. (1992). "From Servitude to Service Work: Historical Continuities in the Racial Division of Paid Reproductive Labor." *Signs* 18 (1): 1–43.

Goffman, Erving. (1979). *Gender Advertisements*. New York: Harper and Row.

Goldman, Emma. (1910, 1970). *The Traffic in Women and Other Essays on Feminism*. New York: Times Change Press.

Gordon, Linda. (1988). *Heroes of Their Own Lives*. New York: Viking.

Gordon, Linda. (1986). "Incest and Resistance: Patterns of Father-Daughter Incest, 1880–1930." *Social Problems* 37 (4): 253–67.

Gordon, Linda. (1976). *Woman's Body, Woman's Right: A Social History of Birth Control in America*. New York: Grossman.

Gottfredson, Gary D., and Denise C. Gottfredson. (1985). *Victimization in Schools*. New York: Plenum Press.

Gramsci, Antonio. (1978). *Selections from the Prison Notebooks*, ed. Quintin Hoare and Geoffrey Nowell Smith. London: Lawrence and Wishart.

Gray, Stan. (1987). "Sharing the Shop Floor." In *Beyond Patriarchy*, ed. Michael Kaufman, 216–34. New York: Oxford University Press.

Greenberg, David F. (1981). *Crime and Capitalism: Readings in Marxist Criminology*. Palo Alto, CA: Mayfield.

Greenberg, David F. (1977). "Delinquency and the Age Structure of Society." *Contemporary Crises* 1 (2): 189–224.

Griffin, Susan. (1971). "Rape: The All-American Crime." *Ramparts* 10 (3): 26–35.

Gross, Edward. (1978). "Organizational Sources of Crime: A Theoretical Perspective." In *Studies in Symbolic Interaction*, ed. Norman K. Densin, 55–85. Greenwich, CT: JAI Press.

Gruber, James, and Lars Bjorn. (1982). "Blue Collar Blues: The Sexual Harassment of Women Autoworkers." *Work and Occupations* 9 (3): 271–98.

Hagan, John. (1989). *Structural Criminology*. New Brunswick, NJ: Rutgers University Press.

Hagedorn, John M. (1993). "Homeboys, Dope Fiends, Straights, and New Jacks: Adult Gang Members, Drugs, and Work." Unpublished manuscript.

Hanmer, Jalna, and Mary Maynard. (1987). "Introduction: Violence and Gender Stratification." In *Women, Violence and Social Change*, ed. Jalna Hanmer and Mary Maynard, 1–12. Atlantic Highlands, NJ: Humanities Press International.

Hanmer, Jalna, Jill Radford, and Elizabeth A. Stanko. (1989). "Policing, Men's Violence: An Introduction." In *Women, Policing and Male Violence*, ed. Jalna Hanmer, Jill Radford, and Elizabeth A. Stanko, 1–12. New York: Routledge.

Harris, Anthony R. (1991). "Race, Class and Crime" In *Criminology: A Contemporary Handbook*, ed. Joseph F. Sheley, 95–119. Belmont, CA: Wadsworth.

Harris, Anthony R. (1977). "Sex and Theories of Deviance: Toward a Functional Theory of Deviant Type-Scripts." *American Sociological Review* 42 (1): 3–16.

Harris, Ian. (1992). "Media Myths and the Reality of Men's Work." In *Men's Lives*, ed. Michael S. Kimmel and Michael A. Messner, 225–31. New York: Macmillan.

Harris, M. G. (1988). *Cholas; Latino Girls and Gangs*. New York: AMS.

Harris, Richard N., and Roslyn Wallach Bologh. (1985). "The Dark Side of Love: Blue and White Collar Wife Abuse." *Victimology* 10 (1–4): 242–52.

Harry, Joseph. (1992). "Conceptualizing Anti-Gay Violence." In *Hate Crimes: Confronting Violence Against Lesbians and Gay Men*, ed. Gregory H. Herek and Kevin T. Berril, 113–22. Newbury Park, CA: Sage.

Hartmann, Heidi. (1981). "The Unhappy Marriage of Marxism and Feminism: Towards a More Progressive Union." In *Women and Revolution*, ed. Lydia Sargent, 1–41. Boston: South End Press.

Hartmann, Heidi. (1979). "Capitalism, Patriarchy and Job Segregation by Sex." In *Capitalist Patriarchy and the Case for Socialist Feminism*, ed. Zillah Eisenstein, 206–47. New York: Monthly Review Press.

Hearn, Jeff. (1992). *Men in the Public Eye*. New York: Routledge.

Hearn, Jeff. (1985). "Men's Sexuality at Work." In *The Sexuality of Men* ed. Andy Metcalf and Martin Humphries, 110–28. London: Pluto Press.

Hearn, Jeff, and Wendy Parkin. (1987). *"Sex" at "Work"*. New York: St. Martin's Press.

Heidensohn, Frances. (1987). "Women and Crime: Questions for Criminology." In *Gender, Crime and Justice*, ed. Pat Carlen and Anne Worrall, 16–27. Philadelphia: Open University Press.

Heidensohn, Frances. (1985). *Women and Crime*. New York: New York University Press.

Henry, Stuart. (1978). *The Hidden Economy*. London: Martin Robertson.

Heward, Christine. (1988). *Making a Man of Him*. London: Routledge.

Heyn, Dalna. (1992). *The Erotic Silence of the American Wife*. New York: Random House.

Hill, Gary D., and Maxine P. Atkinson. (1988). "Gender, Familial Control and Delinquency." *Criminology* 26 (1): 127–50.

Hills, Stuart L. (1987). *Corporate Violence*. Totowa, NJ: Rowman and Littlefield.

Hills, Stuart L., and Ron Santiago. (1992). *Tragic Magic: The Life and Crimes of a Heroin Addict*. Chicago: Nelson-Hall.

Hinch, Ronald. (1991). "Contradictions, Conflicts and Dilemmas in Canada's Sexual Assault Law." In *Crimes by the Capitalist State*, ed. Gregg Barak, 233–52. Albany: State University of New York Press.

Hirschi, Travis. (1969). *Causes of Delinquency*. Berkeley: University of California Press.

Hochschild, Arlie. (1992). "The Second Shift: Employed Women are Putting in Another Day of Work at Home." In *Men's Lives*, ed. Michael S. Kimmel and Michael A. Messner, 511–15. New York: Macmillan.

Hochschild, Arlie. (1989). *The Second Shift*. New York: Viking.

Hollway, Wendy. (1984). "Women's Power in Heterosexual Sex." *Women's Studies International Forum* 7 (1): 63–68.

hooks, bell. (1992). *Black Looks: Race and Representations*. Boston: South End Press.

Hopper, Columbus, and Johnny Moore. (1990). "Women in Outlaw Motorcycle Gangs." *Journal of Contemporary Ethnography* 18 (4): 363–87.

Hornung, Rick. (1990). "The Case against the Prosecution." *Village Voice*, February, 20: 30–39.

Hunt, Jennifer. (1984). "The Development of Rapport through the Negotiation of Gender in Field Work among Police." *Human Organization* 43 (4): 283–96.

Jaggar, Alison. (1983). *Feminist Politics and Human Nature*. Totowa, NJ: Rowman and Allanheld.

Jaggar, Alison, and William McBride. (1985). " 'Reproduction' as Male Ideology." *Women's Studies International Forum* 8 (3): 185–96.

James, Joy. (1992). "Media Convictions, Fair-Trial Activism and the Central Park Case." *Z Magazine* 5 (2): 33–37.

Jensen, Gary F., and Kevin Thompson. (1990). "What's Class Got to Do With It? A Further Examination of Power-Control Theory." *American Journal of Sociology* 95 (4): 1009–23.

Joreen. (1973). "The Bitch Manifesto." In *Radical Feminism*, ed. Anne Koedt, Ellen Levine, and Anita Rapone, 50–59. New York: Quadrangle Books.

Jurik, Nancy. (1985). "An Officer and a Lady: Organizational Barriers to Women as Correctional Officers in Men's Prisons." *Social Problems* 32 (4): 375–88.

Kandiyoti, Deniz. (1988). "Bargaining with Patriarchy." *Gender and Society* 2 (3): 274–90.

Kanter, Rosabeth Moss. (1977). *Men and Women of the Corporation*. New York: Basic Books.

Kanter, Rosabeth Moss. (1977a). "Some Effects of Proportions on Group Life: Skewed Sex Ratios and Responses to Token Women." *American Journal of Sociology* 82 (5): 965–90.

Katz, Jack. (1988). *Seductions of Crime: Moral and Sensual Attractions in Doing Evil*. New York: Basic Books.

Katz, Janet, and William J. Chambliss. (1991). "Biology and Crime." In *Criminology: A Contemporary Handbook*, ed. Joseph F. Sheley, 245–71. Belmont, CA: Wadsworth.

Kelly, Joan. (1979). "The Double Vision of Feminist Theory." *Feminist Studies* 5 (1): 216–29.

Kelly, Liz. (1988). *Surviving Sexual Violence*. Minneapolis: University of Minnesota Press.

Kelly, Liz. (1987). "The Continuum of Sexual Violence." In *Women, Violence and Social Change*, ed. Jalna Hanmer and Mary Maynard, 46–60. Atlantic Highlands, NJ: Humanities Press International.

Kessler, S., D. J. Ashenden, R. W. Connell, and G. W. Dowsett. (1985). "Gender Relations in Secondary Schooling." *Sociology of Education* 58 (1): 34–48.

Kessler, Suzanne. (1990). "The Medical Construction of Gender: Case Management of Intersexed Infants." *Signs* 16 (1): 3–26.

Kessler, Suzanne, and Wendy McKenna. (1978). *Gender: An Ethnomethodological Approach*. New York: John Wiley.

Kimmel, Michael S., and Thomas E. Mosmiller. (1992). *Against the Tide: Pro-Feminist Men in the United States, 1776–1990. A Documentary History*. Boston: Beacon Press.

Kinsey, Richard, John Lea, and Jock Young. (1986). *Losing the Fight Against Crime*. New York: Basil Blackwell.

Klein, Dorie. (1982). "Violence Against Women: Some Considerations Regarding Its Causes and Elimination." In *The Criminal Justice System and Women*, ed. Barbara R. Price and Natalie J. Sokoloff, 203–21. New York: Clark Boardman.

Klein, Dorie. (1973). "The Etiology of Female Crime: A Review of the Literature." *Issues in Criminology* 8 (2): 3–30.

Klein, Malcolm W. (1971). *Street Gangs and Street Workers*. Englewood Cliffs, NJ: Prentice-Hall.

Koedt, Anne. (1973). "The Myth of the Vaginal Orgasm." In *Radical Feminism*, ed. Anne Koedt, Ellen Levine, and Anita Rapone, 198–207. New York: Quadrangle Books.

Komter, Aafke. (1989). "Hidden Power in Marriage." *Gender and Society* 3 (2): 187–216.

Kreps, Bonnie. (1973). "Radical Feminism 1." In *Radical Feminism*, ed. Anne Koedt, Ellen Levine, and Anita Rapone, 234–39. New York: Quadrangle Books.

Lebergott, Stanley. (1964). *Manpower in Economic Growth*. New York: McGraw-Hill.

Lemert, Edwin. (1967). *Human Deviance, Social Problems and Social Control*. Englewood Cliffs, NJ: Prentice-Hall.

Leonard, Eileen B. (1982). *Women, Crime and Society: A Critique of Criminology Theory*. New York: Longman.

Liddle, A. Mark. (1989). "Feminist Contributions to an Understanding of Violence against Women—Three Steps Forward, Two Steps

Back." *Canadian Review of Sociology and Anthropology* 26 (5): 759–75.

Lindemann, Barbara S. (1984). " 'To Ravish and Carnally Know': Rape in Eighteenth-Century Massachusetts." *Signs* 10 (1): 63–82.

Lippert, John. (1977). "Sexuality as Consumption." In *For Men Against Sexism*, ed. Jon Snodgrass, 207–13. Albion, CA: Times Change Press.

Lombroso, Cesare. (1911). *Crime: Its Causes and Remedies.* New York: Little, Brown.

Lombroso, Cesare, and William Ferrero. (1895). *The Female Offender.* London: T. Fisher Unwin.

Lopata, Helena Z., and Barrie Thorne. (1978). "On the Term 'Sex Roles.' " *Signs* 3 (3): 718–21.

Los, Maria. (1990). "Feminism and Rape Law Reform." In *Feminist Perspectives in Criminology*, ed. Loraine Gelsthorpe and Allison Morris, 160–72. Philadelphia: Open University Press.

MacKinnon, Catherine. (1989). *Toward a Feminist Theory of the State.* Cambridge, MA: Harvard University Press.

MacKinnon, Catherine A. (1979). *Sexual Harassment of Working Women.* New Haven, CT: Yale University Press.

MacLean, Brian D., and Dragan Milovanovic, eds. (1991). *New Directions in Critical Criminology.* Vancouver, B.C.: Collective Press.

MacLean, Brian D., and Dragan Milovanovic. (1991a). *Racism, Empiricism, and Criminal Justice.* Vancouver, B.C.: Collective Press.

McMullan, John L. (1992). *Beyond the Limits of the Law: Corporate Crime and Law and Order.* Halifax: Fernwood Publishers.

McNeely, R. L., and CoraMae Richey Mann. (1990). "Domestic Violence Is a Human Issue." *Journal of Interpersonal Violence* 5 (1): 129–32.

McRobbie, Angela. (1991). *Feminism and Youth Culture.* Boston: Unwin Hyman.

Majors, Richard. (1986). "Cool Pose: The Proud Signature of Black Survival." *Changing Men* 17: 5–6.

Majors, Richard, and Janet Mancini Billson. (1992). *Cool Pose: The Dilemma's of Black Manhood in America.* New York: Macmillan.

Malcolm X. (1965). *The Autobiography of Malcolm X.* New York: Grove Press.

Mancini, Janet K. (1981). *Strategic Styles: Coping in the Inner City.* Hanover, NH: University Press of New England.

Mars, Gerald. (1983). *Cheats at Work.* Boston: Unwin.

Martin, Deirdre, and Mark Levine. (1991). "From Matron to Chief: The Status of Women in Law Enforcement." *Law Enforcement Technology* (Feb): 26, 28–29, 52.

Martin, M. Kay, and Barbara Voorhies. (1975). *Female of the Species.* New York: Columbia University Press.

Martin, Susan E. (1989). "Women in Policing: The Eighties and Beyond." In *Police and Policing: Contemporary Issues,* ed. Dennis Jay Kenney, 3–16. New York: Praeger.

Martin, Susan E. (1980). *Breaking and Entering: Policewomen on Patrol.* Berkeley: University of California Press.

Mauer, Mark. (1992). "Americans Behind Bars: One Year Later." Washington, DC: The Sentencing Project.

Mauer, Mark. (1990). "Young Black Men and the Criminal Justice System: A Growing National Problem." Washington, DC: The Sentencing Project.

Merton, Robert. (1938,1969). "Social Structure and Anomie." In *Delinquency, Crime and Social Process,* ed. Donald R. Cressey and David A. Ward, 254–84. New York: Harper and Row.

Messerschmidt, James W. (1988). "From Marx to Bonger: Socialist Writings on Women, Gender and Crime." *Sociological Inquiry* 58 (4): 378–92.

Messerschmidt, James W. (1988a). "Reply to the Schwendingers." *Social Justice* 15 (1): 146–60.

Messerschmidt, James W. (1986). *Capitalism, Patriarchy and Crime: Toward a Socialist Feminist Criminology.* Totowa, NJ: Rowman and Littlefield.

Messerschmidt, James W. (1979). *School Stratification and Delinquent Behavior.* Stockholm: Gotab.

Messner, Michael. (1989). "Masculinities and Athletic Careers." *Gender and Society* 3 (1): 71–88.

Miller, Eleanor. (1986). *Street Woman.* Philadelphia: Temple University Press.

Miller, Walter B. (1980). "Gangs, Groups and Serious Youth Crime."

In *Critical Issues in Juvenile Delinquency*, ed. David Shichor and Delos H. Kelly, 115–38. Lexington, MA: Lexington Books.

Millett, Kate. (1970). *Sexual Politics*. New York: Doubleday.

Milner, Christina, and Richard Milner. (1972). *Black Players: The Secret World of Black Pimps*. Boston: Little, Brown.

Minneapolis, M.N. (1911). *Report of the Vice Commission of Minneapolis*.

Mitchell, Juliet. (1966). "Women: The Longest Revolution." *New Left Review* 40 (Nov.–Dec.): 11–37.

Morash, Merry. (1986). "Gender, Peer Group Experiences, and Seriousness of Delinquency." *Journal of Research in Crime and Delinquency* 23 (1): 43–67.

Morash, Merry, and Meda Chesney-Lind. (1991). "A Reformulation and Partial Test of the Power-Control Theory of Delinquency." *Justice Quarterly* 8 (3): 347–77.

Morgan, David H. J. (1992). *Discovering Men*. New York: Routledge.

Morgan, Robin. (1978). *Going Too Far*. New York: Random House.

Morgen, Sandra. (1990). "Conceptualizing and Changing Consciousness: Socialist Feminist Perspectives." In *Women, Class, and the Feminist Imagination: A Socialist Feminist Reader*, ed. Karen V. Hansen and Ilene J. Philipson, 277–91. Philadelphia: Temple University Press.

Morris, Allison. (1987). *Women, Crime and Criminal Justice*. New York: Basil Blackwell.

Morris, Ruth. (1965). "Attitudes Toward Delinquency by Delinquents, Non-Delinquents, and Their Friends." *British Journal of Criminology* 5 (2): 249–65.

Morris, Ruth. (1964). "Female Delinquency and Relational Problems." *Social Forces* 43 (1): 82–89.

Mort, Frank. (1985). "Purity, Feminism and the State: Sexuality and Moral Politics, 1880–1914." In *Crisis in the British State, 1880–1930*, ed. Mary Langan and Bill Schwartz, 209–25. London: Hutchinson.

Muehlbauer, Gene, and Laura Dodder. (1983). *The Losers: Gang Delinquency in an American Suburb*. New York: Praeger.

Murphy, Patrick, John Williams, and Eric Dunning. (1990). *Football on Trial*. New York: Routledge & Kegan Paul.

Naffine, Ngaire. (1987). *Female Crime: The Construction of Women in Criminology*. Boston: Allen and Unwin.

Newark, N.J. (1914). Citizens Committee on Social Evil. *Report of the Social Evil Conditions of Newark*.

Oakley, Ann. (1972). *Sex, Gender and Society*. New York: Harper and Row.

Omi, Michael, and Howard Winant. (1986). *Racial Formation in the United States: From the 1960s to the 1980s*. New York: Routledge & Kegan Paul.

Pagelow, Mildred D. (1984). *Family Violence*. New York: Praeger.

Pahl, Jan. (1992). "Money and Power in Marriage." In *Gender, Power and Sexuality*, ed. Pamela Abbott and Claire Wallace, 41–57. London: Macmillan.

Palmer, Phyllis. (1990). *Domesticity and Dirt: Housewives and Domestic Servants in the United States, 1920–1945*. Philadelphia: Temple University Press.

Parsons, Talcott. (1947). "Certain Primary Sources and Patterns of Aggression in the Social Structure of the Western World." *Psychiatry* 10 (May): 167–81.

Parsons, Talcott. (1942). "Age and Sex in the Social Structure of the United States." *American Sociological Review* 7 (5): 604– 16.

Parsons, Talcott, and Robert F. Bales. (1955). *Family, Socialization and Interactional Process*. New York: Free Press.

Petchesky, Rosalind. (1984). *Abortion and Woman's Choice*. New York: Longman.

Philipson, Ilene J., and Karen V. Hansen. (1990). "Women, Class and the Feminist Imagination: An Introduction." In *Women, Class and the Feminist Imagination: A Socialist Feminist Reader*, ed. Karen V. Hansen and Ilene J. Philipson, 3–40. Philadelphia: Temple University Press.

Pivar, David J. (1973). *Purity Crusade: Sexual Morality and Social Control, 1868–1900*. Westport, CT: Greenwood.

Platt, Anthony. (1969). *The Child Savers: The Invention of Delinquency*. Chicago: University of Chicago Press.

Plummer, Kenneth. (1984). "Sexual Diversity: A Sociological Perspective." In *The Psychology of Sexual Diversity*, ed. Kevin Howells, 219–53. New York: Basil Blackwell.

Plummer, Kenneth. (1984a) "The Social Uses of Sexuality: Symbolic Interaction, Power and Rape." In *Perspectives on Rape and Sexual Assault*, ed. June Hopkins, 37–55. NY: Harper and Row.

Pollak, Otto. (1950). *The Criminality of Women*. New York: A.S. Barnes.

Porter, Roy. (1986). "Rape—Does It Have a Historical Meaning?" In *Rape*, ed. Sylvana Tomaselli and Roy Porter, 216–36. New York: Basil Blackwell.

Powell, Gary N. (1988). *Women and Men in Management*. Newbury Park, CA: Sage.

Price, Barbara Raffel, and Natalie J. Sokoloff, eds. (1982). *The Criminal Justice System and Women*. New York: Clark Boardman.

Prieur, Annick. (1990). "The Male Role and Sexual Assault." In *Gender, Sexuality and Social Control*, ed. Bill Rolston and Mike Tomlinson, 141–50. Bristol, England: The European Group for the Study of Deviance.

Pringle, Rosemary. (1989). "Bureaucracy, Rationality and Sexuality: The Case of Secretaries." In *The Sexuality of Organization*, ed. Jeff Hearn, Deborah L. Sheppard, Peta Tancred-Sheriff, and Gibson Burell, 158–77. Newbury Park, CA: Sage.

Pringle, Rosemary. (1988). *Secretaries Talk: Sexuality, Power and Work*. New York: Verso.

Ptacek, James. (1988). "Why Do Men Batter Their Wives?" In *Feminist Perspectives on Wife Abuse*, ed. Kersti Yllö and Michele Bogard, 133–57. Newbury Park, CA: Sage.

Quicker, John C. (1983). *Homegirls: Characterizing Chicano Gangs*. San Pedro, CA: International University Press.

Rafter, Nicole Hahn. (1985). *Partial Justice: Women in State Prisons, 1800–1935*. Boston: Northeastern University Press.

Rafter, Nicole Hahn, and Elizabeth A. Stanko, eds. (1982). *Judge, Lawyer, Victim, Thief*. Boston: Northeastern University Press.

Reeves, Margaret. (1929). *Training Schools for Delinquent Girls*. New York: Russell Sage.

Remmington, Patricia W. (1981). *Policing: The Occupation and the Introduction of Female Officers*. Washington, DC: University Press of America.

Reskin, Barbara, and Patricia Roos. (1987). "Status Hierarchies and

Sex Segregation." In *Ingredients for Women's Employment Policy*, ed. Christine Bose and Glenna Spitze, 3–21. Albany: State University of New York Press.

Reuss-Ianni, Elizabeth, and Frances A. J. Ianni. (1983) "Street Cops and Management Cops: The Two Cultures of Policing." In *Control in the Police Organization*, ed. Maurice Punch, 251–74. Cambridge: MIT Press.

Rich, Adrienne. (1976). *Of Woman Born*. New York: W.W. Norton.

Richie, Beth. (1985). "Battered Black Women: A Challenge for the Black Community." *The Black Scholar* 16 (2): 40–44.

Rippey, Clare M. (1914). "The Case of Angeline." *Outlook* 106: 252–56.

Romenesko, Kim, and Eleanor M. Miller. (1989). "The Second Step in Double Jeopardy: Appropriating the Labor of Female Street Hustlers." *Crime and Delinquency* 35 (1): 109–35.

Roper, Michael, and John Tosh. (1991). "Introduction." In *Manful Assertions: Masculinities in Britain since 1800*, ed. Michael Roper and John Tosh, 1–24. New York: Routledge.

Rosen, Ruth. (1982). *The Lost Sisterhood: Prostitution in America: 1900–1918*. Baltimore: John Hopkins University Press.

Rowbotham, Sheila. (1981). "The Trouble with 'Patriarchy.' " In *Peoples History and Socialist Theory*, ed. Samuel Raphael, 364–73. Boston: Routledge & Kegan Paul.

Rowbotham, Sheila. (1973). *Women's Consciousness, Man's World*. New York: Penguin.

Rubin, Gayle. (1984). "Thinking Sex: Notes for a Radical Theory of the Politics of Sexuality." In *Pleasure and Danger: Exploring Female Sexuality*, ed. Carole S. Vance, 267–319. Boston: Routledge & Kegan Paul.

Russell, Diana E. H. (1982). *Rape in Marriage*. New York: Macmillan.

Russell, Diana E. H. (1975). *The Politics of Rape*. New York: Stein and Day.

Sampson, Robert J., and William Julius Wilson. (1991). "Race, Crime and Urban Inequality" Paper presented at the annual meeting of the American Society of Criminology.

Sanday, Peggy Reeves. (1990). *Fraternity Gang Rape*. New York: New York University Press.

Sanday, Peggy Reeves. (1981). "The Socio-Cultural Context of Rape: A Cross-Cultural Study." *Journal of Social Issues* 37 (1): 5–27.

Sartre, Jean Paul. (1963). *Search for a Method*. New York: Alfred A. Knopf.

Schechter, Susan. (1982). *Women and Male Violence*. Boston: South End Press.

Schlossman, Steven, and Stephanie Wallach. (1978). "The Crime of Precocious Sexuality: Female Juvenile Delinquency in the Progressive Era." *Harvard Educational Review* 48 (1): 65–94.

Schneider, Beth E. (1991). "Put up and Shut Up: Workplace Sexual Assaults." *Gender and Society* 5 (4): 533–48.

Schur, Edwin. (1988). *The Americanization of Sex*. Philadelphia: Temple University Press.

Schur, Edwin. (1979). *Interpreting Deviance: A Sociological Introduction*. New York: Harper and Row.

Schwendinger, Herman, and Julia Schwendinger. (1985). *Adolescent Subcultures and Delinquency*. New York: Praeger.

Schwendinger, Julia, and Herman Schwendinger. (1983). *Rape and Inequality* Beverly Hills, CA: Sage.

Seccombe, Wally. (1986). "Patriarchy Stabilized: The Construction of the Male Breadwinner Wage Norm in Nineteenth-Century Britain." *Social History* 11 (1): 53–75.

Seccombe, Wally. (1973). "The Housewife and Her Labour under Capitalism." *New Left Review* 83 (1): 3–24.

Segal, Lynne. (1990). *Slow Motion: Changing Masculinities, Changing Men*. New Brunswick, NJ: Rutgers University Press.

Segal, Lynne. (1988). *Is the Future Female? Troubled Thoughts on Contemporary Feminism*. New York: Peter Bedricks Books.

Shelden, Randall G. (1981). "Sex Discrimination in the Juvenile Justice System: Memphis, Tennessee, 1900–1917." In *Comparing Female and Male Offenders*, ed. Margaret Q. Warren, 55–72. Beverly Hills, CA: Sage.

Sherman, Lawrence W., and Richard A. Berk. (1984). "The Specific Deterrent Effects of Arrest for Domestic Assault." *American Sociological Review* 49 (2): 261–72.

Short, James F., and Fred L. Strodtbeck. (1965). *Gang Process and Gang Delinquency*. Chicago: University of Chicago Press.

Shostak, Marjorie. (1983). *Nisa: The Life and Words of a !Kung Woman*. New York: Vintage Books.

Shover, Neal, and Stephen Norland. (1978). "Sex Roles and Criminality: Science or Conventional Wisdom?" *Sex Roles* 4 (1): 111–25.

Singer, Simon I., and Murray Levine. (1988). "Power-Control Theory, Gender, and Delinquency" *Criminology* 26 (4): 627–47.

Slim, Iceberg. (1967). *Pimp: The Story of My Life*. Los Angeles: Holloway House.

Smart, Carol. (1989). *Feminism and the Power of Law*. New York: Routledge.

Smart, Carol. (1987). "Review of *Capitalism, Patriarchy and Crime*." *Contemporary Crises* 11 (3): 327–29.

Smart, Carol. (1976). *Women, Crime and Criminology: A Feminist Critique*. Boston: Routledge & Kegan Paul.

Smith, Douglas A., and Raymond Paternoster. (1987). "The Gender Gap in Theories of Deviance: Issues and Evidence." *Journal of Research in Crime and Delinquency* 24 (2): 140–72.

Smith, George W. (1988). "Policing the Gay Community: An Inquiry into Textually-mediated Social Relations." *International Journal of the Sociology of Law* 16 (2): 163–83.

Smith, Michael D. (1990). "Patriarchal Ideology and Wife Beating: A Test of a Feminist Hypothesis." *Violence and Victims* 5 (4): 257–73.

Smith, Michael D. (1990a). "Sociodemographic Risk Factors in Wife Abuse: Results from a Survey of Toronto Women." *Canadian Journal of Sociology* 15 (1): 39–58.

Snider, Lauren. (1985). "Legal Reform and Social Control: The Dangers of Abolishing Rape." *International Journal of the Sociology of Law* 13 (4): 337–56.

Sokoloff, Natalie J. (1980). *Between Money and Love*. New York: Praeger.

Stanko, Elizabeth A., and Kathy Hobdell. (Forthcoming). "Assault on Men: Masculinity and Male Victimization." *British Journal of Criminology*.

Stanko, Elizabeth A. (1989). "Missing the Mark? Policing Battering?" *Women, Policing and Male Violence*, ed. Jalna Hanmer, Jill Radford, and Elizabeth A. Stanko, 46–69. New York: Routledge.

Stanko, Elizabeth A. (1985). *Intimate Intrusions: Women's Experience of Male Violence*. Boston: Routledge and Kegan Paul.

Staples, Robert. (1982). *Black Masculinity*. San Francisco: Black Scholar Press.

Steffensmeier, Darrell, and Emilie Allan. (1991). "Gender, Age and Crime." In *Criminology: A Contemporary Handbook*, ed. Joseph F. Sheley, 67–93. Belmont, CA: Wadsworth.

Steffensmeier, Darrell, and Emilie Anderson Allen. (1981). "Sex Differences in Urban Arrest Patterns, 1934–1979." *Social Problems* 23 (1): 37–50.

Steffensmeier, Darrell, and Miles D. Harer. (1991). "Did Crime Rise or Fall During the Reagan Presidency? The Effects of an "Aging" U.S. Population on the Nation's Crime Rate." *Journal of Research in Crime and Delinquency* 28 (3): 330–59.

Stets, Jan E., and Murray A. Straus. (1989). "The Marriage License as a Hitting License: A Comparison of Assaults in Dating, Cohabitating and Married Couples." In *Violence in Dating Relationships*, ed. Maureen A. Pirog-Good and Jan E. Stets, 38–52. New York: Praeger.

Stinchcombe, Arthur. (1964). *Rebellion in a High School*. Chicago: Quadrangle.

Stone, Michael. (1989). "What Really Happened in Central Park." *New York*, August, 14: 30–43.

Straus, Murray A., and Richard J. Gelles. (1990). "How Violent Are American Families? Estimates from the National Family Violence Survey and Other Studies." In *Physical Violence in American Families*, ed. Murray A. Straus and Richard J. Gelles, 95–112. New Brunswick, NJ: Transaction.

Straus, Murray A., Richard J. Gelles, and Susan Steinmetz. (1980). *Behind Closed Doors*. New York: Doubleday.

Sullivan, Mercer. (1989). *"Getting Paid": Youth Crime and Work in the Inner City*. Ithaca: Cornell University Press.

Sutherland, Edwin H. (1947). *Principles of Criminology*. New York: Lippincott.

Sutherland, Edwin H. (1944, 1956). "Critique of the Theory." In *The*

Sutherland Papers, ed. Albert Cohen, Alfred Lindesmith, and Karl Schuessler, 30–41. Bloomington: Indiana University Press.

Sutherland, Edwin H. (1942,1956). "Development of the Theory." In *The Sutherland Papers*, ed. Albert Cohen, Alfred Lindesmith, and Karl Schuessler, 13–29. Bloomington: Indiana University Press.

Swidler, Ann. (1986). "Culture in Action: Symbols and Strategies." *American Sociological Review* 51 (2): 273–86.

Syracuse, N.Y. (1913). Committee of Eighteen. *The Social Evil in Syracuse.*

Thompson, Sharon. (1990). " 'Drastic Entertainments': Teenage Mothers' Signifying Narratives." In *Uncertain Terms: Negotiating Gender in American Culture*, ed. Faye Ginsburg and Anna Lowenhaupt Tsing, 269–81. Boston: Beacon Press.

Tieger, Todd. (1980). "On the Biological Basis of Sex Differences in Aggression." *Child Development* 51 (4): 943–63.

Tolson, Andrew. (1977). *The Limits of Masculinity*. New York: Harper and Row.

Tong, Rosemarie. (1989). *Feminist Thought: A Comprehensive Introduction*. Boulder: Westview Press.

Thrasher, Frederick. (1927). *The Gang*. Chicago: University of Chicago Press.

Tracy, Paul E., Marvin E. Wolfgang, and Robert M. Figlio. (1991). *Delinquency in Two Birth Cohorts*. New York: Springer Press.

Turk, Austin. (1969). *Criminality and Legal Order*. Chicago: Rand McNally.

Ulrich, Laurel Thatcher. (1983). *Goodwives: Image and Reality in the Lives of Women in Northern New England, 1650–1750*. New York: Alfred A. Knopf.

Ursel, Jane. (1986). "The State and the Maintenance of Patriarchy: A Case Study of Family, Labour and Welfare Legislation in Canada." In *Family, Economy and the State*, ed. James Dickinson and Bob Russell, 150–91. New York: St. Martin's Press.

Vance, Carole S. (1984). "Pleasure and Danger: Toward a Politics of Sexuality." In *Pleasure and Danger: Exploring Female Sexuality*, ed. Carole S. Vance, 1–27. Boston: Routledge & Kegan Paul.

Vandivier, Kermit. (1987). "Why Should My Conscience Bother

Me." In *Corporate Violence*, ed. Stuart L. Hills, 145–62. Totowa, NJ: Rowman and Littlefield.

Vertinsky, Patricia A. (1976). "Education for Sexual Morality: Moral Reform and the Regulation of American Sexual Behavior in the Nineteenth Century." Ph.D. dissertation, University of British Columbia.

Walby, Sylvia. (1989). "Theorizing Patriarchy." *Sociology* 23 (2): 213–34.

Walby, Sylvia. (1986). *Patriarchy at Work: Patriarchal and Capitalist Relations in Employment*. Minneapolis: University of Minnesota Press.

Walker, Lenore E. (1979). *The Battered Woman*. New York: Harper and Row.

Walker, Lenore E. (1977–78). "Battered Women and Learned Helplessness." *Victimology* 2 (4): 525–34.

Walkowitz, Judith. (1980). *Prostitution and Victorian Society: Women, Class and the State*. Cambridge: Cambridge University Press.

Wall Street Journal. (1990). "Doing the 'Right' Thing Has its Repercussions," B1.

Weber, Max. (1978). *Economy and Society*, ed. Guenther Roth and Claus Wittich. Berkeley: University of California Press.

Weeks, Jeffrey. (1986). *Sexuality*. New York: Tavistock.

Weeks, Jeffrey. (1981). *Sex, Politics and Society: The Regulation of Sexuality Since 1800*. New York: Longman.

Weisheit, Ralph, and Sue Mahan. (1988). *Women, Crime and Criminal Justice*. Cincinnati: Anderson.

West, Candace, and Sarah Fenstermaker. (1993). "Power, Inequality and the Accomplishment of Gender: An Ethnomethodological View." In *Theory on Gender/Feminism on Theory*, ed. Paula England, 151–74. New York: Aldine.

West, Candace, and Don H. Zimmerman. (1987). "Doing Gender." *Gender and Society* 1 (2): 125–51.

Weissman, Eric. (1992). "Kids Who Attack Gays." In *Hate Crimes: Confronting Violence against Lesbians and Gay Men*, ed. Gregory M. Herek and Kevin T. Berrill, 170–78. Newbury Park, CA: Sage.

Wexler, Judie Gaffin, and Deana Dorman Logan. (1983). "Sources of

Stress among Women Police Officers." *Journal of Police Science and Administration* 11 (1): 46–53.

Wiatrowski, Michael D., David B. Griswold, and Mary K. Roberts. "Social Control and Delinquency." *American Sociological Review* 46 (5): 525–41.

Wikan, Uni. (1984). "Shame and Honour: A Contestable Pair." *Man* 19: 635–52.

Wiley, Mabel. (1915). *A Study of the Problem of Girl Delinquency in New Haven*. New Haven, CT: Civic Federation of New Haven.

Willard, Frances E. (1895). "Arousing the Public Conscience." *Arena* 11 (Jan): 198–202.

Williams, Walter C. (1986). *The Spirit and the Flesh: Sexual Diversity in American Indian Culture*. Boston: Beacon Press.

Willis, Ellen. (1984). "Radical Feminism and Feminist Radicalism." In *The 60's without Apology*, ed. Sonya Sayres, Anders Stephanson, Stanley Aronowitz, and Fredric Jameson, 91–118. Minneapolis: University of Minnesota Press.

Willis, Paul E. (1979). "Shop Floor Culture, Masculinity and the Wage Form." In *Working Class Culture*, ed. John Clarke, Chas Critcher, and Richard Johnson, 185–98. London: Hutchinson.

Willis, Paul E. (1978). *Profane Culture*. London: Routledge & Kegan Paul.

Willis, Paul E. (1977). *Learning to Labour*. Farnborough, England: Saxon House.

Wilson, James Q., and Richard J. Herrnstein. (1985). *Crime and Human Nature*. New York: Simon and Schuster.

Young, Iris. (1981). "Beyond the Unhappy Marriage: A Critique of Dual Systems Theory." In *Women and Revolution*, ed. Lydia Sargent, 43–69. Boston: South End Press.

Young, Vernetta. (1986). "Gender Expectations and their Impact on Black Female Offenders and Victims." *Justice Quarterly* 3 (3): 305–27.

Zaretsky, Eli. (1978). "The Effects of the Economic Crisis on the Family." In *U.S. Capitalism in Crisis*, ed. Radical Political Economic Collective, 209–18. New York: Union for Radical Political Economics.

Zimring, Franklin E., and James Zuehl. (1986). "Victim Injury and Death in Urban Robbery: A Chicago Study." *Journal of Legal Studies* 15 (1): 1–40.

Index

Race: absent in socialist feminist theory, 60; and African American boys, 102–117, 191, 193, 194; and African American men, 67, 72, 119–124, 194, 195, 196; and African American women, 68–70, 197; and Latino boys, 101, 106, 108; and social construction of "whiteness," 190–191; and white boys, 92–102; and white men, 133–142; importance of for social theory, 62–63; state repression of African American men, 184–185; *see also* Corporate crime; Gay-bashing; Hate crime; Pimping; Youth crime

Radford, Jill, 43

Rafter, Nicole Hahn, 14, 170, 171

Rape: as foundation of patriarchy, 36–45; battering, 143–150; by street groups, 113–116; early 1970s radical feminist view on, 35–36; force-only, 150–153; history of, 47–48; in college fraternities, 194

Rebellion in a High School, 104

Reeves, Margaret, 170, 172

Remmington, Patricia W., 175, 176, 179–180, 181, 182, 198

Reskin, Barbara, 125

Reuss-Ianni, Elizabeth, 178, 180

Rich, Adrienne, 40

Richie, Beth, 197

Rippey, Clare M., 167–168, 169

Robbery, 106–109

Roberts, Mary K., 96

Romenesko, Kim, 121, 124

Roos, Patricia, 125

Roper, Michael, 59

Rosen, Ruth, 120, 157, 162, 163, 168

Rowbotham, Sheila, 53

Rubin, Gayle, 73, 74

Russell, Diana E. H., 39, 148

Sampson, Robert J., 110

Sanday, Peggy Reeves, 47, 194

Sanderson, Kay, 58

Santiago, Ron, 107–108, 111, 112

Sartre, Jean-Paul, 102–103

Scarpitti, Frank R., 14

Schechter, Susan, 144

Schlossman, Steven, 168, 171, 172

Schneider, Beth E., 132, 140

Schur, Edwin, 4, 75

Schwendinger, Herman, 88, 89, 90, 91–92, 110, 114

Schwendinger, Julia, 88, 89, 90, 91–92, 110, 114

Seccombe, Wally, 51–52, 66, 68

Segal, Lynne, 39, 48, 71, 73, 74, 75, 76, 82, 114, 115, 132, 142, 149, 150, 197

Sex-role theory: criticisms of, 25–29; in criminological theory, 14–29; in feminist theory, 32–36

Sexual harassment: by corporate executives, 139–142; by police officers, 180–182; by workers, 130–133

Sexual Politics, 32

Sexuality: in cultural feminist theory, 40–50; in "deviant street networks," 124; in early 1970s radical feminist theory, 34–35; in policing, 179–180; in structured action theory, 73–76; in the family, 143, 147–153; in the workplace, 130–133, 139–142; in youth groups, 89–90; state regulation of, 157–174, 182–183

Shelden, Randall G., 14, 87, 95, 168–169, 171, 187

Sherman, Lawrence W., 176

Short, James F., 88

Shostak, Marjorie, 47

Shover, Neal, 25

Singer, Simon I., 13

Slim, Iceberg, 121

About the Author

James W. Messerschmidt is associate professor of sociology and criminology at the University of Southern Maine. He received his Ph.D.
from the University of Stockholm in sociology, specializing in criminology. His research interests focus on the interrelation of class, gender, race, and crime, and he has authored *The Trial of Leonard Peltier*
(1983, South End Press), *Capitalism, Patriarchy and Crime: Toward
a Socialist Feminist Criminology* (1986, Rowman and Littlefield), and
Criminology (1991, Harcourt Brace Jovanovich, with Piers Beirne).